Thor Heyerdahl was born in 1914. Educated first as a biologist, he subsequently turned to anthropology. A prodigious explorer, he has organised numerous archaeological expeditions and ocean crossings in aboriginal vessels. The author of numerous popular and scientific books, his other titles include *Aku-Aku*, *The Ra Expeditions*, *The Mystery of the Maldives*, *The Pyramids of Tucume* and *Green Was the Earth on the Seventh Day*.

Thor Heyerdahl was for twenty years a member of the New York Academy of Sciences and of the Soviet Academy of Sciences, and was awarded the Pahlevi Environmental Prize by the United Nations. After many years in Italy he now lives in Tenerife, but returns frequently to Peru, the scene of many of his excavations.

ALSO BY THOR HEYERDAHL

The Kon-Tiki Expedition
Aku-Aku: The Secret of Easter Island
Viking America: The Norse Crossings and Their Legacy
The Ra Expeditions
Fatu-Hiva: Back to Nature
The Tigris Expedition: In Search of Our Beginnings
The Maldive Mystery
Easter Island: The Mystery Solved
Pyramids of Túcume: The Quest for Peru's Forgotten City
Green Was the Earth on the Seventh Day

In the
Footsteps
of
Adam

Thor Heyerdahl

In a new translation by
Ingrid Christophersen

An *Abacus* Book

First published in Great Britain in 2000 by Little, Brown and Company
This edition published in 2001 by Abacus Books

Copyright © 1998 by Thor Heyerdahl/J M Stenersens Forlag

Originally published in Norwegian under the title
I Adams Fotspor: En Erindringsreise

PICTURE CREDITS
All pictures are from the author's collection except:
7, 21, 25, 27, 28, 32, 33: Kon-Tiki Museum;
18, 19: Forsvarsmuseet; 17, 26: Jan Høst;
10, 12, 13: *National Geographic;* 20, 23: *Life.*

A CIP catalogue record for this book is
available from the British Library.

ISBN: 0 349 11273 8

Typeset in Horley OS by M Rules
Printed and bound in Great Britain by Clays Ltd, St Ives plc

Abacus Books
A Division of
Little, Brown and Company (UK)
Brettenham House
Lancaster Place
London WC2E 7EN

www.littlebrown.co.uk

Contents

1

The Beginning

– Creation or evolution?
– Adam or apes?
– Do you believe in God or Darwin?

I'll pass these questions on. I have been asked them so often – even by my own silent *aku-aku* in solitary moments of conversation with myself.

I got no further in my attempt to relax over my latest manuscript. I was waiting nervously for my bride-to-be to emerge from the bathroom, dressed and ready to go to church.

Church? Was this me, who in my youth was prepared to swear that one marriage would last a lifetime?

I had not lived up to my youthful ideals. Here I was, sitting in a hotel room in a desert town in the Western Sahara, waiting to get married for the third time. This time the venue was a Catholic cathedral in El Aaiún, the disputed former capital, where everyone today – except for the priest – was a Muslim.

My first wedding was in Norway, in the bride's own home in Brevik, where a young Lutheran minister from the State Church married us in the presence of two student friends and our parents. We left the next day and travelled to Fatu-Hiva in the Pacific Ocean, to spend a year living as Adam and Eve in the primal forest, far from the comforts of civilisation. Her name was Liv. An exceptional person. No one else I've met would have had the courage or strength to embark on this adventure, relying on our bare hands in the struggle for survival, isolated from everything and everyone in the rest of the world, and without radio, medicines or matches.

My second wedding was in New Mexico, where the sheriff in Santa Fe married us, his pistol conspicuous on the shelf beside him. Bill, called in from the room next door, was the witness. My bride was Yvonne. She was in a league of her own. I know of no one else with the stamina and courage to stand by my side through those long years of struggle against such ruthless adversaries, who were hostile to new knowledge and clinging to outworn dogmas.

And now the third wedding; I had barely written the first sentences of an introduction to a new book before Jacqueline swept through the bathroom door and I discarded my paper and pencil to follow her down the stairs to the hotel lobby. In my trouser pocket I had a box with the two small wooden rings that I had carved from a small dried branch in the garden. I don't like jewellery on men – or on women for that matter – and I have never owned a ring, but this time it was part of the procedure. Protestant birth, death and divorce certificates from Norway and the United States were also required, all translated into Spanish and certified by both a priest and a bishop in the Canary Islands. These were necessary before I, born a

Norwegian Protestant, could marry a woman, born a French Catholic in Paris, in a cathedral in Muslim, formerly Spanish, Western Sahara.

We hurried down the stairs to the waiting priests. Outside we were met by a world of desert sand, Berbers in long white robes and UN soldiers from sixty nations wearing blue berets with flags on their sleeves. This was the country where King Hassan II of Morocco had sent 250,000 countrymen armed with red flags in the 'green peace march' to prevent a referendum on the independence of Western Sahara. The situation had not changed since Jacqueline and I had been there five years earlier to study rock carvings in the desert. The only significant difference was that the UN peace-keeping force had been reduced to five hundred men.

Outdoors, the morning sun was scorching.

'The bridal bouquet,' said Jacqueline, looking around a world devoid of florists or even green grass. She slipped into the back garden of the hotel and found a cluster of date palms and a lonely hibiscus bearing one large red flower; we then wound our way past Muslims and military personnel toward the large Catholic cathedral that had been left behind in this Islamic desert town by the Spaniards before their retreat from the country after the Second World War — she with the huge red flower, I with the wooden rings in my pocket.

As I was wondering how this was going to work out, avoiding looking at my watch, we caught sight of two white-robed priests waiting at the cathedral, one outside and the other inside the door. I am not a churchgoer, so this was unusual for me, but I had no prejudice against the indoor rituals others might observe in searching for their god.

As could be expected in this part of the world, which had once again reverted to Islam, the cathedral was empty, but on this occasion two of the priests' personal friends had come as witnesses. Only one, Don Enrique, was a Christian. He was the sole remaining representative of Spanish interests in Western Sahara. The embassy had been closed and the UN had unsuccessfully tried to bring about free elections to decide whether the country should be annexed to Morocco or declare itself a sovereign state. Coincidentally he had been born and raised in the Canary Islands, where we were also living; he came from Galdar in Gran Canaria, where Spanish archaeologists had recently uncovered thousand-year-old housing foundations similar to ones in Iceland from the Viking era. They had even found the remains of a Nordic-type sword. The other witness was a highly intellectual Arab doctor, Abdel Hafid. He explained, with a smile, that after experimenting with Christianity during his university years, personal conviction had brought him back to Islam.

I looked around. The pews were as empty as the bare white concrete walls, which were devoid of any sacred pictures or icons. Where was Jesus, whose lifeless form was usually shown on the cross? He was not even represented on the altarpiece. Was this in deference to any Jewish visitors who, lacking a synagogue, might be tempted to venture in for a quiet moment? This church was, after all, dedicated to the God of Abraham. Could this explain why there were no Christian saints along the side walls? There was only one small chocolate-coloured statue of the Virgin Mary standing with her hands folded in humble prayer beside the pulpit.

Neither gold nor any other precious material adorned the altarpiece, but one noticed the very simple outlines of the Almighty Creator looming symbolically on his throne on the seventh day, the day of rest. He sat barefoot in a simple armchair, positioned above the heads of four humble evangelists who were depicted in the same simple way. A single dove of peace crowned the symbolism.

No one could be offended by such neutral motifs, where only the Almighty himself was dominant. The god up there on the wall was the common god of three religions that were still fighting bloody battles among themselves in the space age.

What are they fighting for?

I was roused from my ecumenical contemplation when a voice started singing in the vestry, and the two priests appeared in a small procession, clothed in their beautiful white robes. The congregation, all four of us, rose, the two witnesses over by the long wall, and we – the bride and groom – with the two Catholic priests between us, facing the altar and the Lord God on the wall. Now I realised that there was no face on the painting. They've done it on purpose, I thought, to avoid offending Muslims, who forbid the representation of faces, especially of a Creator God who is described in both the Bible and the Koran as invisible. But then it dawned on me that the face was missing because a leak in the roof had worn away the paint, though only where the face should have been. I decided to ask the priests about it. Later it was confirmed that it was in fact a leak. A coincidence. Sometimes one wonders if coincidences really occur.

I now had to concentrate on the words, in French and Spanish, spoken by the two priests, and the echo over the empty pews behind us. I suspected that the topic would be Adam and Eve, because the thin little priest, Father Loig, had asked me about creation when we came over on the plane from the Canary Islands the day before. Father Loig was interested in all sorts of things, but mostly in archaeology. It was he who had corresponded with Jacqueline, and had enticed us with descriptions of rock carvings in the Sahara, when we went to El Aaiún five years earlier. Now Jacqueline had lured him all the way back from Nouadhibou in Mauritania, where he had been relocated. Because of the lack of road connections he had flown via the Canaries. Standing two steps above us, next to his superior, Father Acacio, beneath the large bare feet etched on the wall above, he seemed to be just as happy as we were, even though he himself had chosen a life of celibacy. The echoing atmosphere in the cathedral was charged. What would the two of them say and ask us to do? They both faced us with friendly smiles, and with the dove of peace above us the turmoil in Africa seemed a distant past. Next to his large and seemingly more formal Spanish colleague, who was like a giant protective teddy bear at his side, our small French friend in his long white clerical gown, almost seemed like a child waiting for baptism. We knew little about the Spanish priest, except that he was responsible for this cathedral, which was Christianity's last outpost in the UN-controlled Western Sahara and faced extremist Muslim terrorists just across the border with Algeria. Father Acacio was aware of the explosive situation in this part of the Sahara, having just attended a congregation of bishops in Morocco with his friend the Archbishop of Oran.

The hatred among different worshippers of the God of Love became a distant problem as the two white-robed priests faced us below the dove of peace. Father Loig's face lit up and seemed to replace the one that had dissolved on the wall. He began to speak about love, the origin of love, the creation of the world.

'The world was created when the Big Bang set the whole universe into motion,' he said, looking down at me with a smile.

I stole a look at the other priest. With his calmly folded hands, he seemed to be perfectly happy and unconcerned.

'The story of Adam and Eve and the creation of the world in six days is not to be taken literally,' we were informed. It is written that for God, a thousand years is one day and one day is a thousand years. The whole Bible is filled with parables. Jesus himself almost always spoke in pictorial language. Adam and Eve are symbols of love, a self-portrait of the invisible god. An Adam and an Eve were necessary to create a visible picture of the God of Love.

Yes, I almost called out several times. I was in such agreement that I was impatient for him to ask me if I wanted to marry Jacqueline. We had in fact spoken about the Big Bang when we were on the plane from the Canary Islands the previous day. I had admitted that, although science had decided that the universe came into existence with a powerful explosion, there still had to be superhuman and supernatural powers to trigger such a conflagration, not least to create order out of ensuing chaos.

'The groom, who is a biologist,' he continued, 'has also said that the heat from the Big Bang would have been so extreme that an act of creation would have been required to make life on earth afterwards.'

I had said that. And I quietly thought that if science could nickname the creative powers 'Big Bang', then early cultures had an equal right to refer to the Great Spirit in place of what antiquity's founders of religions called Allah and God. I had to admit to myself that believing that a Big Bang could create galaxies of stars was more in tune with the philosophy of the atomic age than imagining that a holy spirit hovering quietly over the waters could do so. The priest did not say so, but I thought it. And I wondered how a man who walked about gently in his white robe and lived in celibacy could speak with such warmth about love. To him it was not carnal love; it had to exist freely like a bird within him. Big Bangs can create hatred in living spirits, but they cannot create love in dead atoms and galaxies. We cannot find love with a

microscope or remove it with a surgical knife, but we can
carry it within us, whether we are striptease dancers or wear
the robe of a priest.

Glancing toward one of the witnesses by the wall, Father
Loig had quoted a few passages from the Koran to emphasise
that the prophet Mohammed, too, had made use of the old
parable about Adam and Eve. The invisible Allah created the
world in the course of six *yawm*, and a *yawm* is not only one
day but also a period of indefinite length. Christians started to
depict the Creator God on church walls in the Middle Ages,
but Muslims did not allow these in their mosques. The priests,
one in French and the other in Spanish, were depicting a
Creator God in accordance with the ancient scriptures. They
were not talking about a bearded and wrinkled old man at all,
not even a virgin. The symbolic self-portrait of Our Lord was
a man and a woman together as a couple, the visible symbol of
a creative love. It was the primal power behind all matter,
behind time and space, that set the universe in motion and
spent six of its own days placing human beings on a sterile
planet and giving them the ability to create new generations in
a matter of nine months.

I was hardly able to contain myself. I wanted to say 'yes' to
everything, and when at last I was asked if I wanted
Jacqueline, I answered *Yes!* with such force that the bride's
subsequent response sounded like an echo in the empty cathedral. Then all six of us embraced, and when Jacqueline and I
left, our large wooden rings temporarily set on our fingers, we
felt there was still hope for peace and understanding among all
of us who followed in Adam's footsteps, even though Western
Sahara for the time being was guarded by UN soldiers.

A few hours later, on that same day, there was an explosion in
Algeria on the border with Morocco. The Archbishop of

Oran, Father Acacio's friend, was killed by a bomb planted by extremist Muslim terrorists.

Small terrorist groups and military super-powers believe in both God and Satan. And in big bangs.

Science looks up at a field of stars with telescopes and inspects atoms with microscopes, and finds no hiding place for heaven or hell. Science cannot help us to distinguish between good and evil.

2

Time for Reflection

Our Lord did not have to wait for the next day's papers to read about the murder of the Archbishop of Oran. One of His most loyal servants had blessed His name as he fell to his death under the sign of the cross, while another person had prostrated himself toward Mecca, giving thanks for the success of the deed. The two shared a belief in the God of Love who had breathed life into their mutual forefather, Adam.

This time a Muslim had killed a Christian in Africa. According to the same paper, things were rough in Europe too. In the one-time Yugoslavia, where Tito had established religious tolerance, Christians and Muslims were now slaughtering one another by the thousands. In the Emerald Isle, on the other side of Europe, where there were few if any Muslims, Christians were beating one another to death because some prayed directly to Our Lord, while others called on the Virgin Mary to intercede on their behalf. Christians and Muslims and Jews all agree that we have a common heritage. Adam and Eve had two sons, Cain and Abel, and as soon as there were two contenders, one killed his brother when his burnt offering failed to find favour with the Almighty.

In the Nordic countries we were no longer as passionate about questions of religion. We had got over the worst, we had got rage out of our system in the Viking era. But around the year 1000, when the gospel reached us from the Middle East, it didn't take us long to get into our long ships and sail down to Jerusalem to behead Muslims. As a good Norwegian schoolboy I had heard, admired and read Snorre and the *Sagas of the Kings*, which described how our forefathers set off on pilgrimages to the Holy Land in the eleventh and twelfth centuries, and how in the course of their journey they slaughtered Muslim infidels along the coasts of Portugal, Spain and North Africa. Some of them might have sought shelter in the good harbour of Oran in Algeria, and avenged themselves in anticipation of what took place while we were hearing about Adam and Eve behind the closed doors of the cathedral. It was under the sign of the cross that the mighty King Sigurd Jorsalfar went on a Viking voyage to the Holy Land and raided towns along the coast of Africa before clearing the way for Christian crusaders to Jerusalem. He gave all the gold that his men stole from the followers of Allah to the Patriarch of the Holy City and to the Pope in Constantinople, and placed his whole fleet of Viking ships and most of his warriors in the Mediterranean at the disposal of the Pope in his war against the followers of Mohammed. He himself, and the rest of his party, rode home through Europe on horseback. His predecessor on Norway's throne, St Olav, had already been canonised by the Pope when he Christianised Norway by beheading any countrymen who refused to believe in Jesus. History reveals that Christians are not always concerned about living by the rules of their faith as long as they believe in them.

Jacqueline and I were to return to our new home in the Canary Islands the day after the wedding. Father Loig was returning to his post further south in Africa on the same flight. By a misunderstanding we were informed that there was only one seat available on the plane from Casablanca, so Jacqueline went with the two priests to the airport to see one of them safely onboard. Father Loig was already on board the aeroplane when news of the murder in Oran reached El Aaiún. We did not hear about it until that evening from Father Acacio. He remained calm, showing no signs of hatred or vengeance, and even less anxiety for himself. He was left on his own in a cathedral in a country where he alone prayed to God, and everyone else prayed to Allah. The Church has always had martyrs, he said. Martyrdom did not start with the Arab Mohammed, who was born when Christianity had already fought for its existence for over five hundred years. The Church had been losing martyrs for almost two thousand years. And there was a new Christian ready to replace his friend, Archbishop Claverie in Oran.

My happiness was no less complete when Jacqueline left for the desert airport. The light from the morning sun shone peacefully over the Sahara's eternally young sand dunes, which concealed so much history and human speculation. I suddenly realised that I had no work to complete and that I was as free as a bird. No duties and no schedule. Although this had not been planned, it was an unexpected and greatly appreciated treat.

I found a deckchair in a corner of the hotel's roof terrace, where I could escape from the ever present noise of transistor radios and enjoy a rare silence beneath a blue sky. Only the fringed tops of the garden's date palms and the soundless birds in the sky were high enough to enter my range of vision. Time vanished as it does on a raft on the ocean. No mail. No telephone. Just a perfect silence that invited me to let my thoughts wander.

'Now, for once, you can relax,' Jacqueline had said when she left me at the hotel. She insisted that I hadn't had a single week without some project or other on the go during the five years we had known each other. She was probably right, but it was because my plan of action was just as much a hobby as it was work.

People might have the impression that I'm a stubborn adventurer who jumps from one raft to the other, from one academic controversy to the next. In reality I am a very peaceful person, primarily interested in finding solutions to problems, and getting to the bottom of unanswered questions. The more I do and the more I see, the more I realise the shocking extent of ignorance that exists among the scholarly circles that call themselves authorities and pretend to have a monopoly of all knowledge. This has to be dealt with.

I have to admit that if I had been unsuccessful every time I embarked on a new expedition or a new enquiry, I would probably have given up and found something else to do. But every time I make a discovery that I thought I could and should be able to make, I become even more absorbed and have fun. At such times, it is not only a matter of scientific curiosity, it's a matter of sheer joy.

Nevertheless, Jacqueline was right. I had barely completed an expedition or a book before I started on a new one. There were never any breaks between travels, mail and manuscripts. Crazy, I thought.

Crazy.

I thought I suddenly heard an echo inside me. Maybe it's

my *aku-aku*, I said jokingly to myself. I remembered drowsily that the inhabitants of Easter Island had told me that I had an *aku-aku*. All their forefathers, and many who were still living, had an *aku-aku*, an invisible companion who offered good advice whenever necessary. No one else but a capable *aku-aku* could have told me to visit them on their deserted island and start excavating in the right places in order to find statues of whose existence no one had been aware.

I thought with pleasure about the joyous months working with the first archaeological excavations on Easter Island. At that time it had neither a harbour nor an airport. It was the loneliest island in the world, with a population of barely one thousand and was visited only once a year, when a Chilean naval vessel came on a two- to three-day visit at Christmas, bringing provisions for the descendants of the people who had raised the hundreds of gigantic stone statues that littered the island. Today there is both a harbour and an airport on Easter Island, but when we arrived in the 1950s and anchored outside Anakena Bay, each and every family was living solely on sweet potatoes dug up from the earth, and on such fish as the ocean offered.

Once again I had an opportunity to let my thoughts run free. I could relax and think about the seafarers and former bearers of tradition, while we excavated their works of art or drowsed during the breaks up in the quarry. Timeless days and nights. In my thoughts I floated back there, the same blue sky over me. Soon I was neither here nor there, and allowed my thoughts to wander. I thought I could hear the voice of the *aku-aku*.

Ia-ora-na. Kaoha-nui. Good day. It's been a long time.

I had to smile. We were obviously both in a good mood and ready for a joke. I haven't heard from you for a long time, I thought. Has it been difficult for you to keep in touch after I left that peaceful Easter Island?

I have been with you the whole time; you are the one who has been absent. First you brought me from Polynesia to the jungles of South America, then on timber logs and reed rafts across three oceans, and now you have parked me on a roof in a desert town in the Sahara? What is the meaning of all this? Are you an adventurer or a scientist?

Apart from four years as a volunteer in Norway's struggle against the Nazis during the war, I have never done anything but scientific research, ever since I started studying biology at the age of eighteen. The adventures have simply been added attractions. I never seek adventures, but I gladly accept them as an additional bonus when experimenting with the tools of antiquity or searching for unknown cultures by disproving former dogmas about prehistoric vessels.

People say you've been lucky.

It isn't so much a question of being lucky as a question of not being unlucky.

At this moment Jacqueline returned. It was true, I was lucky. It would have been unlucky not to have met her.

We lay and dozed in our deckchairs on the roof overlooking the Sahara and I could not keep the *aku-aku* away.

Isn't this a little too much? First you go on a honeymoon to Fatu-Hiva, then you go to Easter Island with another bride, and now you are arranging a wedding in the Sahara – as if you had become a Muslim. Three times should be enough!

Yes, this was definitely enough. Nine lives and three marriages; there have to be limits. But I had not become a Muslim. It was here that Jacqueline and I had truly become acquainted, thanks to the priest who showed us the stone carvings.

Do you believe in Allah?

Allah has different names in different languages. I think

that the Christian God is also the Jewish Jehovah and the Muslim Allah.

The issue is not about believing in the Bible or the Koran. It is about believing in the god that the authors of these books believed in, and both books are about exactly the same god. I learned an evening prayer from my father. He was Norwegian and he never mentioned Allah, but neither did he use the word 'God'. It was simply 'Our Lord'.

At school we had a clergyman who taught religion. I was fascinated by Adam and Eve, as well as Noah, and all the animals. And I also paid attention when it came to Jesus, who understood nature and said something like, 'Behold the birds of the air, no prince is more gorgeously apparelled than they.' But when the minister began telling us how Jesus went to a wedding and turned water into wine, I figured he was mistaken and raised my hand.

'Thor,' he said happily, 'what have you got to say?'

My father was the director of the town brewery, so I ached to improve on the story. 'I don't think it was wine,' I said. 'I think it was beer, because it tastes better and is healthier!'

The clergyman did not like that. Furious, he sent me out of the room, and I had to stand alone, freezing in the winter cold, while my classmates heard about all the strange things Jesus had done.

Ever since ancient times we have honoured the same god that Abraham brought with him from Ur. That we shouldn't lie, steal or kill is something we've heard ever since Moses descended the mountain with the stone tablets. But we still argue about whether we should pray to Abraham's god under the star of David, under the sign of the cross, or under Mohammed's crescent-moon; whether we should honour Our Lord's creation on Friday, Saturday, or Sunday; whether it is a sin to eat pork and drink alcohol, right or wrong to consume the flesh and blood of Jesus. Issues like these, which are not mentioned in the laws of Moses, we continue to argue and debate. And by so doing, we show our disdain for everything that Moses, Jesus and Abraham represented.

On the raft voyages, while apparently hovering motionless in the centre of a circle of blue sky and blue ocean, without television or the sound of aircraft overhead, you find time to do some old-fashioned thinking. In 1947, when we set out on the balsa raft, *Kon-Tiki*, on our voyage across the Pacific to Polynesia, the American ambassador in Peru gave me a Bible to keep on board. His equally well-meaning military attaché wagered a case of whisky that we would never return. Although the Bible remained undisturbed in a box beneath my berth, the good Lord helped us safely ashore on the Raroia atoll 101 days later. The attaché had been posted elsewhere, so we never received the whisky, but the Bible came in handy later.

Kon-Tiki's crew consisted of five Norwegians and a Swede, all Protestants, and when the ocean broke over us as we hit the atoll, I heard Torstein yell to Knut, 'All you believers had better pray now.' I think half of those on board prayed.

Twenty-two years later, when we launched the reed ship *Ra* in Morocco in an attempt to cross the Atlantic Ocean, we were seven men aboard with totally different backgrounds. I wanted to show that it was possible to live peacefully together in cramped quarters, under stress, though not sharing the same skin colour, political views or beliefs. For almost two months, Arab and Jew lay shoulder to shoulder in the small bamboo hut; the navigator from the United States lay with his face against the feet of the doctor from the Soviet Union. The Arab from Egypt was not a Muslim, but a Copt, from the world's oldest Christian community. Abdullah, a Buduma from Central Africa, was black as coal and not an Arab but a Muslim. This time, in his honour, we were given a copy of the Koran as a gift from the Pasha in Safi, but Abdullah was illiterate, so it stayed with my Bible until we resurrected it again on our next journey, when we had a Muslim aboard who could read. He was a Berber from Morocco who used the Koran every day.

The Bible and the Koran that accompanied us over the ocean ended peacefully side by side in the bookshelf behind my desk, in the company of other primary sources about the development of the civilisations of the world. They are still with me.

Many wondered why I chose Abdullah, from the interior of Africa, to join us on the first Atlantic journey aboard a prehistoric reed ship. One doesn't normally venture that far inland to hire sailors, and Abdullah had never been closer to the ocean than the point at which the Sahara meets the jungle, right in the heart of the continent. But in Egypt papyrus reeds had become extinct until the Papyrus Institute in Cairo reintroduced them after the *Ra* journeys; boat builders who worked with papyrus reeds were only to be found on the inland seas of Ethiopia and in the Central African republic of Chad.

I have often found the preparations for an expedition more problematic than the journey itself. Sometimes they are also more dangerous. There was political unrest in Chad when I arrived with a French photographer to recruit reed-boat builders. In Fort Lamy, the capital, I rented a jeep in order to follow the long caravan route to Lake Chad, where the Buduma lived, many on floating reed islands in the lake. We were warned against the journey and told that heads from decapitated nurses had recently been found along the roadside.

Dusk had already fallen when we arrived at the village of Bol on the bank of Lake Chad. The village consisted of beautiful dome-shaped huts made from papyrus reeds, and at the end of the road there was a shelter where wayfarers could spend the night free of charge. Three walls, a floor and a roof, all of cement.

We were asleep on the cement floor when I awoke to the low sound of distant music, rhythmic drums and tunes from a wind instrument. The village had seemed lifeless and deserted, and my curiosity was aroused as I stepped quietly out into the dark of night. I stumbled over a camel which responded with a grunt, and stood still for a long time before I felt safe again and edged forward between the hut walls.

The rhythm of the drums grew louder as I rounded a corner and saw an open square. I could make out the shadow of figures in flowing robes dancing around a solitary kerosene lantern. They moved to the music in a staccato rhythm. As my night vision improved, I also caught a glimpse of the two musicians. Standing in the impenetrable African darkness, leaning against the wall of a hut, I was convinced that I was invisible.

To my astonishment I saw that one of the figures slowly detached himself from the circle and came dancing in my direction. I was hoping that he wouldn't come close enough to discover me when I saw that he had drawn a short sword and was approaching me, fencing in my direction without losing the rhythm. An icy shiver ran through me when I realised that not only had I been seen but that my white body was the target he was dancing toward.

Around the kerosene lamp the others continued unconcernedly with their dance. The threatening figure was now so close that the sword could be thrust into me at any moment. I was unarmed and couldn't escape. I saw no way out, but instinctively started moving my feet to the beat of the drums, and before I knew it I was dancing with the man whose sword was held against my chest. He seemed to be under the influence of a drug. Slowly he started to dance backward while I followed closely after him, up against his sword. When we reached the circle it opened and made room for us. The sword was sheathed, and we danced on, behind one another and with the others.

In the glow of the kerosene lamp I caught sight of a generously proportioned female standing with the musicians, and to my amazement I saw that the dancers seemed to be tiring. One after the other they stepped out of the circle, sweaty and panting, each one offering up a little coin. Toward the end there were only two of us left, and finally I was dancing on my own. I had obviously won some kind of competition, and to feel totally safe I put a bill into the bowl where the others had dropped coins. The winner's trophy was the lush beauty, and everyone wondered why I didn't take her with me as I staggered back to the cement floor.

The next morning it was clear that I had won great status in the village, and amongst my many new friends I met the reedboat builder Abdullah.

Abdullah had much to learn on his first journey away from the heart of Africa, and we had much to learn from him. He was the only one who had ever seen papyrus, and he knew how to build a reed boat, with raised curves in the bow and stern, enabling it to dance over and between the waves. Abdullah had never seen any other expanse of water nor any bigger waves than those on Lake Chad at the southern end of the Sahara. On board, Abdullah trusted Allah more than he trusted us, who had never seen a papyrus boat before, but to be on the safe side he also tied a small leather pouch containing magical rocks and leopard claws around his waist. Thus equipped, he scared the wits out of the rest of us by balancing recklessly and fearlessly and without being roped on the slippery edge of the reed boat. If he slipped into the water, he would simply grab laughingly a bundle of reeds and haul himself back on board.

Allah had brought Abdullah into the world in a part of Africa that had seen better days. The Sahara was expanding southwards at a speed of a couple of kilometres a year. Some five thousand years ago, aboriginal inhabitants further north in the desert had decorated the cliff walls in the Tassili Mountains with paintings of people hunting hippopotamus from reed boats. About two thousand years ago, North Africa was still the granary of the Roman Empire. When Abdullah came into the world, endless sand-dunes from the north had already bypassed Lake Chad in Central Africa and were slowly encroaching on the tropical jungle. Not a bush to be seen around the lake, just sand and lush green papyrus reed at the water's edge and on floating islands that drifted about, carrying people and livestock as passengers.

While the rest of us live in a world of skyscrapers and astronauts, Abdullah and his two countrymen, whom I brought to Egypt to build an ancient vessel, had never even walked up a flight of stairs before they boarded the plane in the capital, Fort Lamy. They had grown up in beautiful dome-shaped reed houses with earth floors. When we were on our way up to the third floor of a hotel in Khartoum they lifted their legs as if they were climbing mountain. Flown out of a world where a mat on the floor was the only furnishing, one of them put his head underneath the bed until Abdullah, who spoke French, explained that they were meant to sleep on top. Even after having seen the toilet filled with clean water they were suspicious about its real use. Abdullah reacted to everything with a stoic calm, and before we reached Cairo no one could tell by looking at my three Buduma companions that they had made the leap into the atomic age in less than a week. That was all the time it took. But both their teeth and their eyes glowed in the reflection of the moon when at night we arrived at our camp by the pyramid of Cheops. I had chosen this site in order to build the papyrus ship in accordance with the old Egyptian illustrations. They stared stiffly at the pyramid.

'Who lives there?' Abdullah asked, noticing the difference in dimension to the tents where we were going to live.

'No one,' I explained. 'It's a grave.'

'How many are buried there?'

'Just one.'

That was too much for Abdullah. 'Those Egyptians,' he said with disbelief. His scepticism did not change when he learned that the Egyptians had built it more than 3,500 years before the birth of Mohammed.

According to the Koran, as a Muslim, Abdullah could have four wives. Financial responsibility for the beautiful Buduma woman he left by Lake Chad fell on me. But not many days had gone by at our camp in Egypt before Abdullah invited all of us to Cairo to an Arabian wedding with belly dancing and all sorts of wind and string instruments. I was entrusted with the task of stuffing banknotes down between the bride's breasts, and now, even before our arrival at the launch site in Morocco, I was having to provide for two of Abdullah's women in different parts of Africa. He was already heading rapidly towards his third marriage with a veiled Berber woman in the port city of Safi when we managed to get him on board the reed ship and postpone the wedding until the voyage was over.

This was in the spring of 1969, the year American astronauts were making the final preparations for the first journey to the moon. NASA had offered to install some equipment on our reed ship so that we could talk directly to the astronauts when they landed up there while our journey was still underway down here. To experiment with a papyrus ship named after the sun god Ra, and launch it bristling with antennae in order to talk to people on the moon, seemed too much of a parody, so I declined regretfully but firmly. To my great consternation, the day before we were scheduled to leave, a representative from NASA appeared on the pier in Safi with a box of moon equipment. My refusal had not been taken seriously. I remained firm, and we left the friendly man standing on the pier with his box. He would be flying home across the Atlantic while we started our journey over the same ocean in our reed ship.

On board, Abdullah proved to be an intelligent man, and he had a quicker mind than most. We had barely left Safi before he learned how to use the compass so that he could pray facing towards Mecca. Wind and currents gave us the same steady course westward that Columbus had followed, so Mecca remained more or less in the same direction. On the other hand, an unexpected problem arose at sunrise the first morning out at sea. Abdullah reported that someone had spilt salt in the water. He leant overboard and, according to procedure, washed his face and arms up to his elbows in honour of Allah. Then we heard a scream. Not only was the water salty, it was dirty as well! Black clots were floating on a thin layer of oil on the surface, more visible in the water than on Abdullah's black face. Abdullah's religious cleansing ceremonies required clean water. Owing to our respect for Allah, the problem was first solved by giving Abdullah a small extra portion of drinking water from our clay mugs. In extreme conditions, the Koran permits a traveller to clean himself with sand, but the Sahara was already far behind us and quickly disappearing from our sight.

We assured Abdullah that we would soon be sailing in the same crystal-clear water I had seen from *Kon-Tiki* twelve years before. At that time we had crossed eight thousand kilometres of the Pacific Ocean without noticing a single lump of oil or any sign that there were people on this planet other than the six of us.

It was Abdullah who first alerted us to the fact that the ocean was in the process of being polluted! And there is only one ocean, because the Atlantic Ocean is connected to all the others. The continents lie like islands in one interconnected world ocean. Day after day Abdullah and the rest of us scooped up lumps of oil, some as small as a grain of rice, others as large as potatoes and oranges, often overgrown with barnacles or carrying tiny crab-passengers. Having looked forward to showing my new friends the wonderful crystal-clear ocean world we had grown to know intimately from the balsa raft, I became so alarmed that I sent the first report about the mounting pollution of the world ocean to the United Nations Secretary-General, U-Thant. He had allowed us to sail under the UN flag because we wanted to represent a microcosm of some of what the UN stood for. One world in one ocean.

Abdullah had no other complaints during his first encounter with the ocean. On the contrary he cheered knowingly when he caught sight of the first whale, shouting: 'Hippopotamus to port!'

We did not complete the crossing in our first papyrus boat. We were quite simply amateurs. In the twentieth century the world's leading experts were the scientists in Cairo, who had shown us the ancient Egyptian illustrations and wall paintings of reed ships with detailed rigs, and the Buduma from Lake Chad, who carried on the ancient tradition of papyrus boat-building, but who had never constructed them to resist ocean waves.

None of them understood why the pharaohs had sickle-shaped ships, often with a tall, inward-curving stern. Everyone was convinced that the elegant curl on the stern was there for aesthetic reasons, and since it was structurally independent, the boat builders from Chad removed an important rope, which had been strung like a bowstring down to the deck. Little did we know that this would be the Achilles heel of the reed ship *Ra*. The ship lost its elasticity and could not ride the ocean waves, and the reed bundles began to disintegrate. When we approached Barbados, it was no longer possible to hold the papyrus bundles together.

Exactly one year after *Ra* was launched in Safi, the construction of *Ra II* was completed. We were ready for another go at the Atlantic.

Everyone who had been on the first *Ra* voyage volunteered again: Abdullah from Chad, Norman from the United States, Yuri from the Soviet Union, Carlo from Italy, George from Egypt, Santiago from Mexico and myself from Norway. But this time I had increased the number to eight by squeezing Kei from Japan into the small bamboo hut on the reed deck.

Abdullah had waited at his bride's home in Egypt during that year. Now he was set on marrying the Berber woman who he had left at the dockside the last time. Then, out of the blue, a telegram arrived from the Norwegian embassy in Cairo: Abdullah had become a father. A son! Allah had granted him a gift that no new trip to America could match. Abdullah was back in Cairo faster than an American rocket could reach the moon. When we stood on the reed deck and waved farewell to him, a new crew member was with us waving to the crowd of people on the pier, a Berber from the

Atlas Mountains. The day before, this soon-to-be seafarer had been a porter at our hotel in Safi. He had never seen the ocean before he came down from the Atlas Mountains, but he too was a Muslim, almost the same colour as Abdullah, blackened from the desert winds and the high mountain sun.

Madami could read, and in his sack were his swimming trunks, his bathing mat and the Koran in Arabic. Abdullah had been the first to cry out about the pollution in the ocean, and now Madami was given the task of keeping daily records of the pollution, scooping up the oil lumps we passed with a net. Once again we were sailing under the UN flag, and this time the Secretary-General had asked us for a pollution report as well as samples of the black lumps. We collected large and small lumps of oil for forty-three of the fifty-seven days of our journey across the Atlantic. This time we made it all the way to Barbados. U-Thant enclosed our report as 'Appendix A' in his *Report on the State of the Oceans* at the first UN Environmental Conference in Stockholm that same year, 1970.

I got along well with Neil Armstrong, without the NASA antennae, when we later met to confirm, before a World Wildlife Fund congress in London, that man lives on a very small planet that can easily be destroyed. There is so little land and so much ocean on earth that Neil said that it looked like a small blue planet from the moon. And the world ocean is in itself so small that you can drift across it on a reed boat without a motor in a matter of a few weeks. Just a little faster than the lumps of oil.

3

Out of My Depth

Still drowsy with sleep, I woke up on the roof of the hotel and looked out over the desert. Jacqueline was reprimanding me for having dozed off in the sun.

'Remember the hole in the ozone layer,' she said. 'It's not like when you were a boy.'

When we went on to lunch, I told her how once in my youth I had made a futuristic caricature of what bathing would be like when people had destroyed the thin atmosphere of the planet. There were no 'green' conservationists, but scientists had pointed out something that made me think that the human battle against nature could ruin the perfect balance in the composition of the air, a balance that ocean plankton and virgin forests had created before the birth of humans.

'How on earth could you be thinking about that rather than the team who might win the Norwegian soccer championship?'

Jacqueline asked. During the five years she had known me she had come to think of me as relatively normal.

How had I started thinking along those lines? Not an easy question. When we returned to the roof, we moved our chairs so that our heads would be in the shade and Jacqueline fell asleep before she got an answer.

I was so rested that I had no need for my usual ten-minute afternoon siesta. Instead I lay wide awake and watched the birds circling beneath the blue mantle of sky, reminding me of my boyhood days, when the world was eternal and without limitations. We had plenty of time then. No one was in a hurry, except myself perhaps, when I was late for school. And I almost had to run to keep up with my father on the rare occasions I was allowed to go along with him to his office at the brewery. Swinging his cane, he walked briskly to get exercise and appear fit to those he met and to whom he tipped his hat in passing. Not because he was in a hurry.

Pollution? Not in the small town of Larvik. Its white wooden houses were built on steep slopes, and clean air blew in from the backdrop of forest. Thousands of Larvik's windows looked over the fjord, which in turn opened to the great ocean. The town thrived, from the harvest of the sea and the forest, including extensive shipping across all the oceans beyond the horizon and whaling in Antarctica. Norway's only beech forest lay behind the town, and endless pine forests stretched along the Farris Lake and far into the inland mountains of Norway. The only industries were Treschow's large pulp mill, Alfred Andersen's shipyard and the brewery, emitting its pleasant smells, near the town square. The streets of the town were swept clean with brooms, and a sooty, black chimney sweep kept the chimneys clean. In my earliest childhood the streets had to be swept clean of horse manure. Discarded orange peel, a piece of paper or a rusty tin can thrown by the side of the trails in the woods caused annoyance. We could drink from any running stream.

These were ideal surroundings for children. Almost everyone had back gardens to play in, and there were orchards with wooden fences to climb and, where the town's cobblestone streets ended, unlimited playgrounds in the woods and on the beaches.

My parents had moved there from what they considered to be Norway's major cities; my father from the capital, Oslo, which was then still called Kristiania, and my mother from Trondheim. They must have caused quite a few small-town eyebrows to be raised at a time when divorce was seen as exclusive to the theatrical world. My liberal-thinking mother had already been through two divorces when my conservative father divorced his first wife to marry her.

A competent businessman, my father had started his own brewery. When he began to bottle the local mineral water he received King Haakon's permission to name the spring water after him. Later he went into business with a colleague and they ran what became the town's only brewery. The other one was abandoned and became an exciting playground for us boys, with its large darkened halls, vaulted cellars, empty stables and huge yard behind tall wooden fences. The property reached right up to our own back garden.

It was here that I discovered myself as an individual, separate from my mother's warm body. It was an autumn night at the outbreak of the First World War. I believe I even recall the wail of the autumn storms, accompanied by whip-like cracks from the flagpole lanyards in the garden. I was afraid of the dark and quite cowardly as a boy.

You, who were so overprotected?

Perhaps for that very reason. I had old parents. They were so afraid of something happening to their only child that I was given the impression that everything was dangerous. Other children in the neighbourhood were allowed to go to the docks alone and to play outside after dark, but not me. Other boys were allowed to use an axe to make a bat or a sharp knife to make a bow and arrow, but not me.

If there was any point on which my parents were united – apart from producing and spoiling me – it was in a belief in progress, my father because both his own father and his uncle had been pioneers in bringing electricity and farming machinery to the country, and my mother because she was a Darwinist and believed that all progress led in the direction of something even better. In his family album, my father had shown me that his ancestors came from the large forests bordering Sweden, and that the family could be traced back twelve generations, landowners all, until his father and uncle moved to the capital and established Heyerdahl & Co. They set up the first telephone system in the country between their office and warehouse. My father had saved a newspaper clipping from Oslo from 1880, describing the first time an electric light bulb was demonstrated to the city's inhabitants: 'And from as far up Karl Johan's Gate as could be seen from the fire house, the light glowed like a shining star, in contrast to the gas lamps that shone with a red glow, like an oil lamp compared to a gas flame.'

Two years later they crowned their work when my grandfather, a major in the civilian national guard, led a royal procession up to the palace, while his brothers lit two light bulbs in front of the building. The newspaper *Aftenposten* wrote: 'The facade of the palace emerged from the dark as if by a stroke of magic, and shone in a bright light as if the rays of the sun had fallen upon it. The audience greeted this sudden and unexpected revelation from the world of light with shouts of appreciation.'

And then you turn up two generations later, without matches, in an attempt to return to nature?

I've probably inherited something from my mother as well. Her family's leanings followed a different path, away from city life. Her oldest brother studied theology and wanted to be a country parson. He was very absent-minded. This was during Norway's union with Sweden, and during his first sermon he said, 'Our Father, who art in Sweden . . .' A statement like that did not sit very well with Norwegian farmers at the time, and his father called him back to the city. Two of my mother's other brothers studied philosophy in Germany. When they returned to Norway, much influenced by the writings of Rousseau, they each bought land and built farmhouses in the outback, under the Sylene Mountains. One gave up, but not the other. Mother told me that she received letters from him describing how he was sitting on top of a manure wagon reading Schopenhauer. His children built a road into Tydalen, in order that cars and civilisation might reach their remote valley.

At an early age I began wondering whether the word 'progress' was leading us astray. It was first used to designate something that moved forward toward something better, but the word had barely passed the lips of our forefathers before it grew out of hand, encompassing everything that implied taking a few more steps away from nature. We have reached the point at which we forget our indebtedness to nature, which brought us into this world. We are part of nature, we have it in us and around us, whether we believe that we are created in it or developed by it.

It is not easy to explain why, at such an early stage, I began to suspect that we had to be careful not to damage ourselves by damaging nature. It may be that ever since childhood I had seen the world around me as being something unstable, constantly changing. My mother always spoke about Darwin, about evolution from animals to humans. To me nothing was immutable.

My mother had problems with Jesus after her own mother died while she was still a little girl; her mother had been sickly and spoke incessantly about how she longed to return to Jesus. As a young girl my mother had been sent to England to be educated, and she returned influenced by the teachings of Darwin: everything, including human beings, was constantly becoming better and smarter. My father was not a liberal thinker like my mother. He had been sent to Germany to study brewing and returned with Martin Luther's belief that Our Lord had created the world and that it was impossible for human beings to improve on it. He enjoyed life for what it was and spent no time speculating unnecessarily on problems that could not be solved. He never used words like 'God' and 'Jesus' but directed his Lord's Prayer to the proper address in heaven and seemed to be on good terms with both of them.

'We're making progress,' my mother said, pointing to the vacuum cleaner and the electric stove. To her generation it was still a miracle that someone could boil water for tea without flames from wood or gas but just by way of a few wires. My father was not as convinced that mankind was improving. Newspapers described inventions of new lethal weapons, political unrest and rearmament in many countries, despite the fact that a horrific world war, with mustard gas and explosives in the trenches and mines and submarines in the ocean, had barely come to an end. Norway had been neutral, but many innocent Norwegian sailors had gone down with their ships. The ocean had become a graveyard and appeared to me as something sinister.

One of my first memories is of being outdoors and crawling

up an old, worn stone step on a small hill. It was my first personal experience of something that I would always remember. I had ventured away from my blanket and my nanny, and tried to climb up a step so high that I chose to crawl around it. And there, in the grass, I discovered small ants that were striving just as much as I was. One of them tried to climb up a straw. Even smaller bugs moved like red dots on a leaf, causing a green caterpillar to metamorphose into a huge dragon standing erect on its tail and swaying in all its length to view the landscape. And then suddenly Laura was there lifting me up and away from my newly discovered world.

I was a little older when I was led past a small mound of golden sea sand. I tore away from the hand that was leading me in order to dig my fingers into the fine, loose sand and discovered that, when I was close, the mound disappeared and I was staring into a wonderful world of tiny toys. They were so small that the grown-ups couldn't see them, and my fingers were much too large to grab hold of them. Some looked like dolls' dishes, some like trumpets or other amusing things, and others had shapes like real seashells and snail shells, only much, much smaller. I cried in frustration when I was pulled back. How could I explain my discovery to the grown-ups who were so large that they failed to see the small fantastic things that lay hidden in a plain old mound of sand? For the first time in my life I realised that there were things in this world that neither the largest nor those who knew the most could see.

But then I came to experience the world below the surface of the water. I was five years old, and discovered nothing that made the visit worthwhile. I was not even wearing a swimming suit. It was in the middle of winter and my mother had dressed me in warm winter clothing with heavy boots and a cap pulled down over my ears. I was standing on thick ice, so

thick that my father had assured my mother that it would
support elephants. In fact it supported the weight of a huge
brewery horse and sled standing next to me. Two men in
winter clothing were working at the edge of the white ice,
drawing a huge saw up and down into the black open water,
sawing large blocks of glassy ice and loading them onto a sled.

My father had bought this pond, which lay within the
town's boundaries. During the long Danish occupation of
Norway it had belonged to Count Gyldenløve's estate. Now
the manor had become a town museum and my mother was
the chairwoman of the museum society, but father was more
interested in the pond that provided the brewery with ice.

I was waiting for the grown-ups to drive away. Boys, big
and small, hung with their noses over the wire fence, waiting
for the same thing. The two men with the saw were workers
from the brewery and would be driving the load to the ice
house. All year round blocks of ice were delivered to cus-
tomers along with beer and soda from the factory. There were
no freezers or electric refrigerators then, but those who had
iceboxes had a huge block of ice delivered every week from an
enormous warehouse at the brewery. The ice was stored there
under a thick layer of sawdust.

The two men drove off, the sleigh bells jingling through
town, and when we could no longer hear them I ran to the gate
with the key.

The next thing I remember was watching some of the boys
in wonder. The eldest of them ran, and, one after the other,
jumped from the edge of the ice on to a floating ice floe. In the
same leap they were back on solid ice. They were so nimble
that they landed before the floe tipped over.

This looked like fun. I wanted to show what I was good for.
I got ready, ran and jumped onto the ice floe, but I was too
slow to turn around before it tipped over and my foothold

turned upside-down. With this, I fell into a totally hostile world.

I struggled madly to get back up to the others, but the hole I had fallen through had disappeared. I bumped my head and nose against a solid dark ceiling where I thought the black opening had been. I wasn't aware that while a hole in the ice is dark and the ice is bright when seen from above, everything is reversed when you are beneath it. From this vantage point, the opening in the ice lets in light while the layer of ice is dark. I became totally confused and disoriented, and that is all I remember from my swim. One of the boys must have grabbed hold of a wriggling boot and pulled me up by my feet. I awoke to the sound of my own screaming as I heard someone suggest that I was dead. I was so scared that I managed to convince the others that they were mistaken. Freezing and soaking wet both inside and out, I ran straight home to a warm bed and motherly care. That convinced me that I had indeed survived.

I didn't however feel completely safe until my father returned from the office and asked me to sit up in bed and say the Lord's Prayer. This was a secret between us and it provided a pleasant feeling of calm and warmth. My mother never joined us in prayer. Sometimes when we heard footsteps at the bottom of the stairs, I lay down quickly and my father quietly left the bedroom. Once they met just outside my door and I heard my mother say with a friendly, reproachful voice, 'What is it you're teaching the boy?'

My father never took me to church. He never went himself. He was not that kind of a Christian. His faith was not to be shared with strangers, just with me. For the two of us, faith and morality were a matter between ourselves and the Lord. Father may well have made a special deal with God: if he behaved perfectly in all other respects, he would be permitted to appreciate beautiful women.

Being an atheist, mother believed in Darwin rather than in Jesus, but she adhered strictly to Christian morals. When she returned from England as a young woman, wearing modern silk underwear and carrying a deck of cards in her suitcase, her Lutheran aunts threw the underwear and the cards into the stove. Mentioning the word 'underwear' was not allowed; the term was 'unmentionables'.

How could two such different people stay together?

They probably did it for my sake. But I never heard them argue. I tried to listen through the floorboards in our old wooden house after they had said goodnight and gone downstairs, but all I heard was the old gramophone playing classical music.

After my adventure under the ice, I thought a great deal about life and death. I was more interested in animals and plants than in who had created them, and collected everything that moved. I guess I never doubted that there was something beyond the visible world, and on this point I was on the same wavelength as my father. However, I was more involved in what I could actually see on earth than in the invisible angels of an abstract world beyond the skies that the minister referred to in our religion classes, usually without much conviction.

Laura, my slender nanny, had pictures of chubby little angels framed in glass over her bed, and the plump cook, Helga, sang about angels when she and her girlfriends met for coffee and played string instruments in her room. Once, when quite a young boy, I crept out of bed and peeped through a keyhole. I got quite a shock. I saw the sizeable Helga trying to lower herself into our bathtub one evening when my parents were out at a party. I stormed back to bed in horror and pulled the quilt over my head. I had never even seen my mother in her underwear, and now I had had a revelation. It was unbearably exciting and educational, but for the life of me

I didn't dare take another look. She was just as naked as the angels, but had difficulty pressing her body into the tub. What would happen when she, with her beautiful voice, went to heaven and flew around with wings?

Helga cannot be said to have aroused my interest in the opposite sex, but the water that cascaded on to the bathroom floor stimulated a new version of my daydreams. They were a constant part of my private world when I was left alone in my room at night. If it was summer, I tiptoed silently out of bed and climbed up to the large open window with its view of the Larvik Fjord. We lived on a steep hill, on the side facing the sea; three storeys up I could look over the red-tiled rooftops all the way down to the long jetty and beyond that to the open sea. The voyage continued from there when I was back in bed. If I was lucky, I went on dreaming about native peoples and strange animals in Africa. But now it was winter and too cold to crawl out of bed; my mother always insisted that I sleep with the window open in all kinds of weather. On these nights I pictured myself in the bathroom, without Helga, opening both taps until the water cascaded on to the floor and into the bedroom. It would take the bed with me in it down the hill and out on to the fjord, on and on until we reached a land of palm trees, and playmates who seemed much more exciting than those in the neighbourhood.

In another version, I didn't have to travel at all. I just built a huge glass dome over the old abandoned brewery, turning it into a hothouse, where I could plant tropical vegetation and invite Indian, African and Arab children, two by two, just like Noah in his Ark. And the animals, of course.

A boy pretty much removed from reality?

It was during puberty that I grew shy. I didn't know my classmates at my new school. In our neighbourhood most children left school after the first seven years. Until then I had been the centre of attention in the gang on our hill. I had the key to the pond, unlimited amounts of orange and cherry pop in the icebox, and everyone thought it was fun to go on my expeditions into the forest.

I was probably inspired by my mother's books about great explorations, wild animals and foreign peoples: maybe foreign peoples most of all. You couldn't find any of them in the vicinity of Larvik in those days. I remember a circus arriving in town and everyone running to see a live, black man. The disappointment was great when one of the boys discovered that the palms of his hands were white. We agreed that he was just a fake.

There was a lot of wildlife in the forests surrounding the town; pine forest mixed with all sorts of deciduous forest to the east, and a beech forest along Lake Farris to the west. We put away our pop-guns and bows and arrows and went on expeditions with buckets and nets to capture wild animals. At that time, with the exception of great mammals, no species were threatened. There were no toxic pesticides, and pollution did not exist in our part of the world. There were fish in all our streams.

We caught tadpoles in small lakes and ponds, colourful salamanders and big black water beetles. In the forest we caught hedgehogs, mice, beetles, grasshoppers and snakes. In the air we caught everything from bats to butterflies. And if there were enough eggs in a bird's nest to permit the taking of one, it too would be added to the collection. My father had given me my own newly panelled room in the old brewery stable, and we hung a sign on the door: *Zoological Museum.*

In everyday life I was definitely a coward, but when it came to procuring new species for the collection, I was altogether a different person. My mother almost fainted once when I arrived home with a gaggle of boys at my heels. When I rang the doorbell and she opened the door, I presented her with a live viper, held by the tip of its tail on an outstretched arm. It writhed in evil coils, trying to bite me, but every time it appeared to be succeeding I shook it vigorously. My mother ran to get a glass jar filled with alcohol, and the hissing viper was dropped in, head first. Then it relaxed and fell asleep in a coil at the bottom, looking like a precious treasure. I had managed to capture it with a Y-shaped stick pinched over its neck, and without smashing its head.

You, the shyest and quietest boy in class?

At least that's what Arnold Jacoby wrote. He was my best friend at the new school. Without him I would have risked being dismissed as a nerd. At least that is how I picture myself in retrospect. I had no interest in sport, like the others in my class, I was the last one to be chosen for football teams, and I disliked jumping on the springboard in the gym. I preferred poring over small insects, pinned on needles and framed in glass.

My father despaired. He couldn't even get me to try swimming, certainly not beyond a spot where I could touch the bottom with my feet. As a last resort he tried to trick me. He hired a beautiful young lady who arrived carrying a long pole with a rope coil attached. I was meant to hang in it and swim like a frog in deep water outside the dock. My disgrace has never been greater than when I bid him a curt goodbye and left him to swim with the young lady. I couldn't take one more humiliation like that.

By this time I had school friends who were crazy about sport and who knew to the second how fast Nurmi ran a 1,500-metre race, and to the centimetre how far Rustadstuen had jumped in the Holmenkollen ski jump. When they started cross-country running in the nearby forest, I joined in, in spite of always finishing last. If I saw something beautiful in the woods, I would stop to examine it. Once, however, when three sweet young girls came to watch the start of a race, I thought about the lady with the fishing pole and ran so fast that I passed everyone and crossed the finishing line first.

That I would one day be surrounded by forty thousand sports fans, welcoming everyone to the Winter Olympics in my home country, in the company of a movie star, was as inconceivable to me as the possibility of meeting someone who had just been walking on the moon.

My running in the woods gave my father new hope, in spite of the fact that he never managed to lure me into deep water. He noticed that I devoured books about Tarzan, the king of the jungle, and had a bright idea. He had the carpenters at the brewery raise up two very high masts in the backyard, and connected them with a cross beam at the top. We fastened a thick climbing rope and two gymnastic rings to the beam, and I was able to play Tarzan and swing high over the ground in the jungle creepers. I used the rope and rings every afternoon, and became so strong in both arms that I could let go with one arm and hang by one finger with the other, my elbow at right angles.

But in the gym I was as hopeless as ever and never managed to jump the wooden horse. My interest in football declined even further when my father bribed me into attending the Norwegian championship finals. I was promised a new fishing rod if Larvik Turn won. They lost.

Running in the forest, climbing the rope and camping outdoors with a tent and a sleeping bag restored some of the fitness my mother had worked into me during the first years of my life. She was a fanatic when it came to a healthy diet and fresh air. The maid had to be taught how to milk the two goats that we kept in the backyard, so that I could be fattened up on goat's milk. I had to go out in the fresh air and play alone, even when it was raining. I was not allowed to descend the stairs in the mornings before I could prove that my digestion was in order, which was so embarrassing that once I put a scarf and a hat in the potty, emptied it into the water closet, and pulled the chain.

A lasting memory from that time was my family's reaction when the post office at the bottom of the hill caught fire. The whole town consisted of white wooden houses, and half of Larvik had once burned to the ground before I was born. This fire started at night while we were sleeping and the flames soared above the fjord. A rain of sparks reached all the way up to us. My father declared that if the fire spread we should seek refuge under the old brewery's cellar vault. At this my mother ordered me to the potty so that I wouldn't need to go if we were locked underground. Fortunately the fire engines arrived, bells clanging and horses snorting, before I had finished, and I survived childhood without the fear of fires.

On the other hand, my life almost came to an end for the second time under water.

Beyond the cemetery there was a deep and wide crevice in the hillside that separated an island cliff and its bath houses from the mainland. There was a constant undertow here from the Larvik Fjord that flowed into the crevice and pulled away with the rhythmic waves of the ocean. The son of the janitor at the brewery had drowned here. There were also some horrible rumours about an unmarried woman who had thrown her stillborn baby into the crevice. The bath houses were empty in the autumn, and a small wooden bridge without a railing tempted me to follow a group of boys out to play catch on the island. Proud of my ability to run, I attempted to escape a pursuer by jumping diagonally on to the wooden bridge, but I lost my footing and tumbled into the deep crevice. Not even a good swimmer could climb up the steep walls, which were slippery with seaweed. I twisted with the undertow and flailed wildly and helplessly with my arms and legs in cascading masses of water, and can only remember that I sank deep down into the water twice – and then the world was gone. An insignificant little boy, nicknamed 'the American', sped over to the bath houses and grabbed a life-saving ring with a rope and threw it into the witches' brew. How I grabbed hold of the ring is a mystery, but it was the boys' joint effort that dragged me up. My father saw to it that the insecure 'American' became the class hero, because from then on he always showed up at school with a silver knife in his belt.

After this no one could convince me that I too could float, merely by rhythmically moving my arms and legs. I had tried, but never would again. My father had to accept that I was growing up with a dread of water – until he shook my hand, many years later, after the *Kon-Tiki* expedition. By then I had learned to swim.

4

Head Above Water

Reminiscing about the world of my childhood was abruptly cut short in a flash of blinding sunlight.

'Last day; time to pack up. The plane leaves today.'

I woke up and my *aku-aku* fell asleep as Jacqueline stirred in the chair next to me.

Goodbye for now, I whispered to myself. No more silence and laziness. I pictured the waiting piles of unsorted mail. Yards and yards of unanswered faxes covering the floor of my new home in the Canary Islands. But I was well prepared. I had found ideal working conditions far away from the tourists on an old, secluded and abandoned property. On the property were large trees and the remains of the *finca*'s avocado plantation. It was uncultivated. Its buildings were protected thanks to their old age and thanks to a celebrated local poet who had once lived here in seclusion behind huge trees and high walls.

I still had to get up at six o'clock in the morning to

squeeze enough hours into the day. This was an abrupt transition for Jacqueline, who changed her breakfast routine by
six hours for the sake of her husband. In return, she was
given the sunrise over the ocean as a symbolic wedding gift.
During her years in front of the cameras in Hollywood, she
may never have seen a sunrise. Now, with her strong interest
in painting and archaeology, she could sit by the window
and watch the sun – the first creative artist – ignite the daylight, brush the ocean, the sky and the tall mountains behind
us with a harmonious array of colours, ever changing, playing silent music. If she hadn't been standing by my side, the
aku-aku would probably have made his presence known. It
may have been there, quiet as a mouse, just as enraptured as
we were.

On other parts of the island, whole towns of skyscrapers
had been built for the enjoyment of modern sun-worshippers
who paid a lot of money to spend a few days under a clear,
blue sky. However, it was the ancient sun-worshippers who
had brought Jacqueline and me to this island and this valley,
and it was the pure and uncorrupted symbol of their god that
passed over our heads on its daily journey westward from
Africa to the jungles of America.

Further down the valley were step pyramids that had been
there since time immemorial. They had been there for so long
that no one knew who had built them. Old people had heard
from their grandparents that they had always existed. Younger
newcomers to the island were uninterested and simply thought
they were beautiful but meaningless stone piles, left behind by
the first Spanish conquistadors who had cleared the fields.
Until now the local population had respectfully protected the
whole pyramid area, and the town had developed around the
old, mysterious structures. Tight rows of houses formed a
protective screen from the streets that were built around the

area. Schoolchildren had worn paths and shortcuts across the site without moving one single stone from the perfectly constructed pyramid walls. Consciously or subconsciously, the walls were respectfully preserved, and the only people who had paid them any special attention were groups of individuals with esoteric interests who came here in order to meditate on Atlantis or visitors from other planets. The city council had now arbitrarily decided to open the area to new development, and to allow streets to criss-cross the site, putting an end to both superstition and science.

I managed to save the pyramids in the nick of time. A white patch on the municipal map of Guimar bore the inscription *Las Piramides de Chacona*. These pyramids – no one knew who had built them – were not protected by any act of conservation. There is no provision covering pyramids in the Atlantic. The only conserved item was the wall of an old Spanish building perched on the highest point amid the pyramids. Its many small rooms suggested that it had been a monastery, and it had been preserved as a national heritage, just like the house I had bought.

By sheer chance I was the person who got to know about these pyramids – the sort of coincidence that made me feel like a puppet suspended on a string, gravitating from one island to another in order to 'discover' things known to the local population.

One never discovers anything which has always been there, staring one in the face, ever since birth. It was a Norwegian tourist by the name of Sørvik who decided to send me a cutting from a local paper with a picture of one of the pyramids. The text suggested that it must have been the work of supernatural beings, but the picture revealed that in this case ordinary mortals had been at work – people who had reached the Canaries across the sea and who were familiar with the stepped pyramids built on both sides of the Atlantic in the dawn of world history.

Personally I had twice visited the Canaries in the hope of learning something of its aboriginal population, the people who welcomed the Portuguese and the Spaniards when they arrived. Among the Guanchos in Tenerife there were a great many who resembled the people of Northern Europe – tall, blond and with fair skins; but this was also the appearance of many of the Berbers of North Africa, as well as the legendary seafarers who, according to the Aztecs and the Incas, had introduced the civilisation of their ancestors and taught them to build pyramids. Precisely for this reason I had visited these islands a good deal earlier; I was keen to know more about these seafarers who resembled us Europeans, but sailed across the Atlantic with women and goats and dogs on board, long before the time of Columbus and Leiv Eiriksson. In addition they were familiar with the art of mummification and the trepanning of skulls just as in ancient Egypt.

I was still excavating the extensive pyramid site at Túcume on the coast of Peru, but was on a short visit to Oslo when I received the cutting with the picture of the pyramid. The only person of my acquaintance who knew the Canaries like the palm of his own hand, was my friend Fred Olsen. He had inherited a shipping company and landed property on these islands from his father Thomas, who had sheltered Liv and our boys, just outside New York, during the Second World War, while I was involved in the war in Northern Europe.

Fred had never heard of the pyramids in Tenerife, but happened to be living on the neighbouring island of Gomera, where Columbus set off on his first voyage to America. His daughter Kristine was an outstanding photographer, and together with her mother Kristin, she took the ferry to Tenerife. On this island, where some four million palefaces are annually welcomed to bask in the sun, white and bearded Guanchos resisted European conquerors during Columbus' first voyage, the same conquerors who were welcomed by the beardless Indians, on the other side of the ocean, as gods returning to their original home.

It required a certain amount of courage for two Nordic women to land in Tenerife, among crowds of tourists, and make enquiries about pyramids. But they found their way to the town of Guimar, situated just off the beaten track – without any tourists or a single hotel, and with the pyramids nestling in the middle.

As soon as I received a batch of photographs from Kristine, I boarded the first plane. When I set eyes on the well-preserved terraced pyramids, I was filled with a feeling of awe at the thought that I was face to face with the distant past – just as in Peru three years previously, when I was shown the much larger but equally uninvestigated and forgotten pyramids. The local population was equally disinterested in both places.

'But don't you have pyramids in Norway?' they asked me in Peru.

'They can't possibly be pyramids; they've always been there', I was assured in Tenerife.

That evening I left my guides and made my way back to the pyramids on my own. There I was, a solitary figure between the old walls, and convinced of what I knew, despite the fact that I was in a tourist resort and fully awake.

I gave a start as a fair-haired chap appeared immediately behind me on the temple platform.

'Are you Thor Heyerdahl?' he asked.

'Yes, and who are you?' I asked him.

'I am a Guancho,' he replied calmly.

'They all say that there is no Guancho blood left on the island,' I ventured.

'I am a Guancho on my father's side and also on my mother's side.'

'If you are a Guancho perhaps you could tell me what this is,' I said, pointing at the largest pyramid.

'People say it's a rock clearance site.'

'Do you believe that?'

A smile creased the face of my tall friend. 'They may as well believe it.'

At a house further up the Guimar Valley I was introduced to my friend's mother and siblings. Carlos Campos had been a policeman in the town of Guimar. And his entire family were just as blond and blue-eyed as he was. They maintained that on the slopes of the mountain on this side of Guimar practically all the inhabitants had Guancho blood: it was here that the people had held out longest with their slings against the Spaniards with their muskets. During the Franco regime, insisting that one was a Guancho or knew a single word of the Guancho language was punishable by death. The accepted wisdom was that the primitive aboriginal population had been wiped out by the conquerors; but now the dictatorship was at an end, and Carlos and his likes were able to indulge in freedom of speech.

Before the town council managed to bring their bulldozers into play in the pyramid area, Fred, a man of action, and with the enthusiastic support of pyramid photographer Kristine, had bought up the whole of the extensive white patch on the municipal map. And before anyone realised what was going on, the Chacona pyramids had been fenced off, and plans were afoot to repair and furnish the protected Chacona house for an exhibition of pre-European cultural parallels on both sides of the Atlantic. Fred, who financed the project, was anxious that any revenue from future tourist visits should be devoted to scientific needs. I was to set up an international committee of archaeologists who would be responsible for running the exhibitions and allotting the funds. Kristine enlisted the services of my youngest daughter Bettina as manager of the practical work of getting the project off the ground, whilst I would now start to oscillate between the pyramids in Peru and those in the Canaries. My other daughter, Marian, who was a potter, was assigned the task of making reproductions of parallel items from both sides of the Atlantic. In this way FERCO, the Foundation for Exploration and Research on Cultural Origins, was set up.

It was on top of the largest of these step pyramids that I met Jacqueline for the first time. A newspaper article reported that I had come to the island in an attempt to save the pyramids, and that I claimed they were similar to the ones in Mexico and Peru. Jacqueline's curiosity was aroused, and she came over from the other side of the island to take a look. This meeting marked an abrupt turning point in our lives. The valley of the pyramids would come to be our home.

When Jacqueline halted my conversation with the *aku-aku* on the roof in El Aaiún, we were about to return to this valley. We had decided to risk everything to rescue the pyramid complex and the remains of the burnt out monastery-like building that could easily house a museum or special exhibits. We would also restore the old *finca* in the large garden and make it our home. Jacqueline introduced me to the responsible authorities, who have long since set the wheels in motion for the preservation of the pyramids and the designation of the whole area as a cultural park. 'Las Piramides de Chacona' was to become a centre of research, connected to the Internet and dedicated to the study of the origins of cultures and pre-European sea route communication.

*

The wedding trip to Western Sahara had only been meant as an outing, but it lasted for a week owing to the problem of getting a reservation. Now that we were finally on board, Jacqueline was sleeping and I was enjoying the sight of Africa's golden coastline and the Sahara desert gradually disappearing behind us as we flew out over the blue Atlantic. I was on the verge of dropping off myself when an invisible companion came to life.

Do you recognise this?

I looked out and saw only the blue Atlantic Ocean. We must have reached the halfway point between Africa and the Canary Islands. We had sailed over these depths with both *Ra* and *Ra II*, making the crossing between the mainland and the islands before reaching the open ocean. The vitality of the ocean was reduced to a motionless expanse of blue. We could not even see the white caps cresting the waves, breaking in the direction of the trade winds toward America. To get a proper impression of the planet, it should be seen at very close quarters or from the moon.

Do you believe in the lost city of Atlantis?

Just then the landing gear hit the runway and I forgot the whole question in the noise and commotion that followed. At home in the pyramid valley, a fax was waiting and the wheels were in full motion with the new project FERCO. I had so much else to think about that, even had my *aku-aku* tried to attract my attention, I didn't notice.

'You have to go to a barber,' said Jacqueline one day when I was preparing to shave in the old-fashioned way, shaving cream all over my face. My head has a modest amount of hair, but on my neck it grows incredibly fast. In the afternoon she drove me in to the island capital, where I reclined in the barber's deep chair and made myself comfortable. My companion was there at once.

You didn't answer my question. Are you afraid of science, or are you afraid of being labelled as one of those who seek out the pyramids to meditate on supernatural visitors from outer space or from the depths of the sea?

I am afraid of both. But mostly I am afraid of the kind of expert who tries to make people believe the pyramids are only heaps of stones. The other ones are not taken very seriously. Personally I believe that the pyramids were built by ordinary people who came from Africa with goats and seed aboard simple vessels, long before any Europeans. The legend about Atlantis should not be discarded by science or abused by New Age dreamers. It is far too easy to put on our reading glasses and believe that we can discover everything about the past by researching the printed material in our books, prepared to accept that the ancient authors were only trying to record myths and fantasy.

Like the legend about Noah and the Flood?

It was getting progressively more difficult. The barber wanted to know whether he should trim the hair in my nose, and the *aku-aku* wanted to call my attention to Noah and the Flood.

'Both in my ears and in my nose,' I answered. For believers and non-believers, the subject of the Flood and Atlantis was so delicate that it would have to wait until we had more time.

The next afternoon Jacqueline wondered why I didn't take my usual ten-minute siesta with her after lunch. Instead I stretched out with a notepad and a pencil in the garden hammock, well concealed behind the dense foliage of the avocado trees.

The *aku-aku* didn't wait for long.

How can it be that you, who were afraid of water in childhood, have, as a grown-up, taken to sea on antiquated craft that no one believed in?

I agreed that it didn't make much sense. What was it that had gradually given me self-confidence in my youth? I recalled how I spoke to myself then, such a long, long time ago.

As a young student, I had hiked with determination right into a snowstorm in the mountain wilderness. Alone with a husky, I kept going in defiance of the weather. Snow whipped against my face like sand, and I kept telling myself: This will make the boy a man!

I had grown tired of myself. Tired of being far too timid and shy. Awkward with girls and a loser in competitions and games. I wanted to find myself, force myself out of an inner hiding place. I consciously attempted to liberate myself from my inner bondage, and it actually felt as if the snowstorm were compelling this process.

After I was saved from drowning the second time, I developed the same feeling for deep water that I had for cemeteries and dentists. All my friends became expert swimmers and had fun in the Larvik Fjord all summer. Their parents had either a sailing boat or motor boat. Fortunately we did not, and I thanked providence for the fact that my parents were newcomers to Larvik and that they each had a cabin in the mountains. My father preferred his, located over the tree line at Ustaoset, where there was a railway station and a number of holiday cabins. It afforded a lot of fun. My mother's cabin in eastern Norway was just as far from the sea, far above the tree line between the Gudbrandsdalen and Østerdalen valleys. In those days there were no metalled roads to Hornsjø, but there was a hotel, a primitive one surrounded by a dozen low grass-roofed log cabins, which rarely had guests and was abandoned and half buried by snow in the winter. Half the log cabins were small summer farms that kept goats and produced cheese and were full of life in the summertime. The rest were occupied by city dwellers on their summer holidays. They kept to themselves, fished trout in the mountain lake from rowing boats, or went for walks in the mountain.

Hornsjø became my second home, the place where my mother gathered around her my adult step-siblings and her closest family members during holidays. It lacked the Gulf Stream's influence and warm swimming water of the Larvik Fjord. After brave dips in tarns, edged by mountain flowers and shrubs, everyone else came shooting out of the water just as fast as I did.

Perhaps subconsciously, it was my mother who steered me on to the track my father had tried to show me when he appeared with the woman with the fishing rod. I had gained a little strength in my arms from training with gymnastic rings and from rowing while trout-fishing in the mountain lake.

Then one summer something totally unexpected happened. Right out of the uninhabited, enchanted forest behind Lake Hornsjø, a lone man appeared. Dressed in an old-fashioned and threadbare hunting outfit, with a sack on his back, he knocked on the cabin door and offered us the largest mountain trout we'd ever seen. My mother suspected that this folk-tale figure might be hungry and invited him in for a meal. How this fellow could tell stories! He spun the most marvellous animal tales I'd ever heard or read, about animals that we only caught a glimpse of on a lucky day in the forest or on the mountain. Elk, wild reindeer, wolverine, marten, hare – even ermine, snow mice, lemming, wood grouse, cranes and everything else that plays and dances in the forest without letting the rest of us near them. They were all part of Ola Bjørneby's world. He lived with it all, night and day, and it showed itself in his happy state of mind and easy-going sense of humour.

He earned a few extra shillings by chopping wood for us. My mother didn't even protest when he showed me how to make my own bat. And then something incredible happened.

One day when he came up from the valley with a few supplies
for his home in the wilderness, in a small, deserted mountain
valley, I was allowed to go along to help him carry his parcels.
I was worn out when I returned at the agreed time, but I was
so infatuated with what I'd seen and experienced that one day
my mother, to my delight, let me go back to the Åsta valley
with Ola for a few days to help out. The valley was cut off
from the rest of the world. Only a small path led from Hornsjø
to some dilapidated and abandoned mountain farm buildings
that were called 'Hynna'.

A magical new world opened up as we jumped over the
stepping stones to cross the river where it ran into Lake
Hornsjø, and plunged into the pinewood forest that closed
around us all the way down to Ola's valley. He lived in a small
bothy that had once housed sheep. It had an earthen floor and
old log walls that were raised above the ground, leaving
enough space for sheep to crawl beneath them. He cooked his
food on an open hearth under a hole in the roof that let out
most of the smoke. The furniture was the same inside as it was
outside: large logs, stones and pine branches. The longest log
stretched all the way on to the hearth, and it grew progressively shorter day by day; all I had to do was chop kindling
wood.

In Ola's world, I realised for the first time how simple life
really is. People have made it more complicated because they
have grown accustomed to it. From the moment we learn to sit
and stand, we are taught that in order to sleep we need a bed
and in order to eat we need a chair and table. I discovered
after my first day in Ola's world that even without furniture I
was still alive.

Ola was a willing speaker, but he never talked about himself. In a roundabout way my mother discovered that he had
seen what might be called better days. He was the son of a

wealthy man from a family of landed gentry who had fallen on bad times. His father squandered the family fortune on drink. Refusing the humiliation of any form of charity, Ola took off into the mountains with his father's hunting and fishing equipment. When he stumbled on the hut at Hynna, he decided to stay.

Ola lived with one foot on either side of the law, by and large adhering to the area's fishing and hunting rules. He was a popular man, even among the hunting and fishing police, and the long arm of the law rarely reached into the Åsta valley. In this way, Ola Bjørneby usually managed to procure his daily ration of food, in peace and on his own terms, without having to rely on any assistance, like a Robinson Crusoe.

One time he appeared before the valley's storekeeper with such a large mountain trout that jealous souls sent the fish and game warden on a long trip to Lake Lyng, high up in the Østerdal Mountains. The guardian of the law had placed himself and his binoculars behind some rough shrubbery when Ola and I came trekking past in full view. We launched a small boat onto the lake, and Ola grabbed the oars so that I could try fishing with an otter-board, a device for keeping the mouth of a trawl net open, with a lot of fishing flies connected to it; when we rowed fast enough, the wood cut into the water and pulled the fishing line with the flies dangling side by side out into the lake. In this way we could catch a number of fish at the same time. The method was reserved for the local population, and strictly forbidden for city-dwellers or any other visitors.

Ola scouted eagle-eyed in all directions while he was rowing, and suddenly caught sight of the warden's binoculars in the distance. In an instant he let go of the oars and grabbed the otter-board, while I took over the rowing. It was perfectly legal for me to row, but although Ola could claim permanent residence in the community he would be arrested for allowing me to hold the otter. I braved it out, and rowed as if my life were at stake. 'No,' I answered every time Ola asked if I was getting tired. Finally I was so weary that I could only shake my head. That damned guy with the binoculars was able to take it easy! Blisters were forming and bursting on my palms, and I was becoming so intimate with the hard board I was sitting on that I had to make a cushion out of reindeer lichen and heather. As the hours went on I found I had less skin but more nerves to sit on. Not until evening approached and we rowed ashore did we see that the warden was preparing to leave. We were leaving Lake Lyng in opposite directions. The man of the law hurried to reach civilisation in Gudbrandsdalen before nightfall, while we tried to reach the cabin in Hynna.

We had won the battle of the lake, but it was far from being a triumphant march through the wilderness when I climbed out of the boat and started walking. My tender backside stung as if I were being whipped with every step, and with a small portion of Ola's fifty kilos of fish on my back I struggled to keep up. 'No problem, we'll sleep here and get up early tomorrow,' Ola said as he lay down on his back in the heather and fell asleep. We used to crawl beneath the branches of a pine tree when we slept out in the forest. Stars twinkling through the fringes of branches are so beautiful. There is still nothing like lying on your back beneath the open sky, seeing the entire star-studded universe above you every time you open your eyes. This time, however, I missed that view. I must have been lying on my stomach when I fell asleep on a huge stone slab.

My summer vacations with Ola taught me much that has become integral to my being. But maybe what I learned most was that I am part of nature, regardless of how I dress. Once you have experienced that, you will feel at home no matter how far you are from the nearest house, whether in a forest, on a mountain, in a desert or on an ocean. In the forest with Ola, we not only saw wildlife but also saw where the animals had been and what they had done. We saw where the elk bull had rooted with his antlers, an elk cow had passed with her calf, a hare torn a strip off some succulent bark, or a fox hunted a black-cock. There wasn't much left to find out about nature when I returned to school and the textbooks.

When autumn approached and the cloudberry bogs turned red, it was with a heavy heart that I left the mountain plains to start secondary school in Larvik.

I was now fifteen and although I had reached the age of confirmation, this ceremony was not for me. The others at school had been confirmed, but mostly because of the presents they would receive. I didn't like the minister, and I didn't want him to put his hand on my head.

When Arnold and I were philosophising, much of it was about the girls we liked best in the class and about the mystery of love. Nevertheless, no matter how interesting our female classmates were, they remained – in our inexperienced minds – totally unapproachable. At that time sexual education was unknown in schools, and almost unimaginable at home. Our knowledge was limited to what we had seen in the animal kingdom, and what the larger boys had scrawled on the walls of public toilets. I remember once when I was young and a slightly older boy had attempted to give me my first lesson in the hieroglyphics of sex. With a piece of chalk he drew a round circle on the wall, with a slit in the middle and rays around it, and then he asked, 'What is it?'

'A sun,' I answered innocently.

He sighed. 'It's something ugly,' he whispered in my ear.

'The devil?' I whispered carefully.

For my own part I was so naive when it came to this matter, that I looked upon girls and grown-up women as a different species from us regular people, as something so incredibly exciting that it was hard to find anything to say to them. One of my friends at school had arranged to meet a girl one evening. He carefully read the sports section in the local paper in order to have something to talk about.

Arnold and I were certain that love was something divine. It was at this time that my parents decided to separate. They were never divorced: my father simply sold his share of the brewery and all his other business interests and moved to an hotel in Oslo until my mother and I moved from Larvik to Oslo, when I entered university in 1933. I swore to myself that I'd never divorce the one I chose to be my bride.

And then you were divorced twice, but never confirmed?

I was divorced, but never separated from the belief in love. I was baptised when I was small, but I didn't want to state by being confirmed that I believed in the Larvik minister's vengeful doomsday god. Contrary to the minister, I believed that the god of love would be compassionate to that poor unwed mother who had thrown her stillborn child into the crevice at Kirkebukta, where I myself almost drowned, because she had not been allowed to bury it in consecrated soil.

Arnold and I often discussed religion and morals when we were out walking in the quiet, narrow streets of our little town, virtually empty at night, trying to figure out the mysteries of life. The church had lost its hold on young people, and was attended only during confirmation, after which the confirmees received gifts such as a watch, cufflinks or their first pair of long trousers. Arnold had been confirmed, like everyone else, and he was on good terms with the minister owing to his fine bass voice and his piano playing. Both of us enjoyed music, even though I sang off-key. My only contribution was the huge gramophone at home.

My form of religion gradually developed into a belief in an all-encompassing creative power, a force behind the development of nature and everything that grew and moved on earth. As the son of a gardener, Arnold was fond of flowers and would listen to my theories about civilisation being on the wrong track. When I told other people that I disliked machines and engines and that in the long run this form of progress would do nothing to improve human existence, they thought I was mad.

What made you think that?

Maybe it was an instinctive belief in nature as the progenitor and master of human beings. If there was a god whose invisible powers extended into everything that had sprung up from the ocean and the earth, then why hadn't He himself invented machines to please humans? I was afraid that machines at some point would get the upper hand and take the place of the natural world that Our Lord had given us.

You didn't believe in progress?

Yes I did, but I did not believe that any old step that led us further away from nature could be called progress. I began to feel that we, as human beings, were experimenting with our own way of life: clearing the forests; assuming that moving from a farm to a factory is progress. When I was younger, drawing was one of my hobbies. My subject was often a yellow sun shining on circular native huts, palm trees and monkeys. Later I exchanged my crayons for pencils, erasers and felt-tipped pens, and I sketched cartoons depicting the foibles of civilisation. I liked travelling by train, and was just as impressed as everyone else the first time a classmate brought something he called a radio to school. With earphones wired to some kind of a battery, we acknowledged, one by one and with wonder in our eyes, that we could hear distant music.

I also became more interested in fitness after having tasted life with Ola Bjørneby. I became especially good friends with a huge fellow called Eric, who ran the cross-country races in the forest with us. He was a jovial oddball, totally different from Arnold. They never became close friends, because Eric had decided to go to sea rather than attend high school with us. They were both large fellows, but since Arnold liked music and poetry our only conversations were about philosophy. Eric was a practical outdoors man, and in my last years at high school, having passed my wilderness apprenticeship with Ola Bjørneby and starting to spend all my vacations out of doors in Norway's wildest mountains, it was Eric who came with me.

We weren't ready for each other the first time we met. I was with my own gang of friends, equipped with buckets and nets catching salamanders in the local forest when we met Eric, the leader of a group of boys with toy guns and wooden swords. They had built a pirate ship in the forest. Later, when we started cross-country running, I would go home with him. At first I was startled by the awesome pirate staring down at me from a huge drawing in his bedroom, but later greatly enjoyed his humorous artistry.

When Eric shipped out to sea we lost contact, but many years later, it was Eric Hesselberg I invited to be the navigator on the *Kon-Tiki* expedition.

Like myself, Arnold moved to Oslo after high school. While I chose to study biology and geography at university, he went to art school and became a professional illustrator and author. His book *It Also Concerns You* was a great success. It tells the story of Larvik's only Jewish family. They had twelve children and, with the exception of the youngest, all of them died in the Nazi gas chambers. We, who were Samuel's class-mates, had no idea that he was Jewish, but only knew that he never came to school on Saturdays. It doesn't take much for faith in the god of love to turn to hatred. Although friend and foe alike can believe in the one god of creation, they can also disagree about which day of the week he chose to rest.

I was completely convinced that what we called civilisation had become a dangerous thing, that the machines of war in full alert all over the world, would drag all civilised societies into a new and dreadful conflict. Alfred Nobel had believed in progress and perpetual peace when he invented dynamite. Dynamite took more lives than gas masks saved during the First World War, and when we were in high school we heard about the invention of new, gigantic war vehicles capable of moving over all sorts of terrain without wheels. Eric and I wanted to escape from Europe before all the new, horrific inventions of war were put to use. Eric dreamed about starting an ideal community in Central Africa, far away from the dangers of civilisation. There were many blank spots on the map in those days.

I have often been asked what great explorers like Roald Amundsen and Fridtjof Nansen meant to me in my youth, but it is not an easy question to answer. Both were, of course, great heroes to all of us boys, and they were still alive then. Amundsen had reached the South Pole before we were born, and was way ahead in the contest to get to the North Pole first. I'll never forget when I was at a Boy Scout camp in Åndalsnes in 1928. The Italian, Nobile, had gone down with his airship somewhere over the polar region, and in a brave attempt to rescue his opponent, Amundsen's small plane crashed into the Arctic Ocean. Our camp was told that Amundsen had been found alive, and everyone stormed out of their tents, dancing and cheering. So much greater was our sorrow when we discovered that the news was erroneous.

I was only eight years old when Nansen received the Nobel Peace Prize for his great work with displaced persons after the First World War. We admired Nansen more than anyone. With his polar ship *Fram* he had sailed into the drift ice and, in the cross-polar currents, come closer to the North Pole than anyone before him. He and Johansen left the *Fram* and the crew and skied to 86 degrees north, before returning to civilisation. We all knew that he had crossed Greenland on skis in 1888. When I was a boy no one else had ventured far enough on to the inland ice that covers Greenland to be able to tell geographers whether this huge polar island consisted of wild mountain ranges or a flat glacier.

Then something happened that would have a bearing on my own life. In 1931 two daring Norwegian students had skied right across the widest section of Greenland with a dog team and written a book about it. One of them, Martin Mehren, brought some of the Greenland dogs to Oslo.

My mother was mad about dogs. In one of her previous marriages she had owned twenty white Samoyeds, a slightly more refined relative of the muscular dogs that pulled Greenland Eskimo sleds. Since the time when I drank milk from the only backyard goats in Larvik, I had grown up with a peaceful Chow-Chow to take the sting out of the loneliness of living in a house with two elderly parents. When school came to an end I had moved to Oslo with my mother. The loneliness did not diminish when my father, to make room for all my mother's antiques, bought her an apartment on the top floor of a building on Camilla Collett Street, with a large living room that extended from one end of the house to the other and a narrow balcony on each side. Here, in the middle of town, she emerged triumphantly from the elevator one day with a Greenland puppy that she had bought from Martin Mehren. I was overwhelmed with joy, but as soon as she set the dog free and closed the front door behind her our new house-guest ran into the living room, and like a wild thing, jumped all over sofas and tables. Back and forth it rushed, out on to both balconies, jumping up and down, until finally it came to its senses as, with its well-grown paws on the brick railing, it peered down six floors.

My life was never the same after Kazan came to stay. I skipped university for three days and used all my strength to hold Kazan down every time I said, 'Lie down,' commanding him to stay until I said, 'Up.' My mother excused the beast by saying that its mother, according to Mehren, had been cross-bred with a wolf. The miracle happened: Kazan became the most obedient dog I have known, clean and peaceful and able to understand everything I tried to teach him, and much more.

Kazan was so quiet when he was with me that I allowed him to accompany me to lectures at the university, and on my rare visits to a restaurant he lay so peacefully beneath the table that no one noticed. The dog learned to pull fifty kilos on a sled in uneven terrain during the winter, and in the summer could carry fifty kilos on his back. While I was studying in Oslo we were inseparable, in town and on hikes out in the country. Both the dog and I were happiest when we could get away from everything, as far as possible from the city and as high as possible into the mountains. The dog became so attached to my backpack and my thick mountain boots that he challenged anyone who tried to come near them in my absence. The warning did not always work, and I was forced to keep a supply of sticking plasters and bandages.

Eric came along on more mountain hikes than anyone else; old friends have always meant a lot to me. I planned increasingly difficult expeditions in the mountains. In those days, hardly anyone slept outside when they explored the wintry mountains, but Eric and I were inspired by Nansen and Mehren. We had no need to find shelter before nightfall. We had learned to dig snow-holes in windblown snowdrifts, and we became experts at finding good, hard-packed snow.

My hiking companions believed that I saw myself as a future polar explorer. With the exception of Arnold and Eric, I never discussed my growing resolve to visit other parts of the world. I financed my excursions by writing about them in Saturday papers and magazines, illustrating them with photographs and amusing drawings. Sleeping out of doors in the snow was so unusual in Norway in the 1930s that readers were interested in learning how to carve blocks of ice to build an igloo – and we built them in the most exquisite places.

There was nothing quite like waking up on a wintry morning on top of Stor-Ronden Mountain and creeping from our igloo feeling that all of Norway was within sight. A winter storm might be howling outside, but an igloo or a simple snow-hole was warm and comfortable as long as it had proper air circulation, through a little hole in the roof, and the entrance level was lower than the floor. With a single lit candle, the temperature inside will remain above freezing when the temperature outside is below freezing. This is because the inner walls turn to ice, which in turn act as insulation and provide a reasonable room temperature.

I have always liked to have an alternative course of action in case things go wrong, and I can only remember breaking that rule once. On the raft journeys there would always be a log or a bundle of reeds to float about on if the ropes came apart. But once, on the summit of Glittertind, Eric and I took a crazy chance, which I have always regretted in spite of a happy outcome. With its permanent snowcap, Glittertind was at that time higher than its neighbour, Galdhøpiggen, and thereby

Norway's highest mountain, and this was why Eric and I struggled our way up its steep wall of snow on skis, with Kazan fighting his way after us pulling the sled. We planned to build an igloo on the summit, but before we could reach it we were caught in a snowstorm. Soon we could not even see the tips of our skis. Nor was it possible to see any precipices, and the only way to avoid them was to continue our ascent.

When we finally reached the stone marker at the top of Glittertind, the storm was so violent that we couldn't even stand upright and had to take off our skis. The marker was all we could see, and the snow fell so thickly that it was difficult both to breathe and keep our eyes open. The surface was impenetrable, making it impossible to dig a snow-hole or cut blocks for an igloo. We desperately clung on to our skis, preventing them from being swept away into an unknown world, and there was no time to think of an alternative. We untied Kazan from the sled, took a compass bearing based on the direction we had come from, jumped on top of the sled, and let go. We kept the speed down by digging our heels in as well as we could and several times even managed to stop and wait for Kazan until finally it got out of hand and we lost control. It was the ride of a lifetime! Ever faster, at a wild pace, we ended up rolling over in deep snow on flat ground without knowing where we were. We thought we would never see Kazan again. After waiting for an eternity the dog appeared, limping and struggling to reach us through the deep snow. We knew we were in the midst of a wild landscape, but we could only see ourselves, the sled and the dog. The world disappeared in a white-out, no contours or any means of detecting the difference between over, under or behind.

A map and a compass are relatively useless in an unknown location in invisible surroundings, but we knew roughly where we were and set off in an approximate direction toward the neighbouring valley. Not surprisingly, our course led us into higher terrain and as we progressed it became steeper and steeper. Soon we couldn't even turn our skis. We were forced to sidestep, keeping our minds on the task at hand and trusting that an avalanche would not sweep us away. Poor Kazan struggled to keep the sled upright, and his strength was drained by the time the three of us, through our combined efforts, made it over the ridge and down the other side. The storm had abated and been replaced by thick fog. Once again, everything was white, until what we assumed was a hallucination presented a large house in the distance. As if by a stroke of magic it turned into a small cabin right before our eyes. As the fog lifted, we saw that we had reached the Spiterstulen tourist lodge. Many years later we were told that this ridge had never before been crossed on skis.

Did that turn you into a cautious man?

More careful. Later on I set out on a ski trip alone with Kazan. To some this might seem even more foolish, but it had a specific purpose.

It was in the mid-1930s, and an early Easter snowstorm had been forecast in the mountains. I had accompanied a cousin to a railway station on the Dovre line. We had spent some time in a snow-hole in Trollheimen, and taken Kazan on a hike up to Snøhetta. My cousin was returning to Trondheim, while Kazan and I were going to cross the Dovre mountain plateau and continue down to Gudbrandsdalen. I had only reached Hjerkinn when the storm set in. I sought shelter in a mountain lodge, enjoying waffles, cloudberries and cream and cocoa in front of a roaring fire. The snow beat against the walls of the lodge, and Kazan lay quietly under the table awaiting his turn. A dog should know that he will always be cared for and never beg. Kazan knew that I enjoyed spoiling him, and that his approaching meal would be quite a change

from the dried fish packed on the sled. By the time we had finished our meal, the storm had reached full gale force. It
howled and screeched against the walls and roof of the lodge,
and no one was allowed to venture outdoors without holding
on to the rope that was tied to a door of the outbuilding.

It was then that I realised the storm was a personal challenge. The Dovre plateau had no cliffs nor fences. The whole
mountain lies above the tree line, and bushes, rocks, lakes and
fences all lay under a mantle of deep snow. The men at the
lodge tried to restrain me from leaving, but nothing could stop
me. Neither locals nor storm gusts could prevent me from
strapping Kazan to the front of the sled and my skis to my
leather-lined ski boots. After a few strokes with my ski poles in
the heavy snow, I was out of sight.

I was forced to lean forward against the storm; the pace
was slow. Even Kazan had to struggle and pull with all his
wolf-like might to make any headway. In ideal conditions on
level terrain he could pull a loaded sled and my own weight
effortlessly. Today he had to break through deep powder, and
the snow falling from the sky was trivial compared to the
stinging gusts of ground snow that whipped up around us.
Sometimes Kazan fell behind, and my only recourse was to
wait for him to reappear, often dragging an upturned sled.
Each reunion was a great relief, because we were both terrified
of losing contact.

*What was the point of this wrestling match against the ele-
ments?*

I kept repeating the words: 'This will make the boy a man!
This will make the boy a man!'

I knew I had found my true self in the essence of the
mountains; not yet in the city. When I first returned to the city
and my studies after such mountain adventures, I walked with
self-confidence among the rows of buildings and felt that this

was nothing compared to what I had experienced, but by the next day the buildings were already pressing down on me. They seemed to lean over me, making me feel small and insignificant. All I could do was yield to them and enter their world. Kazan probably felt the same way; he gave me a look, then lifted his leg and peed up against the walls.

It was time to defeat this insecurity – almost cowardice – that overcame me whenever I walked on asphalt or living-room floors. I had to shore up my self-confidence and realise I was the same person, whether I was walking on heather, grass, pavements or living-room carpets.

It must be that I still had some growing up to do. I was surely suffering from the after effects of a spoiled childhood.

'This will make the boy a man!' No reason to go any further. We were still undefeated, in the midst of primal mountain forces, and simply being able to lie down and sleep, was a triumph in itself. It was impossible to dig a shelter or build an igloo in this powder snow. I managed to find the small tent on the sled, but could not set it up in the storm. No problem, I thought. I just crawled through the opening of the tent and pulled Kazan in after me. And there we lay while the storm heaped drifts of snow over us like soft quilts, me in my reindeer sleeping bag and Kazan in his coat of Greenland fur.

Then my heart began to throb. I heard a train whistle. The Dovre line between Oslo and Trondheim was somewhere around here. The whistling came closer. Where were the tracks? The sound grew stronger; I could even hear the loco-motive's engine. The train was bearing down on us at full speed!

Kazan was just as frightened as I was. We had to find our way out of both the sleeping bag and the tent. I panicked when I realised the tracks were buried under deep snow. We could just as well stay where we were, we certainly didn't know which side the train was on. On occasions like this even an atheist finds himself hoping for the existence of a god, and promising to be good if he survives. I was more dead than alive when the hammering of the pistons reached a crescendo as the plough shovelled mounds of snow toward us and the train's car and wheels created an inferno of sound as they passed by. No one on the train knew that outside, in the stormy night, just beside the tracks, a boy lay buried beneath the snow with a dog in his arms, all for the sake of wanting to be a man.

5

In the Footsteps of Darwin

From the vantage point of our orchard in Tenerife, we could see the pine forest reaching right up to where Teide, a snow-clad peak, soared to 3,700 metres above sea level. In my earliest childhood it took us three days to travel from our home by the Larvik Fjord to our Hornsjø mountain cabin. The trip demanded two overnight stops, several changes of train and a seven-hour journey by horse and carriage from Hunder railway station. Today we can get to Hornsjø from Tenerife in a day. But the idea does not tempt us. Bulldozers, new buildings and dilapidated old ones have not left much of the Hornsjø that I reminisced about while relaxing in my hammock under the blue sky, and talking to my *aku-aku*.

You have not said much about girls.

There was pitifully little to say about girls in my boyhood. When we were still in our prams, I had a pretty little brown-eyed girlfriend with black hair, cut like a pageboy. Once I saw her naked and although this was very interesting, I couldn't tell which side was front and which was back. When I turned six and went to school, I started to understand more and realised that it was a disgrace for a boy to play with girls. They had dolls and we had cap-guns. Boys and girls did not attend the same class; we even had different playgrounds, separated by a high brick wall.

The differences between male and female became so overwhelming that I was overcome with shyness when asking a girl to dance at Miss Dødelein's dancing classes. My parents sent me there, wearing patent leather shoes and a sailor suit, for three consecutive years. I was awkward, sneaking out into the hallway to draw the steps of the waltz and the tango on a piece of paper. In spite of my efforts, I tripped over my own and others' feet, and never learned to execute the steps the way I had drawn them on paper.

This awkwardness would give me my first big opportunity with the opposite sex.

Girls and boys were allowed to attend the same class from secondary school onwards, and during my high school years I had more contact with girls. There were dances and other get-togethers, but I missed almost all of them because I declined any invitation that could possibly involve dancing.

So my school years came to a close without any experience with the opposite sex. My anticipation of forming a relationship with the right woman grew steadily stronger. When I graduated from high school, wearing the traditional red-tasselled cap and partaking in the joys of completed exams, I performed in the school play. I helped to write it, and had the lead part as the pioneer balloonist, Professor Piccard, a real person who had recently become the first man to reach the stratosphere in his balloon. In my version, however, he was so absent-minded that he forgot to return and ended up at the pearly gates of St Peter and the angels. This was my first and only theatrical endeavour, and it was a success.

All the graduates from the small towns in the area were invited to the final party for my class in Larvik. We had dinner, wine, a youth orchestra and dancing at a beach restaurant in Stavern, the outermost point of the Larvik Fjord. Everyone danced after dinner, even Arnold. I was left alone with a glass of beer, trying hard to appear above it all and staring coolly at the boats that passed the glass balcony in the clear summer night.

Then Arnold came over and introduced me to a graduate from another town and his dancing partner.

My eyes saw only the latter. Liv had curly blonde hair, bright blue, laughing eyes, lips that were naturally red and a countenance that reflected both wisdom and determination. She wore a flattering white summer dress; had it been possible I would have equipped her with enormous white wings and she could have stepped right into the role of an angel in my school play.

She wanted to dance.

I desperately tried all sorts of excuses.

'Shall we dance?' she repeated.

I was determined to keep her by my side.

'Couldn't we take a walk on the beach?' I asked in panic. To my relief she agreed.

Reflections from the stars and the restaurant lights danced on the water. It was a beautiful evening and she appreciated its beauty too. We went back inside and found a place to sit.

'Would you like to join me in an experimental return to nature?' The words just fell out of my mouth.

'If so, we would have to return all the way,' Liv answered, adding that this was not to be a Hollywood farce.

I was overwhelmed. She was willing to return to a primitive life in a primal forest – and with me. After my planned studies of geography we could find a South Sea island, or any place where such an experiment would be possible.

I sat in silence, savouring the look on Liv's friendly but determined face which convinced me that her answer was genuine. It was a sacred moment. But then the night with Liv came to an end. She would be graduating next year, and had accompanied a gentle young man from the neighbouring town of Brevik who took his defeat like a gentleman and later became a friend. The bus was waiting; some had a long way home, but Liv and I were going to keep in touch.

It was difficult for young people from different towns to keep in touch in those days. How would Liv's parents react to a long-distance call from a boy they had never met? Being a girl, she could not call me.

Almost two years would pass before I saw Liv again.

Meanwhile the boy had become a young university student. After exchanging the red-tasselled cap for the heavier black cap worn by university students, I walked up the grand stairway in the university building in downtown Oslo near the royal palace. Most of my friends were going to study law, medicine or the humanities, at the new university complex that was being built at Blindern, on the outskirts of Oslo. I was the only zoology student among them, and I felt the gravity of what was awaiting me behind the impressive oak door to the right at the top of the stairway. I had no idea that Fridtjof Nansen had also used this door right up to the time of his death only a few years earlier. I did know, however, that he had studied zoology and that, unlike Amundsen, he had been a professional scientist in his field and the author of important scientific dissertations. He had even held the title of professor in zoology, and I was about to meet his successor, who would become my advisor.

Why were you going to study, you who were supposed to return to nature?

I could not just go to Africa, take my clothes off and start looking for food. I had to know more about the blank spots on the map of the world, and work out a contingency plan in case my attempt as explorer failed.

I was filled with anticipation when I pushed open the door into the department of zoology, and recalled the time when the door to my room in the stables had a *Museum of Zoology* sign. I had expected to be confronted by rooms filled with stuffed animals, but the first thing I saw was a human skeleton. It was placed inside the door like a silent butler, with all its bones, including those on the skull, labelled in Latin. It was popularly known as 'Olsen'. I understood that human beings represented the last stage of animal evolution and that this stage could not be displayed as a nude body. The other animals on the floors and shelves were also in skeletal form, except for some stomachs and creepy embryos preserved in jars of alcohol. The first intact creature I saw was my future professor, in her office. A woman greatly admired by my mother, Kristine Bonnevie was one of three women in Norway who had attained the title of professor. I bowed with respect at the door and shook hands with a firm but friendly woman wearing an old-fashioned lorgnette. Silently I hoped that she would have more to offer the ear than she did the eye.

She asked why I wanted to become a zoologist and warned me that there were few positions available unless I planned to teach in high school.

I told her of my childhood dream of becoming an explorer, and about my interest in animal life, from insects to the larger mammals I had been studying in the wilderness over the last few years. She then let me understand that her own interests leaned more toward microscopic anatomy and research into the laws of heredity. However, she welcomed me to her lectures and recommended that I consult with her colleague in the office next door, Professor Hjalmar Broch, a specialist in coral polyps.

As I was leaving her office, she called me back to look at a small amateur photograph. I clearly saw an elk in the background.

'What is this? An elk or a reindeer?' she asked.

My first test, I thought, before answering, 'An elk, of course.'

'How can you tell?'

'By its stance, its overall impression.'

Embarrassed, she explained that someone had sent her the picture for expert identification, but that the table in her reference book for the definition of mammals only said that elk and reindeer could be distinguished by the fact that a reindeer's nostrils were close together while an elk's were on either side of the muzzle. 'And in the picture one can't see the nostrils,' she added with a smile.

On my first day at university I had already learned something important: being a specialist is not the same as being omniscient. On the contrary. The terms are contradictory.

I had looked forward to learning more about animal life from a zoology professor than I had from a man of the mountains, such as Ola Bjørneby. It turned out that the country's leading authority on animals couldn't tell the difference between elk and reindeer without studying their nostrils.

Nevertheless, after my mother, and until Liv came back into the picture, Professor Bonnevie may have been the most important woman in my young life. I was unaware of her importance then, but in retrospect she staked out my future path within a few days. To begin with, she thought of a subject for my thesis that gave me both a reason and an excuse for going to Polynesia. Secondly, since she saw human beings as part of the animal world, she trained zoology students in physical anthropology by teaching us about the indexes of the cranium and the heritability of blood types. Genealogy was her main interest, and chromosome composition was more important to her than animals in their natural habitat. After a while, branching out from pure zoology to the study of human origins and cultural development became a logical transition.

Liv came to Oslo to start her studies the following year, and when we finally renewed our acquaintance, I introduced her to my mother and to Kazan, but not to my professors, as her father had decided that she was to study social economics. We immediately picked up where we had left off that summer's night at the graduation party, and I could tell her that the plan was well on its way.

I had not mentioned my idea of leaving civilisation in order to study it from a different perspective to anyone other than Liv and my two friends from Larvik, but my academic syllabus was organised to provide the knowledge needed to find a suitable location. By then my opinion of my university professor had changed radically. She was extremely knowledgeable, even though her area of expertise was not what interested me most. Zoology had become so specialised that senior scientists using the same laboratory had lost contact with what their colleagues were doing. Research solely for the sake of research. One was only to present what one had found; maybe someone could make use of it in the future.

Liv was shocked when she heard that I spent my time staring into a microscope, counting the number of hairs on the backs of a few thousand small banana flies – flies hatched in jars to control the validity of Mendel's law of heredity. Per Høst, the oldest in our group of seven, earned everyone's admiration when he opened his jar and let all the small yellow flies out of the window, because – as he said – we all knew that Mendel's law was correct, so this was a waste of time. Per had grafted a fifth leg on to the back of a salamander, and the leg moved on its own, independently of the other four. He once placed it on the shoulder of an unsuspecting fellow who had tasted a bit too much of a laboratory cocktail at a hot-dog and beer party at Per's house. The cheerful student did not bat an eye when he saw the monster move the leg on its back. He calmly set his glass down and carefully turned to study his shoulder, but by then Per had removed the creature. It was Per who had to suffer the consequences, because the man suddenly rushed across the room and leaned out of the window. Per lived on the seventh floor, and in the morning the family on the ground floor complained to the man on the floor above, and complaints were passed up from floor to floor until there was no one left for Per to blame. He worked his way down to street level with a bucket and a mop.

Only Per, Yngvar Hagen and Edvard Barth shared my interest in animal life. Per's brother-in-law was manager of the city's main camera shop, and we were able to borrow 16mm movie cameras by trading film clips of elk, viper, owl and whatever we might find in the great outdoors on Sundays and during holidays.

Our other classmates chose to write about more curious subjects. For example, a totally normal and pleasant fellow by the name of Støp-Bowitz decided to study the colour structure of tube worms in the surf. He probably had little use for this later in life, but he did well anyway; one has to study something.

We all realised that specialisation was necessary for the progress of science. There was no point in taking a superficial view; one had to limit the field and plumb the depths. Even then, however, I was beginning to see that something was wrong. Specialists were in the process of learning more and more about less and less, and the price they had to pay was ignorance, gradually eroding their own field of learning. This was bound to happen as the specialists discovered that there was still very much that remained unknown to mankind.

Of course specialists must continue to delve into their subject matter, but they must not lose sight of the wood for the trees. Universities also needed institutions that did not examine small pockets of information, but would bear in mind the overall picture and systematise the findings of other specialists. Someone had to put the pieces together.

By the time Liv came to Oslo I had already added geography to my studies on the advice of both my zoology professors. I had studied enough mathematical geography to understand the consequences of the fact that the earth was round. Ancient geographers had discovered this long before Columbus, but when it came to the Pacific Ocean no one had taken it on board, not even the anthropologists when they presented their theories about migration across the enormous ocean. They drew arrows on the map and talked about the straight line along the equator and the circuitous route along the continental coast running northward from tropical Asia and then back down again to tropical South America. In reality, a straight line from the coast of Southeast Asia to South America would cut through the centre of the earth because the world is round and the Pacific Ocean is so large that it covers an entire hemisphere. Southeast Asia and South America were antipodal at the equatorial line since they were 180 degrees apart, therefore a route over the North Pole was no longer than one along the equator. If one followed what the geographers called the 'great circle', all the curves along the surface of the Pacific from the Philippines to Peru were equally long.

But everything that could float, from coconuts to primitive vessels, would get a free ride with the wind and current, from America to Asia in the equatorial belt, and from Asia to America with the warm Japan Current from the Philippine Ocean and up to the northernmost part of the Pacific.

I would soon learn that this mathematical knowledge of geography was necessary, even though I detested the textbook. When I became better acquainted with my elderly geography professor, Werner Werenskiold, he confessed that he had purposefully written it in such a complicated manner in order to show his colleagues in other fields that geography was also a science.

The geography classes were even more informative and the knowledge I gained there had an immediate influence on my plan. It forced Liv and me to eliminate most areas for our project and only the thousands of islands spread across the enormous Pacific Ocean remained. Werenskiold lectured on the trees in the primal forest, explaining how their closed canopies of foliage high above ground prohibit the passage of sunshine, preventing the growth of flowers and berries on the jungle floor. You have to climb the trees to find sustenance and, once there, you realise that the monkeys have grabbed everything edible and left nothing for their tail-less relatives on the ground. Liv now realised why I had rejected the blank spots that still existed in Africa and the unexplored jungles of South America. In the jungle, food grew at a lever higher than we could reach.

After learning that I was interested in going to the Pacific Ocean, Professor Bonnevie gave me the idea of following in the footsteps of Darwin. Charles Darwin, my mother's great hero, had been on the Galapagos Islands off the coast of South America when he developed his theory on the origin of the species. The scattered islands of Polynesia were even further out in the ocean. Some had risen from the bottom of the sea through volcanic activity, others had been built up by coral polyps, but they had all seen the light of day void of native land animals. How had plants and animals reached these islands? Bonnevie had just read a work published by the Bishop Museum in Hawaii by an American zoologist who had studied land snails on the isolated Marquesas Islands, and observed how they had developed into new species and strains from island to island, in relationship to their elevation above the ocean.

The Marquesas Islands. We were all equally excited – my mother pondering Darwin's theory on the origin of the species, my professor who had had the idea, and Liv and I who had been pinpointing Pacific islands and eliminating them one after the other as they turned out to have been influenced or contaminated by civilisation, lacking in drinking water or uninhabitable for some other reason. It soon became clear that Professor Werenskiold's mathematical calculations of great circles and the effect of the earth's rotation on the ocean currents and winds were important.

Nevertheless it may have been the university preparatory courses in logic and philosophy that were most useful in my later life. The philosophy of ancient Greece was best suited to my way of thinking. I liked Diogenes, who was content to sit in his barrel and enjoy the sun, and Socrates, who peered into a shop window and was pleased to see how much he could do without.

Simple logic allowed me to conclude that a balsa-wood raft could drift from Peru to Polynesia. In the first place, the botanist F. B. H. Brown, the world's leading expert on the flora of the Marquesas Islands, had discovered that several useful South American plants, which could not have reached the Marquesas Islands without the aid of humans, were already growing there when the Europeans arrived. And secondly, the world's leading expert on pre-European navigation had proved that there were no other boats at that time other than balsa rafts. Ergo: the balsa raft had to have managed the crossing even though everyone else – without having tried it – believed the opposite.

You weren't actually thinking of attempting the crossing yourself?

Absolutely not. I still had not learned to swim. I planned a future with my feet planted firmly on the ground, but barefoot.

One summer, when Liv had grown close enough to my mother for me to risk inviting her to Hornsjø, I made her take off her shoes and walk barefoot through the heather and undergrowth just like me. I believed that we should harden ourselves and build up thicker skin on the soles of our feet. We also tried to make fire by rubbing dry sticks of spruce, birch and juniper together, without success. Otherwise I was so well prepared that I was even giving lectures about the Marquesas Islands at the university before we left home.

It was probably one of the first and most fortunate coincidences in my life that Bjarne Kroepelin's Polynesia Library happened to be located in Oslo and was available to me when I was studying. This was the world's largest collection of literature on Polynesia, and my parents happened to know the owner, a prosperous wine importer. Bjarne had visited Tahiti when he was a young man, and fallen in love with Tuimata, the beautiful daughter of the chieftain Teriieroo. This affected my life in two ways; over the years this love affair would lead to the establishment of Kroepelin's collection of books about Polynesia, and Teriieroo became my adopted Polynesian father. Tragically, Spanish influenza came to Tahiti while young Kroepelin was there, and the Polynesians died like flies. He and Tuimata helped load the dead on to wagons, until Tuimata herself fell ill and died. Bjarne Kroepelin never forgot her. He wrote a beautiful little book about Tuimata, which ended with the words: 'And where Tuimata lies, there my heart lies buried.' He dedicated the rest of his life to collecting Polynesian books. He was in contact with dealers and buyers of rare books the world over, and bought everything that was printed about Polynesia, regardless of the price.

During the seven semesters I spent with my fellow students attending lectures in biology and geography, I spent just as much time alone, sitting with a notepad in a leather chair at an old-fashioned desk, surrounded by Kroepelin's bookshelves.

These studies proved useful references during later years when controversy raged. The rest of the world regarded me as a sailor with Viking blood, and the anthropologists in Norway doubted the competence of zoologists when it came to issues about prehistoric vessels. I was well prepared to defend my theories after having read everything that explorers, missionaries, circumnavigators and scientists had published right up until the 1930s, and I had kept up with additions to the Kroepelin library in the years that followed. When Kroepelin died, his entire Polynesia library was moved to the research section at the Kon-Tiki Museum.

Geographically speaking, Polynesia had to be as close as one could get to paradise on earth, even though its population had been partially wiped out and ravaged by diseases brought to the islands by the Europeans. I knew that 80 per cent of the population of the Marquesas Islands had perished of disease, and for this reason we concluded that there would be enough wild fruit trees in the depopulated areas for our survival.

I was fully aware that the question of who the Polynesians

were and where they had come from was still unsolved. And I wondered why the anthropologists paid no heed to the observations of the botanists. I myself planned to collect everything of zoological interest that could be stored in glass containers. The question of how the Polynesians had reached Polynesia did not interest me very much. We had enough on our plate working out how to get there. In the 1930s no travel agency in Norway had heard of the Marquesas Islands. Their expertise was based on Norwegian coastal steamships, a few isolated trips to islands in the Mediterranean and emigration to America. Scheduled air travel did not exist, and certainly not across the oceans. When I said farewell to neighbourhood children who were leaving for America, we knew that it was goodbye once and for all.

This was the situation when Bennet's Travel Bureau in Oslo learned from Paris that the closest one could get to the Marquesas Islands was Tahiti, and that a ship from Marseilles sailed there once a month to unload cargo and passengers going to French New Caledonia. The only other alternative was to take a Norwegian freighter on a scheduled route to San Francisco, Samoa and Tahiti every month or so. We chose to disembark on Tahiti after a six-week voyage on the *Messangerie Maritime*, across the Atlantic and through the Panama Canal.

That sounds easy.

Not that easy. Liv was only twenty years old and still a minor, and I only had fifty crowns a month in pocket money from my father.

I remember Liv and me sitting by a window at the Theatercafé in Oslo, watching drab people rushing past the window carrying umbrellas and overcoats, oblivious to one another. I ordered lemonade and gateau and tried to convince Liv, who looked a little uncertain, that we could successfully persuade our parents to allow us to get married and go to the Marquesas. Liv envisioned her father's implacable reaction, and she smiled and shuddered simultaneously. But together we concocted a plan and I pulled Kazan out from under the table, followed Liv to the trolley-bus and walked home through the palace park to begin working on my mother.

She was easy to persuade. Professors Bonnevie and Broch had confirmed that after seven semesters the zoology lectures would simply start all over again, and their word sufficed. Also, Broch supported Bonnevie's plan that I might obtain a doctorate by studying the origin of the species on the Marquesas Islands – if I went there and collected material. Liv had already captured my mother's heart and, with the seductive South Sea girls in mind, she thought it was very wise for me to marry Liv and take her with me.

Persuading my father was more difficult. With exactly the same South Sea girls in mind, he was of the opinion that marrying before I left was like crossing a stream to find water. He agreed to finance the journey as part of my studies, even though it was unusually long, but my marriage would have to wait until I returned and found a job. For once I made no progress with my father. My arguments simply made no impression on him.

However, I knew that my father's greatest wish was to be reconciled with my mother. The fact that she still refused to see him provided a good opportunity.

'Mamma agrees,' I said carefully.

He answered immediately: 'Then I'll have to speak to her.'

I was already prepared. She had agreed to invite him for coffee, and that was all it took for total agreement between my parents and myself. I've never had a better time sitting in front of the fire.

It was harder for Liv. She wrote a beautiful letter to her

lonely parents in Brevik and told them that she had met a boy from Larvik called Thor, and that we were thinking of getting married and going to the Marquesas Islands. Liv's mother, who was a very intellectual and gentle woman, later described her husband's reaction when she read the letter to him. With a flushed face, he got up from his large and roomy armchair and walked slowly to the bookshelf and picked out the volume *M* in an old encyclopaedia from the end of the last century. Finding it, he read out loud that the Marquesas Islands were remote islands in the Pacific where there were still 'cannibals and immorality'.

My future father-in-law simply refused to lose his only daughter to cannibals, and my future bride almost lost her father to a heart attack. We dropped the discussion for a while, until my father, now satisfied with our scheme, allowed my mother to persuade him to pay a visit to Brevik. Here he would use all his charm so that everyone could agree that the plan was good, and that my father would pay for the honeymoon. We ended up getting married on Christmas Eve, in a simple ceremony in the family's living room. It was snowing the next morning as they all waved goodbye to two youthful newlyweds who took the train south into Europe to board a huge ocean steamer in Marseilles with tickets for Tahiti.

A ticket to paradise, we thought. But by the end of the expedition we concluded that admission to paradise cannot be bought. Those who have found paradise have found it within themselves. Everything I had seen and read had taught me that paradise and hell do not have separate locations on this planet. They are always in the same place, and one cannot simply avoid one by moving away. The two turn up like inseparable companions, no matter how far you have travelled. But they cannot always be seen at the same time, so you have to settle down for a while to be sure you experience both aspects.

With the tickets that my father purchased in Norway we travelled to Tahiti in French Oceania. In the 1930s, Tahiti was just as it had been when Kroepelin had buried his heart with Tuimata. There were no cars in the narrow streets between the small wooden houses in the capital, Papeete, which was dominated by Chinese vendors selling their wares from small handcarts. There was one hotel, where you could sit up in bed and look over the wall into the adjoining room. There was no regular contact with the distant Marquesas Islands, and many weeks could pass before a captain on a schooner was ready to sail there and load his ship with copra. There was still no suitable road for driving cars around the island, but one could make it all the way to the Papeno valley on a picturesque bus filled with colourful *vahines* à la Gauguin, with live chickens and pigs on their laps and on the roof.

We squeezed into the bus and got off in Papeno, the home of Chief Teriieroo, the father of beautiful Tuimata and the most powerful of Tahiti's seventeen chieftains. Large and generous both in spirit and flesh, he was a full-blooded descendant of the ancient Polynesian chieftain families. We arrived with gifts from Bjarne Kroepelin and were received with open arms and automatically declared part of the family. Four weeks were to pass before a bus brought the message that a schooner would be sailing for the Marquesas. In the meantime we had learned a great deal. We were both barefoot and wore colourful *pareus* and Liv spent her time with Faufau and the women of the house around the glowing hearth on the kitchen floor, while I went with the chief and his sons into the forests and the fields.

The most important thing I learned in Tahiti was how to swim. And I did not learn this skill voluntarily.

I fell into the Papeno River as I stepped on a spiny snail

shell and was swept away by the current. I fell in at the deep end, in a large pool, where the water cascaded into thundering breakers at the mouth of the river. I swam automatically to save my life and managed to pull myself onto the turf before it was too late. Swimming was so easy and such fun that as soon as I was on dry land I dived into the pool once more and swam around.

It was harder to learn how to climb a coconut palm. The first time I managed to climb one, I encountered a hornet's nest between the coconuts. Since I couldn't descend fast enough, I slid down the notched trunk and landed on the ground, skinless and bruised and was forced to let Teriieroo pull out the nail on my big toe with pliers.

We finally departed on a schooner for the Marquesas. We were set ashore in a lifeboat on an island without white people, no radios, or any other form of contact with the rest of the world.

Can you remember what you thought?

That the world was incredibly large. The journey alone had taken more than two months. And in Tahiti I had heard that the Marquesas Islands were so isolated from the rest of the world that no one there had known about the outbreak of the First World War in 1914 before it ended in 1918, in spite of Papeete having been shelled by German warships.

Farewells are always a little sad. Had I not been forced to pull myself together for Liv's sake, I would probably have given in to the lump in my throat when we were left alone on the beach, looking out over the ocean and watching the lifeboat return to the schooner. The ship hoisted sail and disappeared over the horizon. Maybe he would return in a year, Captain Barnder had said. We turned away from the ocean and glimpsed brown faces peeping from under the coconut palms along the edge of the forest. They were staring at us. We had so many questions to ask, but no common language. What I remember best is noticing that the crowns of the palm trees were filled with coconuts and thinking that, for the moment, we would not starve.

It was strange to recall all these small details so many years later. It seemed that I had lived many lives since then, though in another sense it seemed as though many of them happened only a few weeks ago.

'What are you lying there thinking about, with a notepad and a pencil on your stomach?' a happy voice asked. When I looked up, my *aku-aku* disappeared into the green foliage of the avocado tree and I was left alone in the hammock with Jacqueline's smiling face peering through the branches.

'I was thinking about Fatu-Hiva,' I admitted, 'my first attempt to find paradise.'

'But you didn't find it with Liv on the South Sea islands. You say that one has to look for it in one's innermost self, and that the closest one can come to an outer paradise is by cultivating one's own piece of land.'

Certainly. Therefore it was not the island Fatu-Hiva and my experiences there that I wanted to recall. I simply wanted to clarify what I had learned after a year of full board and lodging at the open and abandoned guesthouse, the jungle.

Jacqueline didn't want to interrupt; she just wondered whether cheese and salad would be enough for supper. She had barely left before my *aku-aku* reappeared.

So you didn't find the paradise you sought on Fatu-Hiva, even though you say that it's the most beautiful and fertile island you have seen in the Pacific Ocean?

Yes, we found paradise when Fatu-Hiva rose into sight on the ocean like a floating basket of flowers, its wonderful tropical aromas wafted on the breeze to meet us. It was on the beach of paradise that we waded ashore in tropical sunshine towards rows of palms welcoming us to the jungle garden, so much of which was uninhabited.

Small fluffy clouds danced like peaceful white lambs over the high brick-red mountain-wall that divided the island in two, behind the green canopy of the jungle. Even when the magnificent sound of birdsong died down in the afternoon, when the midday heat and magically formed heavy dark clouds concealed the mountains and chased the lambs away, even then the brook continued babbling down the valley, just as happily as before, and we were still in paradise. Weeks passed and we were filled with the same love of nature we had in the wilds of Norway. We never felt lonely or homesick, though our surroundings were totally different from the pine forests we had loved. Breadfruit, bananas, oranges and papaya were ripe for the picking, and there were no monkeys to harvest them before we did. We literally enjoyed the fruits of what had been brought to the island from the east and the west, by people who had contracted contagious diseases and gone off to the eternal hunting grounds sometime in the last century. With the exception of fern roots, nothing that was edible had grown on these isolated islands in Polynesia before humans arrived.

If there was a paradise on earth then we had discovered it in the Omoa valley, and no one prevented us from settling there. We found a tall platform of huge stone blocks – a *pae-pae*. The valley had many of these structures, which once elevated palm-covered huts above the mud in the rainy season. This one was right next to a spring of cold, crystal-clear water that ran into a brook filled with crayfish. The last queen of the island had lived here, according to those who had outlived her and who had now moved to a small village down by the water.

This is where we built our first home of bamboo, covered with braided palm leaves, and with an opening that gave us a view of paradise. It was our own Garden of Eden.

But the real Garden of Eden probably had no mosquitoes, unless of course it was mosquitoes that finally drove Adam and Eve away. Anyhow, it was primarily mosquitoes that chased us out of the valley once the rainy season started. For weeks we had roamed around naked and barefoot in the interior of the valley, which was ours alone. The only four-legged creatures were lizards and small fruit rats, and the descendants of lost domesticated animals, brought by Europeans, that had survived in the wilderness. No snakes. Of all I collected, the only poisonous insects were some huge millipedes that never left the cover of rocks and never attacked, except once, when a drunken and evil-minded native called Napoleon placed a few of them among the banana leaves in our bed, in the hope of pleasing the God of the Catholic priests by driving Protestants away.

The mosquitoes came in thick swarms once the rainy season started, and that was the end of paradise. We were well on our way to perishing in an inferno of itching and stinging. I experienced hell in the Garden of Eden when my fears culminated in the sight of Liv rolling on the floor in the bamboo hut, moaning with pain and covered with mosquitoes. I had never seen her frightened or heard her complain, but we had to give up. Today survival in the garden of paradise on a South Sea island requires mosquito netting. Down in the village we were given some netting by an extremely helpful copra vendor, the island's only half-caste inhabitant. He was a son of Paul Gauguin's friend Grelet, who had lived with the natives in the village at the turn of the century.

But not only were mosquitoes chasing us from paradise. We knew it was only a matter of time before we would become infested with filaria, the worm that causes the dreaded elephantiasis, a disease that had ravaged the villagers. Every tenth person had arms as thick as thighs or humped around on enormously enlarged legs that were as fat around the ankles as the waist. Leprosy had also taken its toll on the coast, and there was no doctor or hospital. Life became intolerable when Liv developed huge boils on her legs which the natives called *fe-fe*, and they burst and turned into open sores that refused to heal. We left the jungle and relocated to the coast in the Ouia valley, on the windward side of the island where small white clouds came sailing with the trade winds from South America. The constant easterly wind blew all mosquitoes into the woods and for a few wonderful weeks we experienced paradise again.

Ironically, it was the villagers who had warned us against moving over to the windward side. The ocean there was rough all year round and nobody could risk getting into a canoe to fish. The only one person still living there was Tei Tetua, the last survivor of the era of cannibalism.

'Your father should have seen this,' I said to Liv as we crossed the mountain ridge and climbed down the cliffs to the Ouia valley. The old man was running toward us, stark naked except for a strip of dark cloth protecting his most precious parts. His face shone with joy at seeing people in his valley, and he welcomed us with the usual phrase: *Hamai te kaikai*, 'Come and eat'. But this was no empty phrase to Tei Tetua. He was a Polynesian of the old school, the only person I would meet who had entered the twentieth century as if the Europeans had not yet arrived in the Pacific. He lived with his adopted twelve-year-old daughter Tahia-Momo in total isolation from the rest of the world.

It wasn't all nonsense Liv's father had read about cannibals on the Marquesas. Officially the last instance of cannibalism

occurred at a large party in the Puamao valley on the neighbouring island of Hivaoa in 1887. The last person identified as
having been eaten was a Swedish carpenter who had been con-
sumed in 1879. Tei Tetua told us modestly that he had only
ever tasted a person who had been beaten to death, from the
neighbouring valley, when he was a child. His father, Uta,
however, had been a veritable cannibal who not only con-
sumed his fallen enemies as a matter of ritual, but because he
preferred the taste to pork.

Hogs grunted and rooted around freely in the Ouia valley,
where Tei Tetua, with his dogs and lasso of bast, was the only
hunter. It is unthinkable to imagine better pork than that the
old man served, accompanied by fresh breadfruit rolled in
banana leaves and baked in his earth oven. He helped us build
our own hut in the shape of an open bird's nest with three
walls. It was raised on high poles to keep the wild hogs from
coming in when we were asleep.

We never made our own food again. The little Polynesian
charmer Tahia-Momo brought us all our meals on large taro
leaves from Tei's hut, which lay just inside the beach of boulders and only a stone's throw away from our pole hut. Food was
plentiful, and there was more variation than in the jungle on the
other side of the island. Tei Tetua kept chickens, and on the
naked bracken-covered hillside on either side of the Ouia valley,
where no one had lived since the inhabitants moved over to the
leeward side of the island in the last century, there were masses
of wonderful cherry tomatoes and *enata* pineapples. The
botanist F. B. H. Brown had concluded that this fruit must have
been brought by people from South America before the
Europeans discovered that there were islands in the Pacific.

And then there was the ocean rising up in mountainous
crests and breaking on to the beach after having rolled unim-
peded in great swells from the coast of South America 8,000

kilometres away. The breakers caused the round stones constantly to roll and rattle on the beach in a rhythmical concert
complete with its own waterfall. The ocean spray provided
fresh circulation in all the saltwater puddles in the lava for-
mations that flanked the valley, and they were filled with life.
Crabs and fish crawled and swam among sea snails, sea
anemone and seaweed. Compared to the jungles of the continents, the ocean was a more suitable foster mother for us
two-legged creatures without climbing skills.

There are countless friendly people on our planet, and I
have met many of them, but none are as incredibly kind and
generous as this former cannibal was. We would shudder a bit
while squatting on our haunches, chewing on a meaty bone,
listening to his stories from another time and another world.
He described how Papa Uta, with a beautifully carved wooden
club that is now a valuable museum piece, went off to war to
extract revenge on enemies in Hanativa, or walked all the way
to the Omoa valley, where Tei now had his only remaining
relatives.

Tei Tetua was no heathen. Everyone in the island group
was now Christian. A priest from the Catholic mission in
Hivaoa had walked over the mountain and converted him. He
had learned that in French Tiki was 'Dieu' and, just to be on
the safe side, he had dug out his own grave next to the wall of
his hut and placed a cross right over it, which he proudly
showed us. Tahia-Momo would help him into it if his strength
failed when he felt death was approaching.

He firmly claimed that according to his own forefathers, the
first people had come across the ocean with Tiki from the
east, from Te-Fiti, where the sun rises. I knew from
Kroepelin's library that the German ethnographer von den
Steinen had heard a generation ago from old people on the
Marquesas Islands that there was a large country beyond the

sunrise that was called Fiti-Nui, 'The Great East'. The American ethnologist E. S. C. Handy, who visited Hivaoa later, heard that the inhabitants' forefathers had come from this large country in the east called Te-Fiti. Handy was so surprised by the assertion that the fatherland was in the east, in the direction of South America, that according to his own words he had to ask twice. Again it was firmly maintained that one had to steer in *te tihena oumati*, 'with a course toward the sunrise', to find the ancestral homeland.

Tei Tetua was just as certain about this. We were mosquito-free, sitting at the edge of the woods, by the fire, and looking over the endless ocean in the direction of where the sun appeared at dawn. The small clouds faithfully followed the wake of the trade winds across the night sky. And when Tei Tetua told us what he had learned in his youth, it was obvious that he had learned his lessons well, without the letters of the alphabet. Without having read botanical works, he could tell me things I myself had learned from reference books. He was fully aware of the fact that the wild pineapple and the tiny tomatoes up on the hillside had been brought by his own forefathers, whom he called *enata*, 'people', as opposed to foreigners. Even the younger generation in the Omoa valley was aware of the source of these useful species. They had two types of pineapple, *faa hoka*, but only one was called *enata*, because it was their original fruit; the other was called *oahu*, because a missionary from Oahu on the Hawaiian Islands had brought it to them. They also had two types of American papaya, the larger one called *vi oahu* and the smaller with the taller trunk called *vi enata*. The nickname *enata* was consistently given to species that botanists had identified as having been brought by boat from their place of origin in South America before the islands were visited by Europeans.

It was Tei Tetua who taught me that what we call oral tradition contains reliable information that is too easily discarded and consigned to the same category as legends, folk tales and myths. Legends in Polynesia are just as dependable as many of the accounts we accept, simply because they were written in pen and ink by medieval historians.

What did you learn about your own world by seeing it through Tei Tetua's eyes?

That we put clothes on in order to fool ourselves into believing we were no longer as primitive as the naked savage. We refused to understand that we had only changed our surroundings, we were the same, no better, no worse. Generation after generation of human beings are born with the same spiritual and physical characteristics described in the legend of Adam and Eve, and which were passed down by Abraham's forefathers. The chromosomes carried by the twins Cain and Abel still exist in us.

We tell ourselves and others that we have made progress in the art of killing our enemies. During the last century we sent missionaries to all the island groups in Polynesia, preaching that it was wrong to club others to death just because we didn't like them. But then, a few decades later, we returned in uniforms, explaining that by wearing such clothing they could kill as many as they wanted – as long as the enemy was wearing different uniforms and saluted a different flag.

We found it difficult to explain that with long-range cannons we did not know who we killed, and that it was better not to know. Tei Tetua was the son of a warrior chieftain who always knew the names of the persons he beat to death.

Anthropologists' dissertations maintained that the tribal wars on the Marquesas Islands were a result of overpopulation, and Tei Tetua's stories seemed to confirm this. He showed no surprise when I admitted to the fear of a new world war; a generation had passed since the last one. Our friend in the Ouia valley also thought this credible. He had drawn his own conclusions from my attempts to describe life in London and New York.

We had multiplied so rapidly that our forests were disappearing, and we had so little space that we built our homes in rows without any room between them, and eventually we built them on top of one another and they became skyscrapers.

I assured him that although we didn't eat humans, we did eat cows and chickens and any animals we thought were tasty. We were fond of animals and didn't like to slaughter them, and we liked fishing. When he heard this Tei Tetua said it was silly of us not to do our own fishing, giving others the pleasure of pulling in the fish and bartering with the fisherman. The idea of money and prices was unknown to our friend, so I didn't complicate the issue by talking about middle men and shops.

Tei Tetua agreed with my criticism of cannibalism. Then, when he asked what we did with all the people we killed in the war, I shocked him.

'We bury them,' I had to admit.

'Just dig them all into the ground?' I could read in the old man's face that I had disappointed him.

6

At the Bottom of Jacob's Ladder

From tribal wars to world war – some progress!

This time my *aku-aku* had ventured into my study, where I was leafing through my notes and papers to recall old memories. It had been a long time since I had seen these papers or thought about these things.

It was quite a twist of fate. After pursuing a course of study that would allow us to avoid civilisation in the certainty that a new war would break out, we let mosquitoes and the danger of infection among peaceful, primitive natives chase us away, only to end up risking our lives among mines and bombs in the very civilisation we had left.

Just a year after our return from Fatu-Hiva, Norwegian newspapers were reporting that German tanks had rolled into Poland. These were the tanks that we thought would make a new war impossible. Better weapons did not guarantee peace.

We bought a nice little log cabin with a peat roof up in the mountains above Lillehammer and turned it into a year-round residence. We had a splendid view of Lake Mjøsa and the town, and an almost impenetrable pine forest behind our cabin that gradually merged with juniper bushes, heather and flower meadows all the way to the mountain plateau near Hornsjø.

I worked in a small outhouse in my own study, which was separated from the woodshed and the outside lavatory by a panel wall. I had total peace. I thanked my lucky stars that I had an education to fall back on. I made a living by writing a book and giving slide lectures about our attempt to return to paradise.

But I was also hard at work on a scientific manuscript. I had files filled with notes from Kroepelin's library, and had left the field of biology for Polynesian anthropology. The manuscript, which was in English, was growing daily, replete with quotations and references. It was called *Polynesia and America*.

I had done something that was totally different from the conventional research of the time. I had tried to solve the Polynesian riddle as a detective would. The groundwork had been done by researchers from totally different branches of science, and I was trying to correlate the results. The method did not follow conventional rules, but it gave good, well-founded results.

Everyone at that time agreed that at least two waves of immigrants had reached Polynesia. The later wave had come such a short time before the Europeans discovered the islands that they all still spoke the same language, in spite of living thousands of kilometres apart, and being spread over the eastern half of the world's largest ocean. Since each individual researcher had attacked the problem within his special field, none of them, so far, had arrived at the same conclusion. The only findings that were not contradicted were those of the philologists, since they could prove that although the types of people and cultures were totally different, the Polynesians had diffuse language roots in common with the Malaysians in Asia.

The route of their migration was still a mystery. The Polynesians and the Malaysians lived at opposite ends of the enormous Pacific Ocean, with the aboriginal Negroid population in the Melanesia islands as a large 4,000-kilometre barrier between them. In all this enormous area, there were no traces of any Polynesian passage. This in itself was a mystery, because the Polynesians arrived on their islands furthest east in the Pacific Ocean with a pure Stone Age culture as late as the European Middle Ages. Therefore they must have left the coastal areas in Asia before the Asian Stone Age ended, between 3000–2000 BC. Where had these seafarers been in the meantime?

This was the crux of the Polynesian problem. Some of their forefathers must have journeyed out into the Philippine Ocean around 3000 BC and continued on to some unknown area, where they remained for almost four thousand years. Where?

Researchers were divided between two theories. Some thought the Polynesian forefathers had passed so rapidly through the Austral-Melanisian and Micronesian island area that they left no traces. But this made no chronological sense. The second and opposite theory maintained that they had spent thousands of years on the journey, moving from one island to the next, sailing into the wind, and in this way metamorphosed themselves and their culture from Malaysians to Polynesians by way of a 'micro evolution'. But in that case, nothing made sense.

The controversy raged at its most intense at the time I was gathering information from the Polynesia library, and went off to the Marquesas Islands to get an inside view of Polynesia as a biologist and geographer. At that time, the most renowned Polynesian researcher was the New Zealander, Sir Peter Buck.

He supported those who thought that the Polynesian fore-fathers must have passed through Melanesia, but admitted that his only reason for doing so was that they certainly could not have come through Micronesia. Buck's prominent col-league, the French ethnologist Dr Métraux, based his views on studies of blood types and wrote that any attempt to place the origins of the Polynesians in Melanesia 'was a crime against known facts'.

This complicated controversy was totally meaningless to me. There was no reason to believe that either Melanesia or Micronesia posed any obstacles. The world was round, and the current from the Philippine Ocean ran to the north of all these islands and reached Hawaii via British Columbia.

British Columbia. No one had thought of a Polynesian stop-over all the way up there in the north. The warm ocean current beyond the Philippines flowed so fast and majesti-cally past Japan to the archipelago along the coast of British Columbia that the canoe people up there went barefoot all the year round, in spite of living as far north as Hudson Bay and Labrador on the opposite side of Canada. After my year in Polynesia, I had to find a way to visit and learn about these American Pacific islands. No Polynesian researcher had con-sidered them. The islands lay slap in the centre of this route and had a maritime population that originated from Asia's Stone Age, and continued living in the Stone Age until the arrival of the Europeans.

The Fred Olsen Oslo shipping company had cargo ships that served British Columbia. My parents knew old Fred, and his son Thomas was the first to hear about my theory. I myself thought it was so obvious that I was afraid others would steal it before I published it. Thomas Olsen agreed with me, and I was given tickets to Vancouver for Liv, myself and Little Thor, who was now one year old, for a token fee.

We had not yet left Norway when England declared war on Germany, so the ship was directed to the north of Scotland to avoid submarines in the English Channel. Tei Tetua's tribal war would pale in comparison to what was about to happen.

My family and my theories received an exceptionally warm welcome in scientific circles in British Columbia, first at the university in the growing city of Vancouver, and then at the Provincial Museum in idyllic Victoria on Vancouver Island. The university still lacked its own anthropological faculty, but I met the foremost expert on local Northwest Indian languages, Professor Hill-Tout. The friendly old language researcher immediately identified two publications that had been written by himself and a colleague in Ottawa and pointed out the marked difference in language between the various tribes along the coast of British Columbia, despite their mutual relationship in both race and culture. The strangest thing, which they each had discovered independently, was that the language of several of the tribes showed a distant but definite relationship to the languages in both Polynesia and Malaysia.

The elderly professor maintained that there was no doubt. He had concluded that Polynesian canoes must have come up to British Columbia, but realised now that canoes from this area could just as easily have made it to Hawaii. Captain Voss from Vancouver had recently sailed a similar canoe from Vancouver, past Hawaii and, with the northeast trade winds behind him, his journey ended on the other side of the Pacific, with the Maoris in New Zealand.

This was a promising start, and, if possible, things went even better at the museum in the capital city. The ethnographic and archaeological collections from all the coastal

Indians were stored in cardboard boxes in the cellar, but the museum's director had the key, and he was a zoologist.

As a favour to a colleague and because I had brought a jar of fruit rats in formaldehyde from the Marquesas, I was given a place to study at Dr Cowan's large desk and access to the excellent library.

For a researcher it could be likened to arriving in heaven, sitting in the director's office devouring source material that I could never have found in Kroepelin's Polynesia library. The islands along the coast of British Columbia lay outside the Polynesian researchers' area of interest, which was the South Sea islands. They had simply forgotten that the earth is round, that the Pacific Ocean curves, and that a flat map tells lies about distances. When considering this, it becomes obvious that the islands off British Columbia are not at the end of a curved and indirect route from the Philippine Ocean, but on a line that is just as straight as the equator.

It was at this museum that I completely understood the implication of Captain Cook and Vancouver's observations and their surprise to see how much the Northwest Indians reminded them of Polynesians in both race and culture. Researchers in the twentieth century have confirmed the same, often convincingly, in their dissertations about the Northwest Indians and their culture.

What others had pointed out, without crossing the geographical border for Polynesian research, I came to see with my own eyes when I left the museum and went to live among the Bella Coola Indians further up the coast with my little family. The winter passed, and then things changed.

My scientific theory had been well received in the local press, and one journalist located me in the Bella Coola valley. Down by the riverbank, under the turf, I uncovered rock carvings and found masks of gods with concentric rings for eyes, just like the ones on Fatu-Hiva. We found the same unusual axe blades of stone and bark beaters as those used on the Marquesas Islands, and we seemed to recognise both our own adoptive father Teriieroo and our old friend Tei Tetua among the Indians in the valley.

The news reached the *New York Times*, but it was accompanied by a commentary from the Polynesia anthropologist Margaret Mead, who had just become world famous for her book on love life in Samoa. She refuted my theory, claiming that I had probably found artefacts left behind by Captain Cook after his visit to Polynesia. I never managed to reply that it was doubtful that Captain Cook had sat down by the river and copied Polynesian rock carvings. More important things were happening, both for me and in the world at large.

I met Margaret Mead, my first academic opponent, in Oslo many years after the war. At that point we could enjoy the fact that our research had covered totally different areas. She had to admit that she knew as little about rock carvings in British Columbia as I knew about love life in Samoa.

Liv and I were about to experience a sudden and totally unexpected change in our lives. I had been bear-hunting with the half-caste Indian Clayton Mack, later to become quite a legendary figure through his book *Grizzlies and White Guys*, which included the story of our adventure. Our hunting trip ended with Clayton shooting and injuring a bear which then chased me in circles around a tree stump. Clayton felled the bear, and its dreadful scream echoed round the mountains, and I was put off any form of hunting for the rest of my life. Clayton and I paddled back from the uninhabited Kwatna valley with the bear in the bow of the canoe. As we swung in between the cliff walls along the long and narrow Bella Coola fjord, someone called to me from the quay.

'Norway has surrendered!'

I cupped my hands in front of my mouth, and called back: 'To whom?'

That anyone could attack Norway, a neutral and inoffensive country, which had not been at war as an independent country since the Viking era, was totally unthinkable to me. Hitler had been regarded as an almost comical figure, and the United States had still not entered the war. The following week, Liv and I and our little boy boarded the coastal ship when it passed Bella Coola on its way south. I wanted to get back to Vancouver and report for military duty at the Norwegian consulate.

In fact I received a rather cool reception at the consulate; after mounting the stairs I read the name plate on the door: von Stahlschmidt.

The consul assured me in English, with a German accent, that Germany and Norway were friends. I should calmly return to my Indians and remain there until the war was over.

I had come to Canada with a student visa and a return ticket to Norway, but now I might just as well throw them away. In addition we only had enough money for a few days in Vancouver, and since Liv was pregnant, the situation was critical.

Worst of all, an American journalist who had been in Oslo on the day of the invasion had written sensational and totally false reports about Norway having welcomed the Germans. His story hit the headlines in both the American and Canadian press. And of course the Germans reported nothing about Norway's sinking of Germany's largest warship, *Blucher*, in the Oslo Fjord with over a thousand men on board, or about the battles that continued for many weeks in Norway's valleys.

Now we were just as unpopular as we first had been popular when we arrived from Norway. We did not even dare speak

Norwegian to one another on the trolley-bus. More than a year would pass before this hatred of Norway died away and slowly turned to admiration, after the United States was swept into the war and President Roosevelt proclaimed, 'Look to Norway!' in a speech to his countrymen. He pointed out that the Germans would have won the battle of Europe if the Norwegian merchant navy, which then was the third largest in the world, had not put all its ships at the disposal of the Allies.

In the meantime, on a personal level, we came to see some of the shadier sides of life. We immediately moved out of our hotel and found an inexpensive room facing a back lot down in the harbour area. A gas light, a horrendous bed, a table, a stool and an old basket for Little Thor made up the furniture. From the curtainless window we looked down on to a large coal shed, illuminated by a single light bulb. Our landlady was suspicious, ill tempered and whiny, and when she heard that we were Norwegian, she grew even more distrustful.

No one knew how long the war would last. I had to find a temporary job. There was work to be found for those who were prepared to queue outside the unemployment office. After observing the people in this line, I stopped shaving, put on an old cap and placed myself at the end. As the queue advanced, everyone was asked about their occupation, and they all called themselves carpenters or plumbers, whether or not they had ever held a saw or a wrench. When my turn came and I said I was a zoologist, they had no idea what that was. Ethnologist made no impression either. When asked if I knew how to use a wheelbarrow, I answered in the affirmative. However, I never did get a job because I had entered the country on a student visa and had no work permit.

The days passed and turned into weeks. Our last traveller's cheque had been cashed, our funds had dwindled dangerously, and Liv was expecting our second child. We had to ration our food. This really helped me understand how fortunate I had been to grow up in a social class where daily breakfast, lunch and dinner were taken for granted.

We had felt hunger pangs on Fatu-Hiva, in the rainy season, but there were still crayfish in the brook and a few coconuts falling off the palm trees. Here there was only concrete and closed doors and windows. Without having experienced it, it is hard to imagine the emotions of a man, with a hungry family at home and an empty stomach himself, staring through a restaurant window at a plump, golden chicken, slowly rotating on a grill while an indescribably wonderful aroma seeps through the door every time hungry people enter or contented diners exit.

When people who have endured this experience join forces with revolutionaries, whether their names are Joan of Arc or Fidel Castro, they are not making a political statement. People who are not hungry never revolt.

Standing there with my last shillings, not even enough to pay the rent, looking at displays of wonderful food in store windows, unable to return home with a juicy morsel for Liv and Little Thor, brought home to me the unfairness of modern society. I wasn't alone in this situation. Thousands and millions, statistically over half the earth's population, were in a situation like this, or even worse. We who have enough, write and speak like prophets about a time when a lack of resources and overpopulation will create a world catastrophe. But catastrophe is already a reality for that part of the world's population who never write newspaper articles and whose voice is never heard, even from the top of a soapbox.

One day while I was standing in front of a bakery shop window, I understood that we, my little family, were actually in great danger.

Liv was incredibly brave, as she was on Fatu-Hiva. Never a complaint, never a sour word. I paced the floor for hours at a time, sometimes in anger and near desperation. And then came the darkest day of them all, a Sunday. The rent was due the next day. Our funds had been reduced to a few coins. Thirty cents. Liv went out and spent all our money on three loaves of sweet bread. With Little Thor between us we walked out into the sunshine and sat down on a bench in Stanley Park, beside the canoe that had sailed from here and all the way down to New Zealand. To hell with the whole theory. The totem pole erected next to the canoe seemed more fitting for the mood of the day. Grotesque characters crawled over one another, and the victor, with clenched claws and the greedy teeth of a beast of prey, crowned the pole. I was ready to repent, to beseech and beg the creative powers of heaven and earth for help, wherever they were to be found, in the universe or within myself.

The next event might have been a coincidence. But coincidences like this have often turned up in acute situations later in life as well, so it pays to pray for them to happen.

When the landlady knocked on the door the next morning to collect the rent, we were flat broke. There was no way out, our time was up, and we were ready to give in.

The landlady had a letter for us as well as the rent demand. It came from the Fred Olsen shipping company, and its agent in Vancouver had us with a telegram from the London office.

Shipowner Thomas Olsen and family had escaped from occupied Norway to England. All his ships were assigned to the Allied convoys through Nortraship, which was in charge of the entire Norwegian merchant navy. The telegram stated that the agent was to trace the whereabouts of everyone who was stranded in Vancouver as the passengers of Fred Olsen and who had no possibility of travelling home. In addition, I was to receive a monthly loan of whatever amount I needed to survive until the war was over.

It was like a wonderful dream. Life could go on. In a rush of joy and with a mixture of gratitude and modesty, I asked to borrow fifty dollars a month. Even then it was a very moderate sum, but we had learned that one dollar consisted of 100 cents. We had purchased three loaves of sweet bread for our last thirty.

With renewed courage I finished my first two articles in English, a scientific article for *International Science* and a popular article for *National Geographic Magazine*. Both were accepted, and from *National Geographic* I received a two-hundred-dollar cheque. Just after this Liv was admitted to the maternity clinic, and the money came in handy for the hospital and for an outfit for the new baby, Bjørn, nicknamed Bamse in honour of a bear cub we had seen climbing up a tree with a daisy in its mouth one day on a trip into the forest in the Bella Coola valley.

The sunny days in the Bella Coola valley were now a distant memory. They were replaced by a new life that was, in a way, totally different. A work permit arrived from Ottawa, and thanks to the father of a Norwegian student I had met at the university when we arrived, I found a job and a sponsor. The father, Robert Lepsøe, worked as an engineer at a factory far up in the Rocky Mountains, employing seven thousand men. It was a frightening complex of factory buildings. Before Lepsøe's arrival, it spewed out so much sulphurous smoke that the forest and green fields in a wide radius around, even over the border and into the United States, had been affected.

Lepsøe had managed to install a filtering system, and now most of the sulphur was collected and driven away in railroad cars. This was an important source of profit. Solely on that man's reputation, I was entrusted with a job in the factory's gang of handymen, and I really did learn how to use a wheelbarrow. We were seventeen men with just as many mother tongues. We worked every day in the factory's so-called 'ball gang' and never got bored because we were assigned different types of work every day, while the employees had assembly-line jobs. My first job was to help load sacks of cement onto a railroad car. I looked around for a wheelbarrow, but the sacks were to be carried on one's shoulder. My knees almost collapsed when a huge giant of a Pole threw the first sack on me. It was even worse stumbling beneath the heavy load and trying to make it up the narrow plank to the railroad car while the others stared and teased the newcomer. I could barely stand when the day was over, and my body had swollen so badly that it was difficult to take off my clothes.

I didn't have to carry sacks the next day. The cement was to be transported in larger containers.

'Come here, Mac, and I'll give you a better job,' the foreman said. I followed him and explained politely that my name wasn't Mac, but Thor.

'I don't give a damn what you're called,' the foreman shouted. 'To me you're Mac!'

The so-called better job was joining a long line of men who fed cement into an enormous, rotating cement mixer. Each man had the contents of a sack dumped into his wheelbarrow as he passed, and the aim was to stay in line while walking up some narrow planks to a scaffold, where the cement was dumped into a mixer, before continuing down the other side with an empty wheelbarrow. The whole operation had to proceed rhythmically and ran at such a furious pace that sweat poured and tempers erupted. Time and again I had to back my wheelbarrow to get more speed to make it up the plank, while the man behind me swore and cursed because I had broken the flow. After half a dozen rounds I was so tired that my wheelbarrow ran off the plank and tipped over the load of cement. The foreman cursed me roundly, but it was time for a cigarette break, which occurred every fifteen minutes on this hard job. While the others enjoyed their foul-smelling cigarettes, I cleaned up the mess and threw myself down on my back and enjoyed every single deep breath until it was back to work again!

But I have never had such good food as then.

Everyone knows that hunger is the best cook. But it is a cook whose services cannot be bought.

Like most people who can afford to do so, I enjoy relaxing and savouring something delicious like oysters or real caviar, or drinking a glass of champagne or a dry Martini. But I will never forget the superlative delight of the meal breaks at the Consolidated Mining and Smelting Company, when we threw ourselves down on a heap of bricks and opened our lunch boxes: bread and butter and cheese, and a bottle of cold chocolate milk.

Hard work takes the greatest toll on those who have never really used their muscles. By the third day I started to feel like a new man. I had built up my stamina and did not tire so easily. But the pleasure of exercising my muscles was short-lived. The foreman picked two of us for a less strenuous job. An experienced fellow whispered that he thought we were being sent down into some huge tanks, and that rumour had it they were only cleaned every fifth year and it was a devilish job.

We were equipped with long-handled scrapers and thigh-high rubber boots. Our first order, when we were already on our way down the ladder, inside the tank, was at all cost to stay on our feet, because the stuff at the bottom was sulphuric acid. If we slipped and fell, the acid would burn away clothing, skin and flesh instantaneously.

Before letting go of the ladder at the bottom of the dark tank, I felt the bottom with one foot. It was covered with a thick layer of slime, slippery as soap. We stepped with great care on to the tank floor, while the foreman leaned over the edge far above us and shouted his orders, which we never quite understood as his voice echoed around like thunder within the metal tank. We surmised that the acid had to be scraped out through an outlet on the far wall of the tank. It was a horrendous job. With our legs apart we slid as if in slow motion, supported by the scrapers that we pushed in front of us, toward the opening, pressing the muck carefully forward so it wouldn't splash. If we pushed too hard, we slid backward, and the slightest loss of balance would cause us to tumble down into the evil brew. I felt that, as if by a misunderstanding, I had landed in a giant cauldron owned by civilised cannibals.

There were worse assignments to come. I was also sent into a furnace. The factory, which first and foremost was a smelting plant, was also running experiments, which resulted in the formation of cinder deposits in some of the smaller furnaces. I was sent inside one of them to remove the metal refuse from the walls, equipped with an air hammer, a chisel and a light bulb as well as a gas mask for my nose and mouth; the inside of the furnace was dark and dusty. As soon as I started hammering the walls, I found myself exposed to a more intense form of one of my early sketches of our progress from paradise: dust, noise and numerous harmful sensory attacks. The air hammer provided an incessant explosion of cannons in my ears and, combined with the dust, lack of ventilation and my dripping sweat, it almost drove me crazy. I could not even hear my own voice, and all I remember is shouting the same two words at each explosive bang: 'I hate! I hate! I hate!'

When I finally finished and crawled out, I contemplated the

fate of tens of thousands of farmers who had voluntarily left their fields to crawl into mines and furnaces. They came to the cities to join in the dance around machines, like the tribes of Moses around the golden calf. But later, in the shower, having removed the worst of the filth, both inside and out, I realised that returning to nature was not the answer either.

Not all the jobs at the factory were as tough as the ones in the tank and the furnace. The best one was assigned to the gang left over after the most important jobs were filled. We were sent to clean old bricks. We sat there, brick in lap, and chipped off remnants of old cement. Whole bricks were then placed in beautiful piles, while broken ones and chunks of cement were thrown onto another heap. We worked our way gradually into the huge pile, and the guys became expert in piling the bricks around us in such a way that we were less visible if someone wanted a cigarette.

I was working with a type of person that was new to me, one not all that different to businessmen and academics as one might think. For most of them work had been hard to come by until the war created employment. The men whose company I enjoyed the most, maybe because they were sea-soned travellers and had a sense of humour, were the so-called hobos, the skilled workers' occupational title for professional vagabonds. They had criss-crossed Canada and the United States by train, often by hanging under railroad cars or hiding amongst the cargo.

As time went by I also came to like the rough foreman, and we developed a better understanding of one another. He had reason not to give a damn what I was called. No one knew his name either; he just went by the name of Mystery. 'Because no one knows who his father was,' it was said. When he was angry, he spoke Italian. I did not realise how clever he was until I discovered he could not read. I caught on one day when

I happened to see someone give him a note that he just stuffed into his shirt pocket. When he thought no one was looking he plunged both arms, down to the elbows, into a barrel with something gooey in it that dripped from his fingers, and then he came over to me and asked me to take the note from his pocket and read what was on it. He was in his element when driving the factory's small locomotive. He had learned what words such as 'Stop' looked like.

Mystery probably meant well when he sent me up into the fresh air on the roof of one of the factory's new buildings after having seen how I hated the stench of all the noxious gases that gathered in and around the factory. A visible layer of clouds, consisting of dust, smoke and poisonous steam, descended into the valley to the small town of Trail, where all the workers lived. Only the white-collar workers lived up on the plateau, on the same altitude as the factory. They enjoyed beautiful houses and green lawns. I chose to commute to the factory, and placed Liv and the two little ones up in Rossland, high above the factory smoke stacks. The sulphurous smoke from the factory was still a health hazard, though conditions had improved after the United States had won a court case when the health hazard literally crossed the border. Older factory workers often suffered from silicosis because of the dust in their lungs. One day, after work, a tall, thin rod of a man with all the signs of the disease looked at me with his pale face and said: 'Another day and another dollar, and one more day closer to death.'

Fresh air was fine, but I was far from happy when Mystery gave me a job as bucket hoister and sent me climbing up ladders and on loose, rickety planks up to the roof of the factory building. I cannot remember whether it was six or eight storeys, but the air was more than fresh enough; it was in the middle of the Canadian winter and we were 1,400 metres

above sea level in the Rocky Mountains. I was already somewhat afraid of heights. As a student, I had almost fallen 1,000
metres from a mountain shelf over the Romsdal valley. My
new job was to hang over the eaves on my stomach, my head
down and my legs in the air, to nail tar paper under the ledge.
A big roof and a lot of nails. My boss was an expert roofer,
and he walked upright, carrying a long pole with a brush, and
smeared glowing hot asphalt along the paper's upper edge, to
enable the next layer to bond with the underlying one. We
gradually worked our way further away from the horrible
eaves, and I had time to notice the temperature. It was
extremely cold and there were strong winds, but my namesake, Mac, who stoked the asphalt over a fire on the ground,
was experienced in the business. He heated bricks over the
fire, and bundled them into a sack that I hoisted up with the
asphalt buckets. I kept a warm brick in my overalls and, when
it cooled, exchanged it for a new one.

Then Mystery remembered that I could write. When the
roofing job was finished, I was given a ledger and a pencil and
was placed outside a furnace like the one I knew so well, both
inside and out. One of the engineers wanted Mystery to keep
a written report that recorded temperatures shown on a gauge
when the ore started melting, and observed the way the ore
behaved, and the colour structure of the melting mass.
Mystery collected the information from me every day and
handed it on. And each time, he looked at the page and
nodded satisfactorily, 'Looks good. Looks good.'

One day I wanted to check whether Mystery really could
not read. I handed the ledger to him upside-down. He didn't
turn it round.

'Looks good,' he said.

However, on another occasion the engineer himself wanted
to meet the person who was writing the reports. Mystery

introduced his assistant. 'You write well,' the engineer said, and I was promoted. Mystery had to find a new assistant, but there were others in the ball gang who could write.

I ended up as a supervisor in a newly built magnesium factory. I had no clue as to what was going on, except that we were making magnesium powder, which was useful in the war against the Germans.

The job did not last long. One fine day my bus pulled up at the factory stop but the factory was no longer there. All that remained was a heap of twisted metal; the whole magnesium factory had exploded during the night shift. I'll never forget the descriptions of the day-shift workers who had been the first to arrive on the scene. A severed hand was seen hanging over one of the iron roof beams.

That was the end of the magnesium powder, but I got a new job.

By then we had moved to Lepsøe's summer cabin beside Arrow Lake, so far from the factory that skunks lived under the floorboards and I had to rise under a night-time sky, while the coyotes howled, and take a bicycle, a boat and a bus to get to work. I never did become a white-collar man, but I made so much money that I paid off the entire loan to the agent in Vancouver. Then I bought a bus ticket and travelled straight across North America to New York to volunteer my services at the Norwegian consulate.

The Norwegian royal family and the whole Norwegian government had escaped to England, and the military high command was also in London recruiting sailors and refugees from Norway to fight with the Allies. As I waited for an answer, I took a temporary job as timekeeper at the Bethlehem Fairfield Shipyard in Baltimore. It was a sedentary job which consisted of checking squares on the workers' time cards that showed whether they had worked on the propeller, the hull, or the superstructure of the ship. I could actually spend the whole day reading American anthropology with a clear conscience, while the others were building ships. I had visited two professors at Johns Hopkins University who guided me towards the most relevant reading material. Both took the time to listen patiently to this timekeeper from the shipyard, who had obviously read a great many books in their field. Professor Ruth Benedict was the first one to give me an important lead. The Polynesians must have come from an area that had a hierarchical society, ruled by a superhuman priest-king. This was a remarkable characteristic that the tribes on all the islands in Polynesia had in common with their neighbours in Mexico and Peru.

I arranged for Liv and the little ones to come to the States. Bjørn should have been baptised long ago. On the day we carried him to the font in the Norwegian Seaman's Church in Baltimore, the Japanese dropped their first bombs on American warships in Pearl Harbor. America joined the war. I thought about Teriieroo and Tei Tetua; bombs were probably raining down on Polynesia as well.

It was bad enough when the island warriors sneaked up on their enemies in silent canoes and clubbed people they disliked to death, and then ate them.

But what would they have said if they had experienced Pearl Harbor?

7

Dance With the Devil

Each and every opponent of aggression and revenge is also a freedom fighter. A man of peace cannot allow strangers to break into his home and darken every corner. When the psychosis of war spreads over the world like an eclipse of the sun, casting shadows over the human soul in country after country, then even your own allies will persuade you that the enemy is the devil incarnate. It was bad enough to know that our country was occupied, even worse to be told that people in Norway were surviving on leaves and bread made from tree bark.

War is a dance with the devil. The hatred of a common enemy becomes more important than any feelings of affection for a friend.

When I was a boy, it was the Russians and the Red Army who frightened the grown-ups. My father never allowed me to stand at the bottom of the hill with the other boys on 1 May, Labour Day, and watch the parade of red banners. The grown-ups' anxiety that this might start a revolution was infectious. The whole free world sided with the Finns during the winter war when they wore white camouflage suits and repulsed the red devils.

But the situation changed rapidly. Only one week after Hitler had made the mistake of attacking the Soviet Union instead of Britain, the words 'Red Army' acquired an entirely different sound. Now it was almost like talking about red angels who were helping us fight the Nazis. Few among my small group of acquaintances could explain the difference between the Nazis and the communists, but Stalin and the Russians were now our allies in the battle against Hitler and the Germans.

Many years later, long after Stalin and Hitler were dead, and I had settled in northern Italy, I finally realised that most Russians and Germans were against both communism and Nazism. It dawned on me that I was living amongst wonderful people who had once been our enemies, and thanked my lucky stars that I had never been forced to kill any of them. And I never met an Italian who had fought for fascism. Those who had a choice went into hiding and worked against what they considered to be a German occupation. Essentially, we had all more or less been on the same side, and I wondered why millions of people ended up fighting one another and, for the second time, starting a world war.

Did you yourself have an answer?

Of course I sided with those who wanted to chase all the aggressors back to where they belonged, but I clearly recall that I never associated the word 'enemy' with any particular nation. In fact, when the war was over, I decided to observe how long it would take before we cut the wings off the Reds and re-equipped them with horns and satanic robes. I had danced with them under the northern lights without detecting either horns or wings. They were frostbitten soldiers just like us, who had learned which uniforms to shoot at and, like us, wanted to return home in one piece.

The warrior's moral code was more forthright among the Polynesians and the Northwest Indians. They never used a bow and arrow. They wanted to look the enemy in the eye when they hit him on the head with a club. On our part, we dropped bombs on to families who were enjoying themselves at the dinner table, or we launched rockets from our own country that killed thousands of women and children in another country. At the same time we made amends for regressing into such barbaric behaviour by becoming humane, initiating regulations for social welfare, even for appropriate conduct at work. The smelting plant at Trail is my best example. From being an inferno of smoke, health hazards, and class distinctions, it has in the course of the past fifty years turned into a model society of green lawns and happy workers. The forest has even returned to the surrounding hills.

As reluctant as I was to stay on as a politician and fight the cause of the workers in Canada, equally reluctant was I to enlist in the armed forces. However, enlist I did. As in my civilian career, I managed to rise just high enough in rank to experience the army from two sides, as an officer and as a ranker. Were I to choose again, under similar conditions, I would rather have been working independently for the good of my country than join the ranks of those who received or gave orders in uniform. Experience has taught me that it is unwise to speak your mind to your superiors when posted to an army camp to learn discipline.

I requested an assignment that would allow me to work with a team of dogs in the forests and mountains behind enemy lines. I explained that I was all butterfingers when it came to technology, that I could not drive a car or change a radio battery.

With this information, they sent me to a communications school for advanced training in electronics.

Special telecommunications equipment had been made in London and was on its way to Canada, for use when the battle for liberating Norway had begun. All was strictly secret, and only ten men were selected to use this equipment. I was one of them, and for unknown reasons, we were given the cover name I Group. We were drilled in the mysteries of 'Right, left, about turn' at a Norwegian army camp in Lunenburg in Nova Scotia. After learning how to march, we were issued with air force uniforms and trained as air telegraphists at Camp Little Norway in Toronto. Armed with certificates attesting that we were also trained navy telegraph operators, we were sent far into the forest to a secluded rest camp for Norwegian army air corps personnel, next to a small, idyllic lake. Together with four technical experts wearing army uniform, the eight of us who had passed all the tests and were wearing air force uniforms, learned every development of modern radio technology, from constructing and using secret transmitters with hidden antennas to television technology, then in its infancy. We rushed around the Muskoka woods with specially constructed megaphones, shouting, 'One-two-three, can you hear me?' so loudly that people in Huntsville wrote us letters saying, 'Sure we hear you, and they hear you all the way down in Gravenhurst too!'

I came closer to drowning than ever before on a canoe trip with some fellow soldiers in the Algonquin National Park. We followed a map that showed the trails where we could portage our canoe between lakes and rivers in the great forest.

The main attraction of the trip, in addition to the possible sighting of bear and moose, was High Falls, a thundering waterfall that fell vertically into a deep gorge where huge, drifting logs were ground to pulp. According to the map, we had to follow a trail for about fifty metres along the riverbank above the waterfall and launch the canoe there. The trail ended by a steep mountain wall. We all thought it looked suspect; the current was unusually strong after the spring floods, and I suggested that we cut the trip short and turn back. Per and Rulle insisted that we had to be in the right place, so rather than abort the trip, I gave in.

We were clever enough not to paddle in the middle of the stream, but used our hands to haul our way along the bank. A few hundred metres further up the canoe was caught by a strong cross-current, and however hard we paddled we could not make it back to land. Rulle saw the danger immediately, and dived into the water while he could still reach shore with a few strokes. His dive capsized the canoe and I found myself struggling in the cold water, dressed as I was in my air force winter uniform and wearing heavy boots. I was a terrible swimmer and, weighed down by my clothing, I experienced a totally new kind of hydrophobia. The waterfall! High Falls roared ever closer. There was no possibility of being saved. Rulle ran along the riverbank like a man possessed, but the current only swept me further away, straight for the cliff where I would be crushed like the logs we had just seen.

I continued to swim for dear life, but I knew that all hope of reaching land was gone. I realised that in a few seconds I would experience death, and find out what happens when life comes to an end.

That thought was enough to ignite within me a search for that creative, all powerful force called God. I looked to myself, not in the air or on land. All Rulle could do was run after me, waving his arms helplessly, but without getting any closer.

A new source of resolve flowed into me. I felt unlimited powers surge into my arms and legs, and I began to swim calmly and with great force, crossing the current at an angle.

The water became increasingly more agitated, the roar overwhelming, but the riverbank stopped moving away – stood still – Rulle's hands almost reached me – a little more – a little . . . There! Our hands locked together. With a united effort I was pulled ashore, dead tired.

But Per!

The red canoe had capsized and was bobbing up and down at the edge of the cliff. A huge boulder kept it from being swept away. We grabbed hold of the bow and pulled. It was surprisingly heavy. When we righted the canoe we found Per wedged under a thwart with the only remaining backpack.

When we had finally revived him, we caught sight of three magnificent deer. They stood perfectly still, like monuments on a mountain ledge, on the far side of the waterfall.

'I take that as a sign that all three of us will survive the war,' said Per.

A few months later he was shot down with his plane over Norway.

The most vivid memory I have from my time as an enlisted man was of 1132 Stenersen. He was full of fighting spirit, but he wanted to contribute to the war effort in his own way and not by standing to attention. The most important thing for a soldier to learn is blind obedience. Your first lesson is standing to attention – heels together and toes at an angle of sixty degrees, body as erect as the barrel of a rifle, eyes fixed straight ahead at a randomly chosen point, your mind empty, awaiting an order, like a row of toy soldiers. Stenersen was in a constant state of flux. Wearing a uniform jacket that was far too long and a cap that was too small, he stood there, staring toward something or other in the distance, with a smirk on his face that clearly told the sergeant what soldier 1132 thought of all of this. The sergeant approached him angrily and pointed to the toes of his huge boots, which were not at an angle of sixty degrees. Stenersen was put in the glass house because he insisted that his feet were at sixty degrees, it was just that his boots were too large. Furthermore, he had no doubt that the Norwegians would manage to drive out the Nazis, even if their feet were at an angle of forty degrees.

Stenersen remained in I Group until flight school, but when he showed up for morning inspection wearing an artist's red bow tie, his uniform was taken away from him and he was ordered to paint a dramatic Norwegian landscape on the side of the link trainer.

The class distinctions I had experienced in the factory reared their ugly head in the armed forces too. There were three different kitchens and three different dining halls, for other ranks, NCOs and officers respectively. As soon as the air force telegraph operators had completed their training and been promoted to sergeants, they no longer ate with I Group, because we were still privates. It was also strictly forbidden for officers and other ranks to have any social contact.

Few men with pips on their uniforms were admired by us enlisted men. I only remember two. The camp commander, Colonel Ole Reistad, was one. From him I learned that respect for a subordinate can be maintained and even increased by giving orders in such a way that the one who receives them still feels he is an equal. The other was Major Viggo Ullmann, the only person in the camp except for myself who had brought his wife and child to Toronto. We lived in apartments in the city. He broke all rules and we visited one another when I had evening leave. While the adults had dinner, my little ones played on the floor with his two girls, Liv and Bitten. Who could have known then that Liv Ullmann would grow up to become a famous film star, and that the two of us would one day sit together in the Olympic Arena in Lillehammer, in a free Norway, commentating the opening of the Winter Olympics in 1994, while a worldwide audience watched?

My clearest memory from Vesle Skaugum training camp in the Muskoka forest was a visit by a six-year-old Norwegian boy who caused just as much of a sensation when he arrived unannounced with his mother, as he did many years later when he took his seat on the royal stand with his two children during the same Winter Olympics. Liv and I, our little boys and Peik, a bear cub they had adopted as a playmate, lived in a small log cabin some distance from the camp. Prince Harald went for his daily run with the camp commandant along a trail past the cabin. They spotted Peik sitting politely at the table, being groomed by the boys. Its black fur was as clean as a fox's pelt, and Liv allowed me to let it sleep at the foot of the bed so it could get used to people. Peik had been anything but friendly when I acquired him from a lumberjack for a bottle of whisky. Liv had more to put up with when the bear grew too heavy, and I removed it from the bottom of the bed and used it as a substitute pillow instead.

I was given the day off to show the prince and princesses how Peik could do tricks. The princesses begged me to take them out in the canoe. They had seen me paddle out with the bear, and how it jumped into the water and pulled me back to shore with a rope. With the Princesses Ragnhild and Astrid on board, and Peik in the bow, I paddled slowly and carefully past the quay where Crown Princess Martha sat on a stool crocheting while little Prince Harald was preparing to film the event with his new camera. Honey was Peik's favourite food;

honey on my finger had made us firm friends. As we approached the quay the film camera started buzzing like a bee, the bear rose up on two feet in the canoe, and we all capsized. I had no way of knowing whether the princesses could swim or not, but it turned out to be great fun for everyone, because the water was so shallow that the three of us could wade ashore.

The worst was yet to come. Peik was dripping wet when he wandered over to the Crown Princess, who had nearly finished her crocheting. The bear shook itself, spraying water everywhere, and with its long crooked claws got a good hold of the crocheting. A veritable battle ensued. Helping the Crown Princess rescue her handiwork was hopeless. Luckily Liv saved the situation with a piece of honey cake.

Then the day arrived when Army Air Corps recruit 2209 Heyerdahl, formerly army recruit 1136, along with his seven colleagues in I Group, knew more about electro-technology than anyone else in the Norwegian forces. The only thing we did not know was how to put our newly acquired knowledge to use. Sadly it seemed that no one else did either.

Now that the war has long been over and I Group's invaluable equipment is lying on the bottom of the ocean, north of North Cape, I think that I can reveal something of our curious contribution to the war effort.

When the ocean liner Queen Mary set a record for carrying passengers, I was one of them. After receiving an urgent telegram from London requesting I Group's immediate presence, we were amongst the eighteen thousand allied troops from camps all over Canada, Australia and New Zealand who were one night secretly transported to an assembly point in Halifax. From here we were squeezed aboard the huge steamship, to be sent into the line of fire overseas. The eight of us shared a single cabin, but only every other night, as we had to take turns with those who slept on deck, leaning against the bulkhead, with no room to stretch out. I will never forget the seasickness and the long lines to the toilets. We could boast about being a high-priority target for German submarines, so the luxury liner raced full speed ahead with all lights out, on a zigzag course to avoid submarine torpedoes.

We arrived after five days and were met by a flight of Allied fighter planes. The priority for most on board when safely ashore was to have a cigarette. Any light from cigarettes had been forbidden during the crossing.

So now we were overseas. But no one knew who had sent for us. Two of our own officers were dressed in army uniform, so we decided to get out of our air force uniforms and into army ones. I was now army soldier 5268. This compounded the confusion; now no one could locate us in any military records. Upon our arrival in London we were greeted by the Commander-in-Chief of the army with the words: 'You have long been awaited and long missed.' Four days later we were told that no one could find out who had missed us. We were therefore sent to the Army School and Training Company in Scotland and told to wait patiently until the problem had been solved. A little later we were issued with new weapons and army gear and sent to a Norwegian communications company in an isolated castle in Scotland.

We were welcomed with open arms by the communications commander, who assured us that he had plenty of officers but far too few enlisted men. Every morning Captain Pettersen lined up all his officers and soldiers in beautiful rows, and sergeants and lieutenants turned snappily on their heels and reported that everyone was present and correct.

I Group had regular army gear and none of its fine technological equipment, so we were either put on kitchen duty or sent to work for Scottish farmers. We only saw the officers during morning inspection, because we ate in different rooms of the castle. After a month we were issued with marching orders and left Captain Pettersen's castle, but only to be billeted in the beautiful Scottish village of Callander. A few days later we were moved to the university town of St Andrews, where we met up with Captain Pettersen and his communications company. We were accommodated in Westerlea House, a huge old castle with wide stone stairways and long corridors with unpainted wooden floors. Here we were ordered to wash the floors and stairs every day – not sweep but wash, because without wet floors no one could verify that they had actually been washed. After a while, the whole castle smelt of rot and mould.

Complaining and begging to be put into the line of fire was of no use. As representative of I Group, I had meetings with the company commander, pointing out that soon we would have forgotten everything we had learned. We were given the key to a Morse code transmitter. As air force and navy telegraph operators, we had learned to send and receive Morse code at a speed that produced a steady drone, and we had to learn to type with all ten fingers in order to get it down on paper fast enough.

My problem now was that not only was I cut off from all contacts in Norway, but also that none of Liv's letters from Canada had reached me. As a soldier I was being paid the same as a recruit was paid at home in peacetime, and it simply was not enough to cover everything, in spite of Liv and the children living inexpensively in the cabin in the Muskoka forest. Before I enlisted I had sold my valuable ethnographic collection from the Marquesas Islands to the Brooklyn Museum. I had lugged the collection around with me since leaving Norway. Among other things it included extremely valuable icons, a king's robe made of wavy black human hair bound with cocoa fibres, and a magnificent crown of carved tortoiseshell and mother-of-pearl. Little did I know that Thomas Olsen had invited Liv and the boys to live with his family in their lovely country home outside New York for the duration of the war.

My days as a scientist seemed distant and unreal. There I was, shoes pointing out at an angle of sixty degrees, staring into space because I was ordered to do so. St Andrews University kept my soul alive by allowing me to borrow stacks of books. My diary entry from that time reads: 'I'm starting to study anthropology again since it seems our mission here has been sabotaged. After dinner the others carry on as before, washing stairs.'

Unrest started to brew among our special secret group from Canada. Morning inspection continued as before. The communications captain did not want to exercise his soldiers under the command of the major of the corps of engineers, billeted in the same castle, so he exercised I Group and his other enlisted men behind the castle. The shouting of orders from both sides of the building resounded in the twilight as if it were battalions rather than six or eight men being handed over from the lieutenant to the company commander and back again to the lieutenant. The captain used a flashlight to inspect every soldier in I Group, making certain the communications emblem was sewn on our sleeves. Afterwards two enlisted men were picked for the daily washing of stairs while the rest were allowed to return to their quarters and relax.

This could not continue. Stair-washing and kitchen duty were bad enough, but there were rumours that the waiter in the officers' mess had been transferred so now we would be expected to do that job too. That was degrading. We agreed that if just one of us were given the job, he would refuse and the rest of the group would support him. It would be the only way in which to bring the problem to the attention of the Army High Command. Earlier, while cleaning Captain Pettersen's office, a letter of complaint that we had sent to London, was found in his wastepaper basket.

The bubble burst during inspection the next morning when 5269 Beyer-Arnesen was detailed to duty in the officers' mess.

The answer rang out loud and clear, as from a man on death row: 'I refuse.'

The words hung in the air. Beyer-Arnesen was ordered to fall out and report to the captain's office. Initially the captain tried to be reasonable. It was an honour to serve in the officers' mess. Beyer-Arnesen stuck to his point. Refusal to carry out an order in time of war is punishable by death. The captain grabbed the telephone and called the military police. The soldier watched calmly. Beyer picked up his gas mask, helmet and toilet kit and was taken to the glass house in St Andrews.

As the group representative I was called into the captain's office to try and bring the soldier to his senses. I told the captain that Beyer was old enough to know what he was doing, that if he were arrested our whole group would have to be arrested, as we had all agreed not to carry out that order. I was informed that the matter would be brought to a military tribunal and that the rest of us had not yet refused to obey the order and would not be given a chance to refuse. Furthermore, if we had been serving in the German army, Beyer-Arnesen would have been shot. When I asked whether he thought the Nazis were good examples, I was simply told that 'war is war'.

I Group met to consult. Since I was in communications, with the proper stripes on my arm, I borrowed a tool box and went straight downtown to the military gaol, where I explained that something was wrong with the wiring in one of the cells. I was let in and went from cell to cell. All the wiring was in order until I reached Beyer's cell. I stopped and slipped him a bar of chocolate and a pack of cigarettes. Beyer told me he was the childhood friend of a lieutenant in the supreme command in London who was the son of the Minister of Defence, Oscar Torp. He gave me a letter to take to him.

Captain Pettersen was pleased to grant me leave to visit London. Lieutenant Torp was shocked when he heard that his friend was under close arrest in Scotland, and immediately arranged for a meeting with his father. The Minister of Defence was, if possible, even more upset when I read aloud from my diary. He assured me that I Group had a truly important role to play and that there must have been some misunderstanding. He would personally take the matter up with the commanding general and the war attorney. My mission was to return quietly and see to it that I Group behaved in an exemplary fashion until the matter was resolved. Even before I left London I learned that orders had already been passed down and Beyer had been released.

Back in St Andrews our enforced idleness continued. Five months had passed since we had done anything more important than wash floors and rake leaves. As we lay like mutineers in our bunks, we discussed the humiliation of doing nothing and not making use of our expensive education while our peers from the flight school had long been in the front line. We had heard about the great contribution that our own air force and the Norwegian navy were making, not to mention all the men in the underground resistance movement behind German lines.

We read in the newspapers how the British Foreign Minister Anthony Eden had pointed out the invaluable contribution of the Norwegian merchant navy, which alone transported 40 per cent of all oil to the Allies. Why were we not called upon, with our telegraph operator licences? British Admiral Dickens said in a speech, 'Our loss of men and ships has been heavy. It is therefore no exaggeration to say that Norway's effort has been indispensable.'

Even when one of us was sent to wash the corps of engineers' latrine, which we never used, we did not protest. Shortly before Christmas 1943, I was called in for questioning by the military police, and asked whether I Group was still unwilling to serve in the officers' mess. If so, we would be accused of mutiny. We remained loyal to Beyer.

I Group received its marching orders just after the New Year, and we were each sent in a different direction. I was delighted to be transferred to a Norwegian mountain company in the Scottish Highlands. They were well-trained soldiers, and the company commander, who was nicknamed Tarzan, enjoyed everyone's respect and admiration. Sporting activities were part of the day and we trained and ran in the mountains. Once again I felt like a human being.

One day during morning inspection we were ordered to stand to attention. When Tarzan took out a document and started to read, we all realised that something serious was about to happen. Orders from the Army High Command in London. Soldier 5268 Heyerdahl was sentenced to sixty days' close arrest, with one year's probation, for – Tarzan paused deliberately – having refused to serve in the officers' mess.

In spite of standing to attention there was unrest in the ranks. Some grinned so openly that Tarzan quickly ordered us to stand at ease while a smile played in the corners of his mouth.

The eight of us had each received a year's probation, and the supreme command now made certain that there would be no more opportunity for creating problems before the end of the year. We were brought together again, not under Captain

Pettersen, but under the command of a small, wiry and stocky lieutenant who wore a British DSO among all the Norwegian decorations on his chest and the communications emblem on his sleeve. Lieutenant Bjørn Rørholt had just returned from a mission behind the German lines and was one of the heroes of the resistance movement. We soon discovered that he was a dedicated soul, bursting with energy, and one who resolutely looked for a new task as soon as one had been completed. He greeted us with a twinkle in his eye; he had heard about us when he arrived in London and had assumed responsibility for involving us in the war.

After a refresher course in electronics with our secret suit-case transmitters and antennas, we were sent off for a few days as guests in private homes. We had to sneak out at night and climb up into trees to transmit messages. We made contact by Morse code with uniformed British servicewomen, 'Fannies', who received our coded messages from their stations at various castles around England. What we encountered at the pub in the evening was not much to write home about. For my part, all I could brag about after the war was that I had not killed any enemy soldiers nor seduced any of the beautiful women Rørholt had bravely introduced me to. I wore the uniform of a private, he was a lieutenant and a member of SOE, so I was probably accepted by these young upper-class women because they thought my uniform was some kind of camouflage.

And then we were promoted to the rank of sergeant and sent to a parachute school.

We were all secretly scared to death as we lined up in front of the plane and Lieutenant Rørholt reminded us that from now on everything we did was voluntary. The one fellow who had the courage to admit that he didn't dare, and then opted out, was probably the one I admired most.

Sitting on the floor beside the open door of the plane and waiting for orders was an ordeal. The parachutes were small and perforated, so we would fall quickly if we came under fire. A thundering noise, rendering us senseless, was all we heard, until finally the parachute opened. When it did, it seemed as if Our Lord himself had grabbed a firm hold of my neck. I descended towards earth with the wonderful feeling of having been a bird in a former life – until the ground came rushing up toward me and I hit it with a jolt as powerful as had I jumped from the third floor of a building.

There were many jumps. On one night jump there were only three lights to mark our dropping zone, and many of the men suffered minor injuries because it was too dark to gauge the target and prepare for landing. I did well because during the flight I kept my eyes shut until the moment I jumped out into the dark. The most difficult part was the initial ground training. Imagine following an order to jump out of a window from a high tower, with a loose coil of rope in your hand, trusting that it would work, simply because one end of the rope was tied to your back and the other was attached to the shaft of a propeller that would spin around and start breaking the fall as soon as the coil started to straighten out. Fortunately it worked.

The most frightening jump of all was when we were used as guinea pigs. We were to jump with our weapons and all our gear in a sack secured with a rope around our legs. Just before we hit the ground we were to loosen the noose and let the sack hang by an eight-metre rope so that it would hit the ground at the same speed but just ahead of us. Two members of I Group ended up in hospital with broken legs. It could have been much worse for me. My parachute didn't open. It simply hung above me like an empty sausage skin. As the earth came rushing toward me, I could hear the instructor on the ground screaming into a megaphone and telling me to pull on the upward risers. I was also trying to manoeuvre the rope attaching the heavy sack to my legs. The parachute opened at the last moment and I kicked my legs free, but everything went black when I rolled around on the ground according to instructions.

One day, between jumps, when I was relaxing on a haystack, a short and skinny officer wearing a lieutenant's uniform covered with war decorations walked over to me. His face was pale, with sharp features, and the powerful setting of his jaw revealed a clean-cut character with a strong will. The man was Knut Haugland, the famous radio operator of the heavy-water sabotage mission at Rjukan that had prevented the Germans from winning the race to produce the first atom bomb. Here was a Norwegian, a member of the underground resistance, who had served his country with great distinction. Winston Churchill had given the sabotage of the heavy-water factory top priority, and Lieutenant Haugland had already met Churchill and our own King Haakon in London. He had also been congratulated and decorated by George VI. When I met him, he had just returned from yet another assignment in Norway. Three years later, when he was the radio operator on the *Kon-Tiki* expedition, he told us how the Gestapo had surrounded him and his radio transmitter in his hide-out in a ventilation shaft at the women's clinic in central Oslo. He shot his way out and disappeared over the hospital wall in a hail of bullets.

We became good friends. Later he insisted that I had been daydreaming about Polynesia in that haystack, and that I had said that if the old greybeards of the scientific establishment were unwilling to believe me then I would build a raft to prove my theory. I made no note of this in my diary, but what is certain is that Knut was going to parachute into Nordmarka on the outskirts of Oslo and co-ordinate one hundred secret radio stations in Norway. He asked me to be his second in command, and I accepted.

These were the days when Soviet troops were marching through Finland into the northernmost part of Norway. Two hundred thousand men of the 20th German Gebirgsarmee were in full retreat from easternmost Finnmark, but they had dug themselves in, having scorched and burned everything in their path, including the whole town of Kirkenes. For the time being, there was no contact between the Soviet and German forces. The situation on the polar front was extremely unclear, and in great haste a small Norwegian force had to be sent over from Britain to look after Norwegian interests.

The 1st Norwegian Mountain Company was sent to Murmansk on an Allied convoy, and Lieutenant Rørholt received orders to follow after with two men to establish communications between the scorched earth area of Finnmark, which the Soviets had liberated, and the Norwegian government in London. All of I Group were immediately promoted to the rank of ensign, and Ensign Heyerdahl and Ensign Stabell were ordered by Lieutenant Rørholt to accompany him.

So the parachute mission with Lieutenant Haugland never took place, but war is war, as Captain Pettersen would have said. Furthermore, I still had the sixty-day sentence hanging over my head.

After the war, when I invited Haugland and Rørholt to join the *Kon-Tiki* expedition, they both agreed. Later Rørholt withdrew but it was Rørholt who organised our communications on board by supplying a suitcase radio transmitter left over from the war and setting up an amateur radio network. Haugland joined the expedition and manned our communications systems.

The mission with Rørholt proved more dangerous than the

journey on the raft with Haugland would ever turn out to be. In November 1944 Rørholt, Stabell and I travelled to Scapa Flow in the Orkney Islands, and then further north to Murmansk on an enormous American aircraft carrier in a convoy consisting of about eighty Allied ships. Half of them were warships, the others were Liberty cargo ships, which I recognised from my time at the Bethlehem Fairfield shipyard.

We had barely stepped aboard before a telegram arrived stating that Ensigns Heyerdahl and Stabell had been promoted once again, this time to lieutenants. Lieutenant Rørholt was promoted to captain. This was to cause unexpected complications when we were set ashore on Soviet territory.

We sailed northward into the Norwegian Sea and the polar night, which loomed dark and sinister as the convoy crossed the Arctic Circle. All the ships' lights were extinguished and the sky and the ocean were indistinguishable in the night-time darkness. In the afternoon, a patch of red sky appeared to the south, and we could make out the shadowy black silhouettes of large and small ships on the endless ocean. Two heavy locomotives were on the deck of the nearest cargo vessel, on their way from the United States to the communists in the Soviet Union. The world was transformed into steel and ice, cannons and black water.

As an experienced outdoor person, I was shocked at the standard of winter equipment we had been issued with as we left England. I had barely enough time to buy a few rolls of chewing tobacco, which I could barter for a reindeer-skin sleeping bag from the Laplanders. The one I had been given consisted of loose filling that fell into the bottom if I held it upright. We were told that arctic gear was being sold in a small depot somewhere in the bowels of the aircraft carrier. We were led down companionways through two open watertight bulkheads, and as Rørholt and I were trying on long, fur mittens there was a loud bang on the iron hull. Instinctively we made for the companionway, but the bulkheads were immediately closed and sealed over us. Another loud thud resounded against the outside hull, and explosion after explosion echoed through the iron ship. We heard depth charges from our own escort ships; there were enemy submarines in these waters.

I had always thought that being enclosed in a submarine during warfare would be the worst thing imaginable, and my suspicions were confirmed while we cowed in the interior of the ship, closed in like rats, and the battle raged above and below us. Suddenly, silence reigned. After a while the bulkheads were opened and we were let up into the cold polar night. The convoy was on its way into the Murmansk Fjord with its priceless cargo. We learned that Soviet warships had put to sea and joined the battle.

We left the Americans in Murmansk. I went over to a bearded hulk of a guy in a fur coat, eager to practise the list of fifty Russian words I had compiled during the voyage. The man understood none of them. He was English, and had escaped from German captivity and managed to get through the Soviet Union to reach the convoy in Murmansk without knowing one word of Russian. 'Just smile to them,' he said, 'and they'll help you.'

I met my first Russian when we boarded a Soviet torpedo boat that had been badly damaged by German cannon shells. It was on its way to Petsamo in Finland, the port that the Soviets had captured from the Germans. On a long six-hour journey in rough seas, I sat next to a Soviet officer who looked as though he were tough and suspicious. I was cold and hungry. I followed the Englishman's advice and smiled in a friendly but perhaps uncertain manner, as I had never seen a Communist before. The Russian beamed a large smile, grabbed my arm, and dragged me down into a cabin. He lifted the blanket off the bunk and pulled out a huge loaf of black bread, broke it in two, and gave me one half. We perched on the edge of the bed, chewing dry bread and smiling at each other while the ship pitched heavily through the icy sea.

At midnight we arrived in Petsamo, the Soviet's only ice-free harbour. The small Norwegian corvette *Tunsberg Castle* was moored there, waiting to transport thirteen large boxes of valuable technical equipment for I Group to the front in Finnmark. There was only room for one of us aboard, so I gladly let Stabell board the ship with the equipment while Rørholt and I took to the road. I climbed up next to the driver of a Soviet military vehicle, which had been riddled with bullet holes and had no windscreen. It was freezing cold and we were accompanied by flickering northern lights.

We sat in silence after greeting each other with smiles. Though neither of us could sing in tune, we sang 'Volga Volga' and Norwegian and Russian folk songs. I tried to make use of my fifty Russian words along the way, but they never quite fitted the situation. The vehicle bumped and jolted through the polar night, and we kept on going without seeing anything to indicate that we had crossed into Finland and were no longer in the Soviet Union. We stopped for a rest in some Russian mud huts, where we were served hot millet soup and huge lumps of coal-black bread. Everyone in the convoy was clothed in fur and we huddled close together to keep warm. I shall never forget the grim atmosphere and yet intense joy one afternoon as we rattled over a long Russian pontoon bridge and the Russian pointed to an isolated little house barely visible in the dark.

'Norvjeskij dom,' he said triumphantly. I understood those words. Norwegian house!

Home again. My mother and my father lived in this country. But southern Norway was far away, a few thousand kilometres still held by the Germans. I had never been in northern Norway, the land of the midnight sun, and now I was to experience it as a smoking pile of ruins. Here and there fires were still smouldering. The Germans had withdrawn and set fire to everything in their path; scorched earth tactics. Only one house remained in Kirkenes, everything else had been destroyed. The fleeing Nazis had force marched all the civilians they could find southward with them. This called for a good three days' march through the no-man's-land of minefields between the Russian and German fronts.

I found Rørholt billeted in an abandoned German bunker with Colonel Arne Dahl, the chief of the Norwegian Mountain Company, who had arrived with another Murmansk convoy just before ours. They had had no direct link with London, but had to communicate through the Russians, who had their own headquarters in the vicinity. We all waited for the arrival of the *Tunsberg Castle*.

A few days later the sad message arrived that the *Tunsberg Castle* had been sunk. Five Norwegian sailors had been killed, and the thirteen boxes belonging to I Group were lying at the bottom of the ocean.

Surprisingly, Stabell showed up just before Christmas, in Russian clothing, but without as much as a wire-cutter saved from the equipment. He had been on the afterdeck when the alarm sounded on the *Tunsberg Castle* and had rushed up to the captain on the bridge and stood firmly to attention to receive any orders. At that very moment, thirty metres of the aft deck was blown away. Further explosions followed, and before he knew where he was he was struggling for survival in the ice-cold water. A Soviet vessel rescued him before he froze to death. He also reported that when our huge Allied convoy had steamed back up the Murmansk Fjord, the Germans were waiting for it and attacked with a flotilla of submarines and fifty Junker 88s. The English reported that twelve German submarines had been sunk or damaged, but also that several of the convoy's cargo ships had been lost, including two Soviet ships. The destroyer *Cassandra*, with a loss of sixty-one men, was towed back to harbour with the bow blown away and corpses still stuck to the twisted iron on the wreck.

Our joy at seeing Stabell again was great, and we duly celebrated on Christmas Eve. A Lapp came down from the mountains with a reindeer roast, and the Soviet commandant who had heard about Norwegian Christmas feasts brought a keg of vodka and a sack of Russian rice to celebrate with us. We were informed that the Russians would pull out of the country as soon as the German troops had been evicted; then we sang Norwegian Christmas carols and Russian folk songs and wished one another peace on earth.

On Boxing Day, a messenger from the Soviet High Command appeared with orders for Lieutenant Heyerdahl to return to England immediately. He was not listed on the personnel record that the Norwegian High Command had cleared through the Soviet embassy in London. Colonel Dahl, as the Norwegian in charge, immediately sent a message back that Heyerdahl's name was on a supplementary list, and that in any case the lieutenant could not be spared owing to lack of officers. The Russians found a Sergeant Heyerdahl on the supplementary list, but no officer. Something was obviously wrong, and the lieutenant had to return immediately to England. Orders from Moscow.

This was pure lunacy. I worked out a plan with Colonel Dahl. Hoping that the Russians would accept his explanations, I was ordered to participate as second-in-command of an elite Norwegian commando group, consisting of tough characters. The order was, 'Attack on your own initiative.'

On the last day of 1944, our small seven-man commando group crossed the mountain by the Smal Fjord and, with a requisitioned truck, reached the furthest outpost of seventy men from the Norwegian mountain company. No-man's-land lay behind us, and the Germans were ahead of us on the opposite side of the fjord. We were well hidden in abandoned German dug-outs, and we rested before carrying out our commando raid. Three German destroyers lay at anchor by a lighthouse on the other side of the fjord, and our assignment was to row undetected across the fjord in a small dinghy, surprise the guards while they were asleep, and blow up the lighthouse.

I suffered intense mental agony in anticipation of the raid. The German soldiers who were sleeping in the guard house were strangers to me. Of course they were enemies, but probably not volunteers, and they would be court-marshalled and shot if they refused to obey an order. It was bad enough to refuse to serve food to one's own officers. I tossed and turned that night, arguing with myself about what was the better of two evils: throwing hand grenades through the window on to a defenceless, sleeping enemy, or waking them first with a scream and exposing my own friends to mortal danger. Then a message came on our field telephone. Colonel Dahl had been given an ultimatum by the Soviet high command: the Norwegian troops were to split up into patrols and search for Lieutenant Heyerdahl.

The message was clear and left no alternative. I bid a quiet farewell to the leader of the commando group, Lieutenant Alfred Henningsen, who was left to do the job alone with five men. I jumped on to the truck with the driver, who had to return through the minefields in no-man's-land in the winter

darkness. Pure insanity! But I had to push on and reach
Kirkenes before being held responsible for splitting the
Norwegian front line into patrols sent to find me and send me
back to London for a Soviet visa!

We heard nothing more from Henningsen and his five men
for the duration of the war. Later we learned that the Germans
had spotted the dinghy and opened fire. The boat sank and
half the crew drowned; the rest were captured by the
Germans. Henningsen was one of the survivors. He later
became a member of the Norwegian Parliament, representing
Troms.

It had started to snow and the heavy truck got stuck in a
snowdrift. The driver and I stumbled on an abandoned snow-
plough stuck in the frozen ground, and we pulled and tugged
until we suddenly noticed that a mine was attached to it. We
spared ourselves any further efforts.

We managed to keep on going, constantly having to dig
ourselves out of snow drifts; we never saw a single snow
marker. The bridges over the Guljok and Tana rivers had
been blown up, but we made it through birch thickets and
open fields down to the frozen rivers and up again on the
other side; except once, after we had crossed the Tana a
second time and the truck got bogged down and would not
budge. In the end we found a Lapp's turf hut and borrowed
a horse to pull the truck clear. On the following day we broke
through the ice in the fjord outside Nesseby. I was on the
verge of experiencing once again my childhood fear of water
and ice, but we were still close enough to the riverbank to
make it to shore, soaking wet. We heard horses' bells, and
three small Lapps came to our aid, but even before we had
started to rescue the truck, the Lapps' horse and sled also
went through the ice and its runners broke. We contrived
new runners from birch brushwood and, after toiling for six

hours, we managed to save the horse and sled. The truck was abandoned for good.

I reached Vardø on foot one morning, and fell asleep on the kitchen floor of the first house I entered.

Before I managed to cross the fjord on the final stretch to Kirkenes, I met a mysterious unshaven private who had hidden in a snow-hole during the German retreat. When he left his place of hiding he found himself, like me, in no-man's-land. As we warmed to one another, he introduced himself using a cover name, Torstein Pettersen. We were immediately on the same wavelength and developed a lasting friendship. Later he would be part of the *Kon-Tiki* crew under his real name, Torstein Raaby.

Torstein kept his experiences close to his chest during the time we were together that winter in Finnmark. Later I learnt that, after his training in England, he had been secretly parachuted into the Tromsø area of Norway. He had stayed under cover close to the place where the German cruiser *Tirpitz* was based, and for several months he sent daily reports to England with a small hand-carried transmitter, connecting his set to a receiver antenna at night that belonged to a German officer. He was also, like Rørholt and Haugland, highly decorated by the Allies. His messages finally helped RAF bombers to sink the *Tirpitz*, the second of Germany's proudest warships.

When the Norwegian headquarters learned that Lieutenant Heyerdahl was back in Kirkenes and preparing to join a Soviet transport back to Murmansk to catch the next convoy to England, there was both relief and commotion in the camp. Since the loss of I Group's equipment, there had been no communication with any country other than the Soviet Union. I was buttonholed by military personnel and civilians who wanted to send messages or give me assignments in London. Someone claimed that on the most recent shipment to

Murmansk, boots for left feet had arrived at the military depot without any matching ones for right feet. Whether or not that was a dig at the communists will remain a moot point, but a lieutenant could confirm that on that very day he had gone out on patrol with eight men and one sleeping bag; the eight had been picked because they fitted the eight pairs of boots that he had been supplied with. Furthermore the patrol had only three rounds of ammunition and cups and cutlery for only four men. The military police wanted to report the number of Norwegian Nazis who had been taken prisoner in the Kirkenes area. The divisional doctor sent information about health conditions and a plea for sanitary equipment, while the depot manager lacked the most basic things, from weapons and ammunition to boot polish, mittens and snow goggles.

On 11 January 1945, a Soviet military vehicle arrived at the Norwegian headquarters to pick me up, and to my amazement I was not alone. With me were two lieutenants from the Norwegian navy whose presence in Russia was also undesired by Moscow. The three of us were to be returned to London on the same convoy. Moreover, three Norwegian staff officers joined the transport vehicle. They did not look like military personnel, but wore their officers' distinctions on a blue uniform; they were important civil servants. They were accompanying a military deputation back to London and the Norwegian government with important observations on the civilian population. We rattled along together in the freezing cold and dark, six Norwegian officers and one Soviet driver, heading eastward, over the pontoon bridge and out of Norway. Day and night was indistinguishable and we saw only snow and endless rows of military trucks and fur-clad soldiers. On and on we went, and every once in a while we stopped to eat and drink tea in snow-covered bunkers in the company of half-naked Soviet soldiers who sat on benches along the walls.

We finally saw lights and realised that we had crossed the border between Finland and the Soviet Union and must have reached Murmansk.

A Soviet naval officer tore open the car door and hurried us off the truck, because we were late and the convoy was already on its way out of the fjord. He pulled out the three lieutenants first and let the three staff officers remain in the car; he had good news: they had been given permission to return to Kirkenes! One of them, in fact a bank director representing the Bank of Norway, smiled indulgently and tried to explain to the friendly Russian that this was a misunderstanding: it must be the three staff officers who were returning to England, and the three lieutenants who had been given permission to remain.

'No misunderstanding, is order from Moscow,' the Russian answered firmly. And the incredible thing happened. The car door was shut, and the three staff officers, frozen stiff and in despair, were sent on their way back to Kirkenes.

We, the lieutenants who had taken it for granted that the permission to remain was for us, were equally confused and disappointed. Nevertheless, with all our gear, we were firmly ushered on board a Soviet submarine chaser that sped at full throttle northward up the Murmansk Fjord to catch up with the convoy that had already left Polyarno. The first thing I noticed when I came to pick up my gear from the truck was the bag belonging to one of the staff officers placed next to mine. It contained secret reports, a pistol and personal effects, and I quickly grabbed it as if it were my own.

The submarine chaser sped up the fjord, and in less than an hour we caught up with the two English destroyers at the rear of the convoy. Without slowing down and in high seas, one of the naval lieutenants was hoisted aboard the *Zebra*, while the other lieutenant and myself were hoisted aboard the *Zambezi*. We both immediately fell asleep in the officers' lounge.

The ship tossed about when we left the entrance to the fjord, but German submarines were lurking below and I woke up to the booming thuds of depth charges. The first ones came from the *Zebra*, but then a submarine turned up abaft of the *Zambezi* and sent coded messages across the Arctic Ocean. Soon many more escort ships in the convoy felt the impact of German submarines. My fellow countryman from the navy was incapacitated by seasickness; the transition from the Finnmark plateau was sudden, but I soon got my sea legs and followed an English officer into the chart house where I could study the composition of the convoy. The escort, protecting a large number of cargo ships that were returning home empty, consisted of one aircraft carrier, one cruiser, eight destroyers, nine submarine chasers and a number of smaller escort vessels. We slung our hammocks in an open passage on deck with orders to sleep with our life jackets on, close to our designated 'dive-in' spot should it become necessary to jump into the sea.

There were many reasons for not sleeping well; one was that the passage was so narrow that when the ship rolled the hammocks thudded from one bulkhead to the other at such a speed that as soon as we fell asleep having hit one bulkhead we were woken up by the other.

We soon heard close and distant explosions in the sea around us, coming from all directions. The English took it all with a wry sense of humour: 'We've got mixed up in a school of mackerel,' the captain said.

Our Lord would never have allowed this kind of fish into the ocean. These devilish, mechanical monsters had been devised by human brains with the sole purpose of sending human souls into oblivion. I wondered what Tei Tetua would have thought about the bearers of culture from the outside world if he had been lying in a hammock beside us.

A loud explosion interrupted my thoughts. The ship shook and a spout of water shot up in the air.

'That was us,' a proud sailor exclaimed, and I rushed up on to the bridge to see what was happening. There was intense activity on board. Orders were shouted and repeated. From catapults on deck, heavy barrel-like depth charges were slung in wide semicircles out into the racing grey waves of the Arctic Ocean. A few moments later the water rolled over and around us as if it were boiling, and spouts of water shot up over the bridge. To minimise the risk of being hit, the *Zambesi* constantly changed course without leaving the convoy.

To mislead the main body of the German submarines, which was lying in wait submerged a good bit further out, the aircraft carrier ordered the convoy to change course and steer eastward along the Kola peninsula in the direction of Siberia, rather than westward. Then the course was changed again, and we pitched terribly as we sailed some hundred nautical miles on a course due north. Now we hit heavy seas, and the following night the ship rolled thirty-five degrees either way.

It was almost impossible to keep a tight convoy. We changed course and sailed two days on a south-westerly course, but rather than abating, the storm increased. On the third day I heard the cry 'Man overboard!' Three crew members had been swept overboard by heavy seas, but they were tossed on board again by the next wave and managed to hold on. The rolling was intolerable. On the bridge they measured forty degrees in each direction, and it was almost impossible to hang on to anything. In a heavy snowstorm we spotted a German reconnaissance plane five kilometres away, before it disappeared.

An attempt to set the mess table for the three of us was a complete failure, ending in pure farce. We tried to hold on to dishes and cutlery until a giant wave sent all tableware, chairs

and rugs flying through the mess. At the last moment I managed to hook my legs around the mess table which was
screwed to the floor, but the ship's doctor came sailing through
the air and crashed onto the bulkhead, followed by a naval
cadet who came charging in, arms flailing, carrying a knife full
of marmalade. As if this were not enough, the galley boy shot
through, clad only in his shirt, dancing around the broken
dishes, with sandwich-spread between his toes. Before realising what had happened, I heard the ship's doctor's dry
comment about the galley boy's dance: 'Is this supposed to be
a striptease, or what?'

The next great wave sent the galley boy back from whence
he came, and the door closed the performance with a dramatic
clap.

The next day the seas were calmer. A U-boat surfaced, new
messages went out over the airwaves and the U-boat trailed
behind in our wake at a constant distance of thirty kilometres
and with a speed of eighteen knots. It submerged when an
aeroplane took off from the aircraft carrier. Submerged, it
could only manage about six to eight knots, so when the
convoy stepped up its speed to twenty knots, we escaped. But
our position had been detected, and before long we were spot-
ting U-boats on all sides. The *Zambezi* was the first to feel the
impact.

I was on my way up to the bridge after having inspected the
watertight bulkheads with the second-in-command when I
heard a strange metallic sound and the hull shuddered and
heaved. My first thought was that we had been hit by a torpedo, but the opposite was true; we were the ones doing the
firing. The crew on deck working the mine launchers sent out
one depth charge after the other, whilst the sonar screen on the
bridge was laboriously tracking a submarine, picked up by
the echo sounder, to starboard. Nevertheless the convoy

commander ordered us to break away from the convoy and chase the other U-boats. *Zambezi* rolled and tossed in the deep troughs, while the look-out and the instrument crew were vigilantly checking for acoustic torpedoes. Soon we got an echo bearing and changed course toward a U-boat that appeared on the screen. We maintained course until the U-boat was positioned immediately below us, then the navigational instruments failed and before we could adjust them we had lost contact with the convoy. We increased speed to twenty knots and caught up with the rest of the convoy as we crossed the Arctic Circle going south. At the same time the wind increased to a howling storm. The waves grew to mountainous masses of water that raged and thundered against the destroyer so that it reared up like a stallion battling with a sea monster.

Toward evening it was reported that the aircraft carrier had been forced to turn and ride out the storm. Shortly thereafter orders came that any able ship was to continue southward, maintaining convoy stations. By ten o'clock we also gave up, and the *Zambezi* left the convoy with most of the escort ships and turned north to ride out the storm. For a while this led to pure chaos. *Zambezi*'s navigational instruments failed again, and in the darkness we cut straight through the convoy, barely avoiding a collision with a transport ship that suddenly loomed out of the towering waves. The heavy seas were now more dangerous than submarines, so lanterns were lit on all ships.

It was impossible to get any rest in the hammock. I had to protect myself with both hands against the bulkhead, so I was awake when a colossal wave washed on board and the ship's only motor boat was lost. When one of the bomb launchers that had been riveted fast on deck broke loose, it left a large gash and every new wave sent water rushing in over the crew below deck. We had become our own worst enemy. Depth charges that had been cleared for detonation had broken loose from their moorings and rolled freely around. They were no longer weapons of defence, but uncontrollable enemies tumbling wildly from one railing to the other while the ship rolled and masses of water flooded the deck. It felt as though we had been taken by surprise and cast into a meaningless game of life and death. I think everyone on board felt as helpless as I did. For a moment I calculated my chance of surviving if I jumped overboard and tried to swim away from the doomed ship.

Just then some metres of deck railing broke off and the first of many heavy barrels rolled overboard. Normally, when a depth charge is launched the destroyer sails full speed ahead in order to put as much distance as possible between itself and the ensuing explosion. The *Zambezi* was only making three knots into the storm, and the bomb rolled into the sea along the ship's side. The result was what might be expected. One by one the bombs rolled off the deck, splashed into the sea and, owing to the pressure of water, exploded and sank. The sea, which was already wild, became an indescribable inferno, and with each explosion I thought the hull would crack under the strain. The crew made heroic attempts to stop the bombs that were still loose on deck, but when someone was washed overboard they gave up. This time the fellow was not washed back on board, and all attempts to save him failed. It was a horrible experience, watching him struggling and bobbing in a crazy eddy of icy water just a few arm-lengths from the side of the ship. I heard the cry 'Man overboard' and then he was gone. Impossible to find him in such conditions. In a matter of minutes he would be coated with ice and literally frozen stiff.

'Too bad,' one of the officers said quietly when he heard who the man was. 'He . . . he was such a good accordion player.' The officer could find no better way to express the hopelessness we all felt.

The seas now crashed over the destroyer with such force that it was impossible to send anyone out on deck, even with a harness. In all twelve bombs rolled slowly overboard. The cruiser ordered all ships that were still together to change course and continue to the Faeroe Islands on their own. Two cargo ships collided in the snowstorm. The side of one was ripped open and it reported that it was sinking. Before we reached the Faeroe Islands the bridge announced that we were registering echoes on three sides. The captain wanted to save our remaining valuable bombs, so *Zebra* took over and, with another destroyer, launched depth charges all the way to the entrance to Torshavn harbour.

I flew from the Faeroe Islands over Scotland and on to London in order to get a visa from the Soviet embassy to enable me to return to the front. I also took the opportunity to deliver the documents and other items the staff officers had involuntarily sent with me to the Norwegian government.

I never knew why my original papers were not approved by the Russians until long after the war when I was invited to the Soviet Academy of Science to defend my theories against opposing Soviet scientists. I shared a stage in Moscow with the chief of staff of the Russian liberation army in the north, and we were presented to the public as comrades in arms who had fought together on the northern front. It then dawned on me that my mismanaged promotion from 'ensign' to 'lieutenant' had confused the Russians. The word 'ensign' is just as unknown in Russian as it is in English, where the equivalent would be 'second lieutenant'. In the Cyrillic alphabet, Ensign Heyerdahl became Henrik Heyerdahl. And how could they possibly be the one and same person?

In London, as the first soldier to return with an account of the northern front, I broadcast a report over the BBC in English, French and Norwegian. It turned out to be a dramatic experience for my old mother. She spent all the war years sharing her house with one of my nieces, just beside ours on the hillside above Lillehammer, and had fitted out a secret hideaway in her attic for paratroopers in the underground resistance movement. One of them had just completed his mission and was planning to escape over the border to Sweden and back to England the next day. When the Norwegian BBC announcer reported that Lieutenant Thor Heyerdahl was going to file a despatch about Finnmark the next day, the paratrooper postponed his journey, and on 6 February 1945, my mother heard my voice for the first time in six years and knew that I was alive. As a reward for her contribution during the war, this seventy-two-year-old woman received a signed picture from Winston Churchill with a personal note of gratitude for what she had done for the Allies.

My next mission was to return to the front with a valid visa, but this time I was not forced to wait for a convoy to Murmansk. In London, to my surprise, I was met by Captain Rørholt. He had managed to get back to London via neutral Sweden in the hope of finding new communications equipment for the Norwegian forces in Arctic Norway. We made plans and, with Rørholt's blessing, I wrote a report from Finnmark containing an order to myself to make my way to Sweden to train Norwegian refugees in the use of parachutes and radio transmitters. Rørholt read the report at a meeting of leaders of the Norwegian army and navy, American air force officers and British SOE. The orders I had written myself were signed by the general and the day after I spoke on the BBC I flew over German-occupied Norway to Stockholm as the sole passenger in a small blacked-out British plane. In a borrowed civilian suit, and with a pistol and a Norwegian lieutenant's uniform in my suitcase, I was driven to a camp for Norwegian military police just outside Stockholm. Officially

Sweden was neutral, and although, unlike much of the European continent, the country thereby avoided German occupation, it also provided a haven of safety for Norwegians and refugees and contributed all sorts of undercover help.

Rørholt had discovered that there were about ten thousand Norwegian soldiers disguised as 'policemen' in Sweden, and that they were prepared to move into action as soon as they could emerge safely. My task was to select a suitable group for assignments employing parachutes and radio equipment on both sides of the northern front. Rørholt was later to provide radio equipment and we would get it up to the isolated forces in the extreme north of Finnmark.

I was received with enthusiasm everywhere in Stockholm. Just outside the city, at the Norwegian police post in Axvall, I donned my Norwegian army uniform, creating quite a stir. I was able to select sixteen of the best police soldiers, all students who had also recently finished a five-month radio course, and in addition, eleven trained cryptographers. I began training them in receiving and transmitting Norwegian and English radio procedures, and they were put through hard physical training.

Rørholt called three weeks later. He had the equipment with him, and had established contact with two independent officers who had been told of our secret plans. One was Ensign 'Pettersen'. He was the man with the portable transmitter, whose final report back to London had led to the bombing and subsequent sinking of the *Tirpitz*, and who I had met on his own in Finnmark. He became our contact on the Norwegian side of the Swedish border. The other officer was the renowned Norwegian-born pilot Bernt Balchen, who had flown with Admiral Byrd on his Antarctic expedition, and was now an American colonel. He had six Allied planes at his disposal, and operated out of a secret air base on

Swedish territory. I was to transport my soldiers there, and the group was to be ready to move at 0600 the following morning.

Meanwhile, the group had expanded, and I carried the responsibility for command and training thirty-five men. It would be impossible to move thirty-five police soldiers through Sweden in civilian clothes. I gambled that most people in a neutral country would not notice the difference between a bluish Norwegian police uniform and a khaki-coloured Allied uniform with a Norwegian flag on the sleeve. And I was quite right. No one raised an eyebrow when our little detachment marched through the streets of Stockholm to the central station, where a railway carriage had been reserved to carry the company to the extreme north of Sweden.

My little Norwegian force was billeted in secrecy at a remote Swedish air base at Kallax, near Luleå, close to the Finnish border. The Swedish air force soldiers were not a little surprised one morning to find a long row of Eskimo igloos skirting the edge of the runway. I had started to teach the soldiers wilderness survival, and had every reason to be sceptical about our equipment.

While awaiting Rørholt's arrival, we spent the time on ground training, preparing for parachute jumps, and hard physical endurance training. Cut off from any communication with High Command in England, I promoted the brightest of the fellows to sergeant and some of the others to corporals, in order to have a proper chain of command.

When Rørholt arrived with the equipment, Balchen assisted us in training some of the men in trial jumps from one of his Dakotas before we dropped the men with their transmitters behind the German lines or near our own isolated liberation forces. Balchen then personally flew me to Kirkenes, where I was immediately embraced by the same smiling Soviet officer who had sent me back to London four months earlier.

'Welcome back, Lieutenant Heyerdahl,' he said. 'Now your papers are in order.' He had received a message from Moscow.

It was a small but well-trained communications troop that now camped outside the ruins of Kirkenes. The gear was first-rate, a mixture of American polar equipment, good British and Soviet weapons and wonderful Swedish provisions. I was in the unusual situation of not being under the command of any particular military unit. Colonel Dahl and the Norwegian High Command in Finnmark still maintained their head-quarters in the Kirkenes area, but the Norwegian Mountain Company had advanced alone down into no-man's-land after the Russians had halted their advance on the far side of the wide Varanger Fjord which divided Norway from the Soviet Union. Rørholt and I agreed that I maintain the command of the former 'police soldiers', and he continue with the respon-sibility for equipment and the co-ordination of all outposts. With the go-ahead from the Swedish High Command he remained in the barracks we had been given permission to use in the Swedish air force camp, and this is where he established the main base for our operations.

After landing on the Norwegian side of the border, I started a crash course boot camp for a score of volunteers from Finnmark, and continued to establish small radio stations. Rørholt received a message from one of our stations behind the German lines that armed Norwegian Nazis were on their way north from Narvik to intercept the advancing Norwegian forces. If German intelligence had uncovered how thin on the ground these troops really were, the large German forces would move northward again and wipe them out before the Russians could make it through the mine-obstructed no-man's-land.

With the blessings of both the Russians and Colonel Dahl, I ventured down to the front line again. Just then Ensign 'Pettersen' reappeared, like a lone wolf, and with Lieutenant Stabell, who was now back in Norwegian uniform, he joined my little troop. The spring thaw had not yet set in on the mountain plateau, and to avoid a third journey through the minefields of German no-man's-land, we requisitioned two fishing boats to transport us down the coast.

We put a radio patrol ashore in Båtsfjord to keep a lookout for Norwegian Nazi spies. No Allied warship had made it further than this point. We were in mine-stocked waters, still patrolled by German submarines, and we kept hourly radio contact with Stabell, who was out of sight, following in another fishing boat. We had agreed to meet in Hopseidet, but on the outskirts of Hopseidet I had a sudden premonition that we might fall into a trap, and sent a coded message to Stabell to continue beyond Nordkyn and into the long Porsanger Fjord. This would seem like utter lunacy to everyone, including the Germans, who were positioned on the west side of the fjord and would not suspect that a platoon could enter the fjord right before their eyes.

German observation posts or spies must have guessed at our destination before we changed course. That night, three German U-boats slipped into Hopseidet and landed navy troops. They disarmed the few Norwegian guards, and eye-witnesses reported that some drunken sailors took six civilians into custody and eventually shot them because they failed to extract any information from them. By then we were already far beyond Hopseidet and on our way along the eastern bank of the Porsanger Fjord.

Just as it had been pitch black night and day when I arrived at the front in January, it was now light round the clock. Turning off the lights of the two fishing boats was of little help as we stole into the seemingly endless fjord, immediately ahead of the German front lines. Now, in May, the night was so light that one could see for miles both at sea and on land.

We went ashore from both boats at nine o'clock in the morning. We were met by an incredible array of barbed wire obstructions and landmines. Only the day before two men had stepped on a landmine. We found two parachutes that had hit the ground without opening, and a smashed generator revealed that this was part of Rørholt's airdrop from Balchen's plane. We returned to the boats, and continued all the way in to Hamnbukt, at the head of the fjord. Here we stole ashore and set up camp near some Lapps. When I contacted Rørholt in Sweden later that evening, we were told that the German forces in Denmark had capitulated.

We celebrated the news with the Lapps, who treated us to tots of their special drink, klonk. It was a silent celebration since the cannon on the other side of the fjord were still loaded and our closest neighbours were probably not in as jubilant a mood as we were.

During the days and nights that followed I witnessed modern warfare at first hand. We think with disgust of the time when barbaric heathens chopped off each others' heads with swords. We like to believe that warfare in our days is cleaner. In fact, for those who launch rockets and lay mines, war can be waged wearing white gloves.

I recalled the rain of rockets over London when I came to the minefields of Finnmark. I had seen V-2 bombs fall at random, while London's innocent, civilian population sought cover in underground stations or shelters, like Christians in the catacombs in the Roman Empire. I also saw the Allied squadrons fill the sky, like some prehistoric dragons on their way to extract revenge, using the same tactics, with the blessings of the padre.

One night I had been able to view almost five thousand years of technological progress in one single image, never to be forgotten. I had always dreamed of seeing the famous, ancient ruins at Stonehenge, and while in London on leave from stair-washing, I took a train to Salisbury and thumbed a lift in my Norwegian army uniform to a barbed wire fence that surrounded the whole area, protected from a neighbouring military base.

Firmly intent on not returning without having experienced the prehistoric megalith temple, I decided to make use of my commando training in a peaceful manner among allies. I found a large cardboard box thrown in a ditch and, when night came, I squeezed myself through the barbed wire fence between two layers of cardboard. After admiring the thousand-year-old stone giants reaching skyward in a protective ring around me, I crawled on to the altar stone. After eating the supper I had brought along, I rolled out my sleeping bag and lay down to meditate on the passage of time. In the night sky above I saw the same unchangeable constellations that Our Lord had placed there before life was created on earth. They were all there, with the sun and the moon, and may have been a greater source of fascination to the ancient engineers of Stonehenge than they were to us. Then a single star moved slowly among the others, from horizon to horizon. This one had been created in my own time; it was a V-2 on its way to London.

I saw modern warfare from a new perspective on the altar stone at Stonehenge. When I went ashore deep in the beautiful Porsanger Fjord with Lieutenant Stabell, Ensign 'Pettersen' and our soldiers, we walked on to a stage set for modern man-to-man combat, but we also had our cunning technological equipment to fight it for us.

We landed in a partially snow-covered valley, similar to the Bella Coola valley in British Columbia. This time, however, we were not hunting bears. The valley's entire beautiful birch forest had been vandalised and razed to the ground. Only a few scattered giant spruce remained. The Germans had planted an incredible amount of mines and booby traps. They must have had many men up here. As we advanced, we encountered many abandoned camps surrounded by minefields, and littered with twisted metal, cars, tanks, posters, paper, broken glass and huge piles of bottles.

Norwegian reinforcements had arrived with new convoys via Murmansk, and they had advanced southward over the mountain plateau to the Lapp city of Karasjok, which was closer to Sweden than we were. Rørholt had airdropped a communications patrol to them from Balchen's planes, and these men were in the process of clearing the airport, which was completely covered with mines. There were daily reports of civilians and soldiers being killed, and both the snow and the white birch trunks bore witness to a bloodbath. Up here in the north the war was not fought against living enemies but against the diabolical mechanical equipment they had left behind. A tempting bottle, a useful item, anything at all could have invisible threads connected to an infernal booby trap that had been placed to tear off an arm, ruin a face or shatter a body.

The true heroes on the modern front line were the men who detonated these devilish toys and the medics weaving their way through invisible and terrible mazes to save lives. The enemy can become a friend the instant he receives the ceasefire order, but to the mechanical wizardry that remains buried underground without any other purpose than to maim or kill, peace is an unknown concept. It continues in the service of evil until it has been detonated or defused. A long week had passed since soldiers of flesh and blood had ended their armed engagement. I made a note in my diary to remind myself always to support those who work for peace. In this way I would be able to enjoy a future life with fellow human beings from all countries and all sectors of society. Never again would I join in a dance with the devil.

On the northern front, the line of demarcation between war and peace went unnoticed. My entry for 6 May reads the following: 'Stabell was shaving . . . when we heard an explosion from the field. Everything became eerily still, then the mountains echoed the boom. When I emerged from the tent, Lieutenant Asbjørnsen and two medics were on their way right out into the minefield where hidden devilry could explode anywhere under the sand or in the junk piles above ground. We ran toward the explosion. When we had run a few hundred metres, a cry came to us from some twisted bits of red iron, remains of what had once been a hangar. "Rolf has hurt himself," he moaned. He had fragments from the explosion in his eyes, and his nose was badly cut . . . We climbed over a hill of sand and found a man on his back about eight metres from a hole in the ground. The white birch trunks were stained with mud and splashed with blood. The poor man's face was no more than soot, mud and blood, and his hair was a wet mass . . . He was fully conscious and complained of pain in his legs. Blood gushed through his torn pants. We took a knife and cut off his pants, underwear and socks. Large open sores were filled with mud. No use cleaning anything here. We bandaged him as well as we could to stop the worst bleeding, and then the medics carried him back, carefully retreating back in our own footprints.'

As early as 7 May we heard a vague rumour on the radio that the Germans in Norway had capitulated. The bugle player ran out to the campground and blew 'cease fire' but we managed to calm him down immediately, because the German vanguard was just the other side of the hills to the west.

On 9 May both we and the German vanguard still had weapons ready on either side of the hill, but we were the only ones having to cope constantly with newly wounded personnel. Then we heard thousands of jubilant voices on the radio from Oslo: Norwegian troops from England had just landed and were on their way to the capital; liberation was being celebrated ecstatically by the Norwegian people. We rejoiced with our countrymen but exchanged smiles when we heard the announcer's triumphant comment from the south: 'At this very moment, the first Norwegian troops are returning to Norwegian soil!'

We had crawled out of the tent and were dancing around with joy when I caught sight of a solitary Lapp running down the hillside with a reindeer carcass on his back.

'Peace has come! The war is over!' I shouted to him in joy.

He took the pipe out of his mouth and asked: 'Who won?'

Yes, who won?

Many of us soldiers have asked each other that question since. The Red Army had quickly changed from devils to angels when the Germans marched into Russia, but as soon as the Germans left they reverted to being devils. We needed the Germans in NATO to defend us against our former liberators on the northern front. No one reacted when a few years later I settled for a longer period of time amongst our former enemies in Italy, and it was considered just as natural that a German, a Russian and an American were with me on the expedition with the reed boat *Tigris*.

What became of the enemy?

We carry the enemy within us until the next time the devil,

with his magical powers, releases it to participate in his diabolical dance. Just who we choose as our enemy is unimportant as long as we have someone to vent Cain's legacy of hate upon. If we are to believe the word of the Bible, Cain beat Abel to death, then Adam had no more sons for us to be likened unto.

War and peace became one and the same thing those first days. A 'cease fire' order came over the radio on 13 May, but it had the surprising adjunct that it only applied to companies with at least one division. Since there were not that many soldiers in Finnmark, the instruction did not apply to us. That day I noted that seventy mines had been found around a single bomb crater that was to be repaired in the road.

Stabell, who had been thrown into the Arctic Ocean by a mine when we first came to Murmansk, could have been blown sky-high with 'Pettersen', alias Raaby, and myself during the two weeks we shared a tent on the banks of the Porsanger Fjord. On 22 May I wrote in my diary: 'Moved to new campsite. The corps of engineers has set up camp by our old site. They had a mine-clearing exercise today, and great was their surprise when they found a large teller-mine under the sand in the middle of our old tent.'

In theory a teller-mine would not explode with the pressure of something as light and 'expendable' as a human body, but theories do not always hold true. An experiment by one of the newly arrived officers in Karasjok proved this point. He placed a German teller-mine on the ground and explained to his soldiers that it adjusted to the weight of a tank or a heavy car. To prove it, he stepped with both feet on to the mine and it exploded. Twenty-two men were killed and nine wounded. One of our paratrooper telegraph operators was there and he contacted Rørholt at the main base in Sweden. In record time, he and Balchen managed to get two doctors and a nurse down to us. They landed, uninjured, in deep snow. Before a mass funeral could take place in Karasjok, the church graveyard itself had to be cleared of land mines.

On 13 July, about two months after the liberation was announced on the radio, I applied to the Army High Command in Oslo for an honourable discharge. My request was turned down. They needed me in Finnmark. I then requested two weeks' leave to visit my wife and children who had come home from America and my old parents who I had not seen for six years. Leave was granted.

I went south via Sweden to Oslo. With two lieutenant's stars on my collar I went straight to the office of the High Command. I was met by two ensigns with one star each, and ordered them to get the discharge forms, told them what to write, had it stamped and sealed and delivered to the neighbouring office.

A few days later, in the bosom of my family, I received my discharge forms in the mail, signed by two high-ranking officers.

I was a civilian again, a free person, with my own name and no number or rank.

8

No Time to Think

Once again I was lying in the hammock in my garden in the Canary Islands. My eyes were open, and memories of the meaningless days of war disappeared into the surrounding foliage – or maybe they simply withdrew into the endless labyrinths of the mind, where they remain hidden, like invisible strips of film footage.

When I closed my diary containing the notes I had made of the manhunt in the Arctic Ocean, my *aku-aku* disappeared. I thought he had been shaken and scared by my recollections of friends and enemies who were possessed by orders to kill, but when I glanced at my watch I knew that it was the haste within me that had chased my invisible companion away. A clock has a scarecrow effect on an *aku-aku*, to whom time does not exist and who lives in a world where one day is like a thousand years and vice versa – just like the story of creation and Einstein's calculations.

Life had never before been so busy, and time had never flown so quickly as it did now, fifty years after we had drifted from Peru to Polynesia aboard the *Kon-Tiki* raft. As a creature circumscribed by time, I climbed out of my hammock and frightened my two faithful four-legged friends Kan and Oro, who had been sleeping peacefully at my feet. We ran to the house. They had more than enough time to spare, but I had things to do. My travelling schedule had been unusually hectic, and I had barely managed to unpack after a visit to Japan and the United States before having to head back to Peru and Easter Island. There was no chance of a moment's peace with my *aku-aku*. With time passing faster than jet planes and faxes, I was barely managing to keep up.

The fiftieth anniversary of the *Kon-Tiki* journey was observed and celebrated on a far grander scale than the journey itself had been. Back then we were satisfied just to have survived the expedition, but that was nothing compared to the fact that fifty years had passed. I often felt guilty about leaving our two dogs and the wonderful pyramid valley in Tenerife to drag Jacqueline through this commotion of festivities and journeys. We were crossing our shrunken planet in all directions, flying far above all the oceans I knew so well from first-hand experience. All of this was to mark the fact that a long time had passed since the raft voyage to Polynesia.

It is always relaxing to sit back in a comfortable aeroplane seat and realise that no duties and no appointments can be taken care of before the plane touches down. I felt that I was approaching home when we crossed the Andes toward Lima, and the endless Pacific Ocean appeared ahead of us. It was impossible to count all the times I had visited the Pacific Ocean, especially the stretch along South America's coast from Chile, Peru and Ecuador and further north along Central and North America all the way up to the Canadian archipelago, off the coast of British Columbia. It was here that I thought the Stone Age people from Asia had stopped by on their way to the New World, before currents and winds swept them straight down toward Polynesia. I had travelled there both by boat and balsa-wood raft and, in later years, often by plane. I was now familiar with the opposite shore as well, the other side of the ocean and of the planet itself. I had studied the remains left by the earliest navigators on Okinawa, on Che-jo outside South Korea, and especially in Japan. Just a few weeks ago I had lectured at the University of Tokyo on the significance of the ocean currents on migration in the Pacific. After that I packed in three jubilee lectures at the National Geographic Society in Washington on the way to our new home in the Canary Islands. Once home we had to pack our best clothes for the Kon-Tiki Museum's royal dinner in Oslo and all of this was on our way to Lima, where the plane now touched down and rumbled along the runway. Here we were to celebrate *Kon-Tiki*'s launch from the naval port on 28 April, 1947.

More than any other time when I had returned to Peru, memories flashed before my eyes in rapid succession. Back then, I was just out of uniform, a wolf's clothing from another life. I had conquered my childhood fear of water just a few years earlier. Joining me on *Kon-Tiki*'s voyage were the war veterans Knut and Torstein; Erik, whom I'd played pirates with in childhood; Herman, who I bumped into at the Norwegian seaman's restaurant in New York; and Bengt the Swede, who ran into me as he came paddling in his canoe up the Amazon River just as we were ready to leave from Lima. Today they were no longer with me. Torstein had ended his days on the barren Greenland ice cap, Herman in the empire of the sun god *Kon-Tiki* by Lake Titicaca, and Erik in our birthplace, Larvik, where we had both dreamed of distant voyages to foreign lands. Only Knut and Bengt were still alive.

Knut had retired in Oslo after being instrumental in the creation of both the Kon-Tiki Museum and the Norwegian Resistance Museum.

It was hard to believe that so many years had passed, and that I had survived intact, both the ocean crossing and the following storm of attacks from all those people whose anger was vented by one single fact – the raft's buoyancy. The Pacific Ocean remained unchanged, and it curved westward beyond a blue horizon the way I had first seen it when I flew from Ecuador to Peru to find a suitable location to cut the jungle logs that were to carry us across the ocean. But Lima and the port city of Callao had grown into a huge metropolis, with a population twice as large as that of Norway. Crowded rows of skyscrapers and tenement buildings now covered the barren area one used to pass through to get from the hotel to the harbour. Missing in this ocean of skyscrapers was our old, traditional Hotel Bolivar, which in my memory still soared majestically above low houses clustered around a colonial plaza, against a blue sky.

Even the impressive presidential palace was now disrespectfully overshadowed by towering concrete walls, the captive of a network of congested traffic that coiled snake-like around the residential areas. From here the roads, greedily and insatiably, made their way across the plains, pushing growing smog and slum areas toward the desert mountains. Wealth and poverty grew side by side at the same rate, as in developing countries elsewhere in the world. Party politics and changing governments tried to solve the problems of big cities with more industry and more machines. In addition, the rich built more skyscrapers and the poor built more slums, unfazed by the experts' calculations.

As manager of the Kon-Tiki Museum's archaeological excavations in Túcume on the northern coast, I had been back to Peru numerous times in recent years. After many years in Italy, Peru became a new home and I had a long list of good friends among both the very rich and the very poor. The changes were therefore not too shocking when I returned to this fantastic one-time Inca empire for the *Kon-Tiki* celebrations. Still, this was hardly the same country or the same people Herman and I met when we arrived to build an Inca raft with our nine huge balsa logs, and were denied permission by the Naval Minister. Agreeing with the view of the National Geographic Society's scientific council, and all other nautical experts, he thought it would be suicidal to venture out on the ocean in such a craft. Now, fifty years later, it was this navy's turn to celebrate the anniversary of the launch of the raft. The National Geographic Society had celebrated a few days ahead of them, in Washington. The first event would be a reception in the presidential palace, since the country's president at the time, Bustamante y Rivero, had been the one to finally order the naval minister to allow us to build the Inca raft in the dockyard.

A head of state with Japanese blood running through his veins now ruled from the magnificent old palace. President Fujimori was an unknown quantity, but as in so many other countries, he had been elected as a result of the people's loss of confidence in the old politicians. He won the election as a complete outsider, the election billboards showing a face that bore no resemblance to the Spaniards or the Incas.

Governing a country with such a diverse population and history as the former Inca Empire was not an easy task. So far I had met five of the presidents who had tried. Only the first one, who let me build the *Kon-Tiki*, had survived his elected years with dignity. After the meeting with Bustamante y Rivero, my next encounter with Peruvian politics occurred in my own home in Oslo. One afternoon, a few years after returning unscathed from the *Kon-Tiki* expedition, someone rang my doorbell. I was delighted to see my jolly artist friend, Stenersen, from the boot camp days in Canada. I recognised him by his wide smile and his wide tie, but I did not recognise the short foreigner standing beside him.

A nice guy, I soon learned. They had met at a bar and he wanted to meet me because the *Kon-Tiki* had been launched from his homeland.

Over a cup of coffee, our new acquaintance wanted to know who I knew in his native country. Not wanting to seem like a braggart, I had to admit that I could only name the naval minister, who at first had refused me permission to travel, and the athletic young air force minister who had arranged for my audience at the palace.

'Two of my best friends,' the little man answered humbly. I was sceptical and pretended to believe him. After this I couldn't resist mentioning the president's name.

'I am the one who got him elected,' my guest answered just as calmly. I had to ask him to repeat his name; it was a difficult one.

'Victor Raul Haya de la Torre,' was the answer. This was the man who had founded APRA in the 1930s; for several years it had been the largest political party in Peru. He was a refugee in Norway and had been here long enough to speak broken Norwegian.

APRA, and the charismatic young hero Alan Garcia as president, had been in power when I returned to Peru in the late 1980s and applied for permission to start archaeological excavations in Túcume. Neither the president nor the other government members had heard of Túcume, and when the minister of culture rolled down his wall map neither the village nor its huge neighbouring pyramid complex were marked on it. However, when we started digging, and found the mummy of the Inca period's last local viceroy buried on the top of the largest pyramid, the president's curiosity was aroused. The former vassal king was dressed in his colourful robe of feathers, sitting in his grave, high above the plain, with *tumu* sceptre and receptacles of food, wearing a silver crown and displaying huge silver plugs in his elongated earlobes. According to the legend recorded by the first Spanish conquistadors to have reached the area, these pyramids were built by the grandson of King Naymlap, who had sailed down the coast from the north on balsa rafts with his whole entourage. On a temple wall we found magnificent illustrations of large reed ships navigated by mythical men with bird-like heads – just like those on the temple walls in Egypt and on the cliffs of Easter Island.

It was all too exciting for the inquisitive young president. Alan Garcia and his immediate staff came to stay the weekend in the simple but roomy adobe dwelling by the pyramids. I had built this house for myself and my foreign workers, using sun-dried clay bricks.

None of the inhabitants of Túcume or in the whole desert valley of Lambayeque had ever seen so many police and military men in so many different uniforms. They all spent the night around and inside our compound, some on the roof, behind the bushes, and in the stable, barn and chicken coop. Six kilometres of telephone wire wound its way to Túcume and into the president's bedroom. At mealtimes there was barely room between the walls or at our long dining table for all his servants and special musicians. In the kitchen our own little Túcume cook disappeared amongst all the professional master chefs who created dishes she had never seen before.

Early next morning, our loyal local driver Pizarro was sent off to the neighbouring town to get the president's favourite bread for breakfast. When the whole convoy was ready for

As a child I was brought up on goats' milk. I am pictured here with my father, a
wery manager also called Thor Heyerdahl.

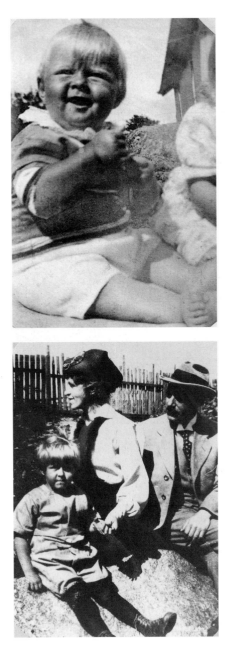

2. Me during the summer of 1915.

3. With my parents in 1918.

4. With my mother Alison in front of my childhood home in Larvik, 1920.

5. My wildlife mentor, Ola Bjørneby, in 1932.

6. With the catch of the day.

7. Me in 1935, aged nineteen.

8. My faithful Greenland dog Kazan, 1936.

9. With Liv at a carnival onboard the *Messangerie Maritime* on our way to Tahiti, 1937.

10. Chief Teriieroo and his wife in Papeno, Tahiti, 1937.

11. Liv at Fatu-Hiva, 1938.

12. Liv chewing on sugarcane, Fatu-Hi 1938.

13. In January 1941 I published my first article in *National Geographic*.

14. The soldier and artist Bjørn Stenersen and Thor Jr on a boat trip by the camp in the Muskoka forest, Canada, 1942.

5. The baby bear, Peik, plays with Bjørn Bamse') outside the Vesle Skaugum amp in the Muskoka forest, 1942.

16. Father, sons and bear.

17. A winter exercise in Little Norway, 1943.

18. With Peik, 1943.

19. Lieutenant Heyerdahl in uniform.

10. Clipping from an article on the *Kon-Tiki* expedition in *Life* magazine, 1947.

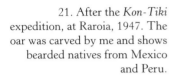

21. After the *Kon-Tiki* expedition, at Raroia, 1947. The oar was carved by me and shows bearded natives from Mexico and Peru.

22. During the twentieth anniversary of *Kon-Tiki* in 1967.

23. The crew on board the *Kon-Tiki*: Herman Watzinger, Knut M. Haugland, Torstein Raaby, Bengt Danielsson and myself. The photo was taken by Erik Hesselberg.

. 'To my friend Thor
eyerdahl. Greetings from
ieif Teriieroo.'

25. Receiving the Vega Medal from the King of Sweden, Gustav VI Adolf, in 1962.

26. On a turtle's back during the Galapagos expedition, 1952–53.

27. Marriage to
Yvonne Dedekam-
Simonsen, 1949.

28. In front of the Colla Micheri estate in Italy, with daughters Anette (born 1953), Marian (born 1957) and Helene Elisabeth, called Bettina (born 1959).

29. In the watchtower at Colla Micheri.

30. At work on the unknown *rongo-rongo* text in about 1955.

31. At the Kon-Tiki Museum in Oslo: King Haakon, Prince Philip, Queen Elizabeth and me.

32. Shaking hands with the Soviet leader Nikita Khrushchev, in Oslo, 1964.

33. At a science conference in Moscow, 1964.

34. Receiving the Lomonosov Medal in Moscow.

35. Decorated as Commander of the American Maltese Order after the arrival in Barbados after the *Ra II* journey, 1970.

36. Raisa and Mikhail Gorbachev with me and Jacqueline in The Hague, 1994.
37. Testing samples of goats' milk with Fidel Castro in Cuba, 1985.

38. A window display of the book on the Túcume pyramids, 1995. Oxford University Library is seen reflected in the window.

39. My childhood fear of water was conquered a long time ago.

. Marriage to Jacqueline at El Aaiún, Western Sahara, 1996.

41. With the President of Peru, Alberto Fujimori, and Cabinet Minister Grete Knudsen during the fiftieth anniversary of *Kon-Tiki* in Lima, 1997.

42. On Easter Island with Jacqueline and Yuri Senkevich, 1997.

43. On a horse in Túcume, Peru.

the morning visit to the pyramids, Pizarro sat behind the wheel of the big expedition truck that would lead the procession. We were barely out of the house before the president wanted to know which vehicle I would be in, and when I pointed to my four-door pick-up he hurried over and pulled the alarmed Pizarro out of the driver's seat. With me at his side he started the engine, and the ever responsible Pizarro jumped into the back seat in order to keep some control over the situation. The car-happy president sped off in a spray of desert sand, and the motorcycle escort took a roaring short cut through the algarobe trees in a desperate attempt to stay ahead. The guard at the gate had already managed to swing it open, and the whole population of Túcume had gathered outside to catch a glimpse of their president and to welcome him. The cheering crowd will never forget their surprise when the escort came racing through the gate, with the president himself behind the wheel of the first car and their friend Pizarro sitting sheepishly in the back seat waving shyly to his friends.

Just a few weeks after the popular president had visited us, there were re-elections in Peru. The APRA party lost, and owing to the accusations heaped upon him by the opposition, Alan Garcia had to flee the country to avoid imprisonment. Among all the election posters showing pictures of Garcia and other well-known politicians, a completely unknown Japanese face appeared and he won the majority of the votes. In Peru, as elsewhere in the world, people had stopped believing in promises made by politicians they knew.

Therefore, on 28 April 1997, fifty years to the day since the *Kon-Tiki* was towed to sea from the naval harbour in Peru, I met President Alberto Fujimori in his palace. It was an exciting time. Only six days had passed since he had ended the terrorist coup at the Japanese embassy. Hostages had been held for 126 days. No one had seen him in public since this dramatic incident. Not surprisingly, the man who received the Norwegian Ambassador and myself in the inner sanctum of the presidential palace could hardly be described as a jovial or relaxed individual. President Fujimori, erect as a soldier and with an inscrutable facial expression, asked us to sit down and partake of refreshments. A little time usually passes before conversation warms up at such a purely official courtesy visit, but a smile broke through when I reminded the president that we had met before, when we sat together eating raw fish from the same dish, owing to a misunderstanding.

That had happened some years before; I still had not met Jacqueline. It was while the cholera epidemic raged in Peru, and rumour said it was spread by eating fish. This was not a happy time in Túcume. The kitchen assistant was down with typhoid fever, and Pizarro had just recovered from an attack of cholera when he drove me to a farewell dinner for the village priest. He had been forced to leave because of bomb threats. The Shining Path terrorist group had signalled its presence in Túcume by planting a flag on the nearest pyramid, and after Padre Pedro had received written warnings about bombs at his home, the bishop ordered him to leave the village.

I was just leaving my place at the farewell dinner for the priest, feeling pleasantly full after eating kid and drinking corn beer, when flutes and drums started up and I was expected to start off the dancing with a *marinera*, a mixture of Spanish bullfighting and Norwegian folk dance. I escaped by the skin of my teeth, as a message came from the fishing village Santa Rosa, down on the coast. It was an invitation to 'a surprise' at 1500 hours, signed by 'Nicolas, President of the reed-boat fishermen's union'.

Pizarro was already waiting with the car, and I invited the woman who had been seated next to me to come along. She was a local architect who sketched plans of the ruins we excavated, and who believed like me that we were on our way to see a regatta of fishermen sitting astride their reed *caballitos* and paddling out to sea. I had forged a special relationship with these men, as they had now been granted public aid to cultivate the nearly extinct totora reeds used to build their traditional simple fishing vessels.

The police had set up roadblocks on the way in to Santa Rosa, and no matter how much Pizarro argued that I was the guest of honour we were not allowed to pass. Pizarro found a detour and we made it to the main street from a side road. The street was jammed. A brass band with a tuba and kettledrums came marching along, but we were too late to join in. I couldn't see a thing, but pushed my way through the crowd, dragging my friend behind me. We managed to squeeze in right in front of the band, and we joined the procession, keeping step with a small group in front of us. We then saw that one of them was President Fujimori, marching next to the mayor of the village.

It was too late to get away. We were surrounded by cheering onlookers, with no way out but forwards with the parade, flanked by waving people and with the band at our heels. Only the president and the mayor were allowed to enter the town hall, and there we were, engulfed by the crowd. I looked up, and saw the two standing on a little balcony right above our heads. The mayor looked down, straight into my face, as I dutifully waved like everyone else. In a second he was gone, and suddenly showed up at my side whispering that I must go to the village restaurant. Then he returned to the president. We managed to push through the crowds and into the restaurant, where there were two long tables and many people. Everyone crowded around the same table, but there was no room for us there, so we placed ourselves at the other table where no one else was sitting.

We remained there, declining any offer of food or drink. We were still replete from the priest's dinner. The door opened and in came President Fujimori and his young son, escorted by the mayor, who seated them opposite us before stepping back respectfully and leaving the room.

Quite a surprise, I thought, before realising that this had to be a misunderstanding. Fujimori obviously did not think the same, and looked far from happy when I introduced myself. He thought this was part of the programme and broke into Japanese with his son while they both ravenously attacked their portions of the president's favourite dish, *seviche*, raw fish marinated in the Peruvian manner.

An embarrassing silence ensued, but suddenly the president seemed to catch on and asked me whether I had been on the *Kon-Tiki*. When that fact was confirmed, the son was given a quick and lively briefing in Japanese, and then Fujimori pushed his own dish toward me so that we could eat together. I tried in vain, both in Spanish and with simple gestures, to assure him that I was not hungry, that I had already eaten, but to no avail. There we were, eating raw fish from a shared dish in the middle of the cholera epidemic, and it became more and more obvious to me that this was a misunderstanding. Nevertheless, the conversation flowed easily, about seafood and the exploitation of ocean resources, and I scored several points when I supported his theory that cholera was not carried by fish from the ocean but by insanitary overland trucking transportation. Túcume and all the roadside villages had been infested, but the fishermen along the coast had escaped the epidemic.

Then I happened to look out of the window and saw the woollen caps belonging to Nicolas and the fishermen. They were outside, peering in; obviously only the village elite were seated at the other long table. Slowly it dawned on me that the 'surprise' for me was not my meeting with the president. He had only come to eat fresh fish with his son. They had arrived by helicopter, hoping to be alone, and then the mayor had mistakenly placed me right next to his plate full of delicacies because during the march I had been part of the president's entourage.

The comedy started to get out of hand when the door opened slowly, and a tiny old woman came tiptoeing toward me, virtually crawling behind the table. It was Doña Perla, an activist from a totally different social class than the one she championed when she fought to improve the rights of the reed-boat fishermen. Almost imperceptibly she placed a note in my hand and I only managed to nod in agreement before she sneaked out.

'Can you introduce Nicolas to the president?' the note said. I could not refuse, even if my life depended on it.

Then Nicolas himself appeared at the door, standing respectfully, cap in hand. He walked over to the president who got to his feet when he saw that I did. What was I to say now?

'This is the president of the reed-boat fishermen's union,' I said, 'and this is the president of Peru.'

Not much else was said. But Nicolas was walking on cloud nine when he returned to the others. Since the president by now had had almost as much to eat as I had, he headed for the helicopter, while I was carried on the shoulders of the fishermen down to the beach. In fact, the surprise was the sight of all the magnificent reed boats, ready for the regatta. But first, we went into the fishermen's bar, because Nicolas was now accepted as an acquaintance of the president.

Fujimori did not forget his presidential colleague, Nicolas. He presented him with a brand new truck to transport fish from the *caballitos* fishermen. Doña Perla was given government aid to re-cultivate the *totora* reeds, and the pledge of an official ban on permits for rich people to build on land where Nicolas and his colleagues had always harvested reeds.

Fujimori had loosened up and regained his human characteristics when the ambassador and I expressed our gratitude after the meeting. We hurried over to the National Museum, where a special exhibition depicting models and pictures from the *Kon-Tiki* and *Ra* journeys was to be opened that morning, on the occasion of the anniversary. Half jokingly, I asked whether the president would attend, and as expected, received a crooked smile for an answer.

The exhibition was displayed inside the museum's large entrance hall, and it was crowded with people who had to make way for us when we arrived. Jacqueline waited on the podium with the museum director and our good friend, Consul General Stimman, fretting that we would be late. The public had just managed to close ranks when shouts of police and a roar of motorcycles caused everyone to turn around once more and move aside. President Fujimori arrived unannounced, and went straight to the museum director, who escorted him up to the podium. He was just as surprised as the rest of us.

This is how President Fujimori, who had not shown himself in public for a long time, came to open the exhibition, first with a speech about the *Kon-Tiki* expedition, its goals and results, and then with scissors that cut the silk ribbon.

The anniversary celebrations were still not complete when we gratefully put down our champagne glasses and the president returned to his palace. The departure of *Kon-Tiki* had taken place at the naval harbour in Callao, and we were now on our way there. To celebrate the fiftieth anniversary of the expedition, the navy's historical institute had published a short book I had written about pre-Columbian navigation in Peru.

The admiralty had arranged for a ceremony at the exact place where the raft had been launched.

In the consul-general's car, we took the bends in the road so rapidly that we held on for dear life, and when we passed through the large gate to the naval harbour, at the exact spot where *Kon-Tiki* slid into the ocean, the marine band was waiting, ready to play.

This was a serious occasion. A small stand of seats had been erected at the upper end of the slip, and it was already occupied by naval officers in starched white uniforms with epaulettes on their shoulders and medals on their chests. Jacqueline and I found our reserved seats between the admirals in the first row.

In an opening speech by Admiral Arrospide, president of the navy's historical institute, our attention was drawn to the historical fact that it was from this harbour that the Pacific islands were discovered, or as he expressed it himself, 'were first visited by Europeans'. After the conquest of their country, the Spaniards heard from the historians in the Inca Empire that uninhabited islands that no Europeans had visited were a few months' journey away in the ocean. The historian Sarmiento de Gamboa gathered such precise directions for the journey to these islands that he persuaded the Spanish viceroy in Peru to fit out two expeditions under the command of Alvora de Mendañas with himself as guide. The first Mendañas expedition reached Melanesia in 1567; the second reached Polynesia in 1595.

The admiral pointed to a bronze plaque with an inscription to the memory of the Mendañas expeditions on the brick wall to the left of the slip. On the opposite side was a curtain that he asked me to pull aside. I did, and the inscription was in memory of the *Kon-Tiki* journey from Callao to Raroia in Polynesia in 1947. The military band thereupon started playing the Norwegian and Peruvian national anthems.

This was too much for my *aku-aku*, who had kept calmly to himself both at the palace and in the museum.

What more can you ask for now?

I too, noticed a lump in my throat.

There is, however, never any reason to feel perfectly safe. The celebrations nearly came to a premature conclusion. A television crew of eleven Russians had come from Moscow for the occasion. My good friend Yuri from the three reed-boat journeys was the interviewer. I had promised to accompany them up to the pyramids in Túcume and out to the statues on Easter Island. For the trip to the pyramids, the Russians had rented their own little plane. A Norwegian journalist managed to bribe his way to a seat on the plane.

Night fell and I sat enjoying the view over the dark Pacific Ocean while we flew northward with the lights from the mainland on our right. After a while I discovered that the lights had disappeared from the right side and were now showing up on the left. I realised that we were flying full speed back to where we had come from. I only hoped we would reach the airport before we ended up in the ocean, where there were no balsawood logs to rescue us.

When we were safely on the ground we were informed that another plane was ready to take us up again, but we had to wait for a new pilot. While Jacqueline and I sat patiently with the Russians and waited, the journalist went over to our plane to take a look. Via his newspaper we later learned that fuel had been pouring out from under the engines. Without being prepared for it, we had been closer to death than when we sailed on the raft from Callao fifty years earlier.

9

David and Goliath

The celebrations were still going on when we made an emergency landing at the airport in Callao. When we got on the next plane, we made a brief detour northwards to the pyramids in Túcume, and then south to Santiago de Chile and out to Easter Island, all in the space of two days.

According to the legends of this most isolated of places, the forefathers of the present inhabitants of Easter Island had taken two months on their westward journey toward the sunset. They were escaping with their king, Hotu Matua, and his queen, Ava-rei-pua, after being defeated in war in their homeland. Times change, but not people. It is as difficult for people of today to believe that people back then could manage a journey lasting two months as it would have been for them to accept that we could fly up and down the entire coast of the Inca Empire and out to Easter Island in two days.

The giant statues stood patiently waiting for us, as they

had before, and they kept the Russian film crew busily occupied with their cameras in every corner of the island. I managed to find time to relax in familiar surroundings, and once again to climb the abandoned stone quarry by the volcano of Rano Raraku.

When I first came here with my own expedition ship and four professional archaeologists, it had taken us many months to become acquainted with these stone giants in the mountain wall and down by the foot of the volcano. Up on the side of the mountain and in the extinct volcano's crater wall, they lay twisted in all directions, with their hands on their stomachs, staring blindly up at the sky like the unborn children of a sculptor. But at the foot of the mountain, they stood upright and with pursed lips, ready to move onward as soon as their backs had been polished.

I found a rocky shelf with a view of the plain where I had slept one night, stretched out beside a stone statue. What a masterpiece of art and technology! Ever since their first period on the island, King Hotu Matua and his men had mastered the art of sculpturing and transporting these massive stone statues, erecting them on platforms around the terrain. Our excavations had shown this. Memories of how the descendants of the 'long ears' had shown us how their forefathers had created these giants, with the help of sharp hand-held axes made of hard basalt, and jacked them up to standing position with the aid of boards and rocks, flooded back. Many years later our own experiments had confirmed their legends, that the statues had 'walked' where the sculptors had wanted them to go. All they needed was a little support from a very modest number of transport workers, who slowly nudged the upright statues forward with ropes.

Jacqueline climbed up to my hiding place to enquire about the location of the statue that had a reed ship with three masts carved on its body. She knew that it was the discovery of this petrified sailor, here on Easter Island, bearing a tattoo of his own ship on his chest, that had inspired me to sail with reed ships across the Atlantic and Indian Oceans. And she had been present when the reed ship cycle had been completed in Peru. This was the time when Alfredo called to us while he was digging his way along a temple wall in Túcume to tell us he had found a carving. First he found bird-like heads, which were soon seen to be attached to human bodies, and then, while he carefully removed sand with a digging spoon and brush, we saw that these bird-men were on the deck of a reed ship with rows of oars.

I saw how coming to Easter Island was important to Jacqueline. It had been such an essential part of my earlier life. I saw how thrilled she was to experience all the places I had told her about and described in my books. More than anything else, she appreciated meeting those of my original Easter Island friends who were still alive. She became best friends with old Lazarus, who in a much younger version had led the 'long ears' when they re-erected the huge statue that had been lying face-down at the foot of his own temple platform in Anakena Bay until 1956. This was the first of the island's roughly six hundred *ahu* statues that were re-erected after they had been toppled over by the 'short ears' in their uprising against the 'long ears' only a few generations before the arrival of the Europeans.

A shout of joy told me that Jacqueline had found the statue with the ship carving. Luck was with her, and with me too. By pure coincidence we had come to Easter Island with the Russians the day before a huge three-masted reed ship was to be launched in Anakena Bay, where King Hotu Matua had landed. It had been built by my Spanish friend Kitin Muñoz and modelled after the reed ship on the statue. It was exactly the same size as the caravel that belonged to Columbus, the Santa Maria. Now the golden reed ship Mata Rangi bobbed gently on the waves in the bay, like a reincarnation of the three-masted ship on the chest of the stone giant.

A few weeks later it became obvious that my worries had been justified when I pointed out that the thick rope along both sides of the gunwale was absent from Kitin's reed ship. This rope would prevent the short reed stems from being pulled apart in heavy seas. After studying illustrations from the temple carvings in Egypt and on stone statues in Easter Island caves, I had reproduced this type of rope in the construction of my three reed ships. Three days after Kitin and his crew from Lake Titicaca and Polynesia had set sail, they were caught in a violent storm with mountainous waves which broke the vessel in two. In the normal course of events, and on an ordinary boat, the crew would have gone down with their ship, but the skipper on the Mata Rangi left the afterdeck to its own devices and gathered his crew on the foredeck. They stayed afloat on half a boat for three weeks until they were rescued and returned to Easter Island with plans to harvest more reeds for a new voyage.

In the early days of seafaring, in the days when kings of Peru and the Middle East had workers and time enough to build pyramids as large as mountains, it was also cheap to build large ships. In fact, they had reeds and time enough to build sturdy vessels as large as the Santa Maria. Today, time is money, both on land and at sea, and haste has lowered standards of maritime safety. More people lost their lives on sinking ship hulls in the Middle Ages than in ancient times, when they could stay afloat on bundles of reeds.

Lack of time is one of the foremost drawbacks of civilisation, and it might be the most difficult product for us to export to people who live under an open sky. We, who are on the cutting edge of progress, accept noise, polluted air, canned food and heart attacks as long as everything moves fast enough for us to accomplish even more. Things move too quickly. Future generations will find it impossible to digest all the entertainment and all the leisure. They will lose their peace of mind in search of a quiet, normal life. Our nervous system is not constructed to tolerate so much noise and so many fleeting impressions, so much murder, sex and constant excitement.

You can eat yourself to death, but you can also amuse yourself to death.

Peace and quiet reigned in the abandoned quarry, among all the lifeless statues. I could barely hear the wind whispering behind the rock wall, or the muffled sound of the distant surf. Then time disappeared too. I remained there, stretched out and staring into the clear blue sky of eternity.

Here we were, celebrating the fiftieth anniversary of the *Kon-Tiki* expedition. So much had happened since then. My memories from after journey's end were not only good ones. I encountered unexpected attacks from scientists from all over the world, and at the same time my marriage to Liv started to fall apart. When we finally met after the long years of separation at the end of the war, nothing was the same. We no longer had the same view of life, and our experiences had been totally different. I had seen the dirty reality of war face to face. She had, without me knowing it, had a carefree life with the children as a guest in Thomas Olsen's wonderful country home outside New York. She saw heroism and patriotism, where I saw meaningless death and suffering among friend and foe. Liv had lost faith in the existence of a god who had allowed a horrendous world war to happen; I was reinforced in my faith in a god who forbade mankind to kill, whether voluntarily or under orders. In the end we agreed that, rather than argue, we would part as friends. And were we to find new companions, we would use one another as sounding-boards in our choice.

I met Yvonne a short time after the *Kon-Tiki* journey at a dinner party with friends in the Norwegian mountains. When I presented her to Liv, the judgement was immediate: 'You have found yourself a real angel!'

I could attest to that. Yvonne was not only beautiful, but the incarnation of peace and friendliness. She finished her penicillin studies in Glasgow and moved with me to New Mexico, where we married in great haste at the sheriff's office in Santa Fe. We found a stone cabin in the mountains, where I worked on an enlarged version of my comprehensive *Polynesia and America: A Study of Prehistoric Relations*. From my study I could look out over the valley to Los Alamos, where Oppenheimer and his colleagues had produced the first atomic bomb. Nobel had had little success in creating lasting peace with his invention of dynamite, and now, it was hoped, the atomic bomb would produce better results.

I started my first, and in time ongoing, co-operation with professional archaeologists at the Museum of New Mexico in Santa Fe. Yvonne developed an absorbing interest in my theories of Polynesian migration, and from the very beginning was my most ardent supporter in the battle against academic opponents.

When we moved home to Norway, I bought a group of old historic houses in the Majorstuen district of Oslo. The red wooden buildings, dwarfed by huge chestnut trees, formed a horseshoe around a large courtyard. Yvonne and I lived here while I planned and later revised the results of the Easter Island expedition.

In the meantime, Liv had met James Stillman Rockefeller, popularly called Pebble, who had just visited the Marquesas

Islands on a trip around the world in a small sailing boat. He was so impressed that Liv had lived there for a whole year that he fell for the brave woman. Liv had my unconditional blessing and ended up in the United States as his wife.

The attacks from my academic *Kon-Tiki* opponents found new sustenance in the publicity surrounding the Easter Island expedition. The attacks became so intense that two young Norwegian archaeology students, who suggested that I had sailed the *Kon-Tiki* onto a reef on purpose, in order to create a sensation, had entire pages placed at their disposal in the Oslo newspapers. At this point I decided to find a peaceful place to work abroad.

In 1958 Yvonne and I discovered the small village of Colla Micheri on the Ligurian coast in northern Italy. High on the ridge of a peninsula, we found the ramshackle remains of old medieval houses, with a view over wooded hills running all the way to the ragged peaks of the maritime Alps and over the blue Mediterranean to the wild mountains of Corsica. The old Roman road that had once been the sole link between the two papal cities, Rome and Avignon, passed through one of the houses. A memorial plaque over the door of the tiny local church stated that Pope Pius VII had rested here and blessed the inhabitants when he passed through in his papal chair on his way home from Avignon in 1814. The chair, that he had supposedly used, lay abandoned inside the house, a forgotten relic, beside old figures of saints.

After Napoleon had constructed a new coast road and an earthquake had ravaged the countryside, the village remained virtually deserted. We bought and restored all the uninhabited houses. At one end of the property was a huge Roman watchtower, at the other end a medieval bird-hunters' tower, which became my workplace for many years.

*

When I first arrived on Easter Island with Yvonne, we had our two-year-old daughter Anette with us. She trudged along and called the statues that now surrounded me in the quarry, her 'big dolls'. It was my life's greatest sorrow when we lost her whilst in the prime of her life. It was painful to think about, lying here and looking up into the sparkling galaxy of stars.

There had also been a clear starry night the last time I was here. I could see all the stars of the southern sky at the same time. There is something strange about time. We can see all the stars at once, but there are thousands of light years between them. We see the past of everything out there among foreign celestial bodies, but not at close range, on this planet, where we ourselves live. We see farthest into the past when we look at the stars that are most distant from us. Maybe the starting point is even closer, but still beyond the scope of vision. Perhaps the future is stored in a place we cannot see, in the chromosomes, and time is unleashed by genes that are programmed for all development, whether from a seed to a tree or from plankton to a human being.

Science has discovered that rays from the sun impregnated lifeless particles in the ocean that eventually triggered the development of simple cells into complicated genes and chromosomes and finally led to the creation of all the species of the world. Could the sun have created time that comes and goes as well?

Are you asking me?

I should have expected the *aku-aku* to show up at such a peaceful moment. This was where he belonged. It was here, when we excavated a kneeling statue that no one had seen before, that the former mayor Pedro Attain and Lazarus introduced me to my *aku-aku*.

But of course I knew the answer. I realised that no modern scientist had made the discovery that the sun was the father of all life. Every culture that built pyramids in honour of the sun was aware of this, in the time when our Christian fore-fathers were worshipping Baal and my own ancestors were praying to my namesake, Thor with the hammer.

Sumerians and Hittites and the creators of the ancient cultures, from the Indus valley to Egypt, had been sun-worshippers and honoured the visible sun as the symbol of the invisible god of creation. It was a bloody act when the Christian European conquerors murdered the Incas because they claimed that the sun was their father, while the Europeans themselves introduced the cross, the forerunner of the electric chair, as the symbol of the god of love. I think Christ himself would have preferred the sun to the cross they nailed him to, as a symbol of his teachings, and of the toler-ance between us all, who are born under the same sun.

On our first expedition to Easter Island, Ed Ferdon had excavated the ancient place of worship, Orongo, on top of the Rano Kao volcano. He uncovered a sun observatory and relief carvings of three-masted sickle-shaped reed ships from the oldest period. These revealed that the people who had painted the reed ships portrayed their most important god Make-Make with the huge, round eyes of the sun. On Fatu-Hiva I had learned from old Tei Tetua that Tiki was a human god, while Atea, 'The Light', was his creator. Just like the rela-tionship between the three identical human gods Tiki, Kon and Viracocha in ancient Peru.

My philosophising about a connection between time that passes and the sun that has put everything on our planet into motion, was just as old as the act of sun-worshipping. Legends about the attempts of their forefathers to capture the sun in order to stop time can be found in the mythologies of both Polynesia and Peru. This task was too much even for the pyra-mid builders, who had to be satisfied with devising the calendar we have inherited from them, based on years, months and days.

You should be happy as long as time passes. If it stopped one day when you were in pain, you would regret it. And if it stopped while everything was going well, you would be bored to death.

The *aku-aku* was absolutely right. Memory is finely attuned when it comes to preserving the past in our thinking; the ability to remember and the ability to forget; the art of using both for the benefit of oneself and others. The ability to forget evil and remember goodness. I had to smile when I thought about how carefree my fifty years in the limelight seemed to myself and my friends today. Fifty years filled with excitement, adventure, meeting wonderful people, good friends, good food, sunshine and joy, both at home and abroad. It was all true. But it was not the whole truth. Were I to dig deep into my memory, I would, after all, be glad that time had passed.

I remembered the storm that raged from all directions following our safe landing in Polynesia. And it only increased in strength in the years that followed, when I introduced archaeologists into the Pacific Ocean, and after each expedition grew ever more convinced that the Polynesians were right to insist that all the islands of Polynesia had been discovered from the east. The Europeans, who themselves had arrived in Polynesia from the east, claimed that the Polynesians must have discovered them from the west.

I have always considered native legends as possible guidelines and scientific dogma as possible false leads, but I have never relied entirely on either. When I have doubted the accuracy of dogma, I have tried out various seagoing vessels and excavated and searched wherever oral tradition has suggested there might be a solution.

The first lead I followed, when I was preparing for my

voyage to the Marquesas Islands at Kroepelin's Polynesia library, was that all Polynesians agreed that their forefathers had come from the east, whereas all the experts disagreed as to where in the west the Polynesians had come from. Missionaries, who recorded Polynesian beliefs and legends in the last century, found complete agreement among the Polynesians, from Hawaii in the north to New Zealand in the south, from Samoa in the west to Easter Island in the east. One missionary, Ellis, wrote in 1827: 'It is a remarkable fact that all the journeys that are spoken about in their stories of sea voyages, whether they are part of the natives' oral traditions or from more recent times, have without exception gone from east to west.'

The foremost scholar on Polynesia at the time when I decided to build the *Kon-Tiki* raft was Sir Peter Buck. In his popular bestseller *Vikings of the Sunrise*, which I read with fascination when it was published after I returned from the Marquesas in 1938, he quotes the text of a Maori song about the direction to the Polynesian's homeland:

> *Now I steer the bow of my canoe*
> *Toward the opening where the Sun-god rises,*
> *Tama-nui-te-ra, Great-son-of-sun,*
> *Do not let me stray from my course*
> *But sail direct to the land, to my homeland.*

This was why Peter Buck called the Polynesians 'the Vikings of the Sunrise'. But at the same time he believed that the Polynesian homeland lay in the west. In New Zealand, as in the rest of Polynesia, as well as Peru and Egypt and wherever evidence of sun worship had been found, it was believed that the souls of the dead followed the sun to the west. What he forgot was that in the whole of Polynesia they believed that the sun set in a tunnel that led it through the underworld and back to its own home in the east, where it rose. This journey with the sun was only for the dead. The living headed eastward, as the song told them to do.

Buck had published his textbook *An Introduction to Polynesian Anthropology* only two years before the *Kon-Tiki* expedition. Here, like all other researchers, he accepted the dogma that a balsa raft could not reach Polynesia. Therefore he started by reinforcing the idea of a boundary between Peru and Polynesia that could not be crossed: 'Since the South American Indians had neither the vessels nor the abilities to navigate right across the ocean between their coast and the closest islands in Polynesia, we can rule them out as the possible first settlers.'

When the *Kon-Tiki* voyage tore down this academic iron curtain towards the east, showing that the whole ocean around Polynesia lay open without protection of any kind from the wind and currents from South America, we, who had experienced the incredible seaworthiness of the balsa raft believed that all interested parties would be delighted. After a week of commotion and publicity, I was very pleased to receive a telephone call saying that the first reaction from the academic world had come in the shape of a newspaper interview with Sir Peter Buck.

I was a little less pleased when I finally saw the clipping from the *Auckland Star*, which made it extremely clear that Sir Peter Buck thought the raft voyage no more than a joke. He threw his head back and laughed aloud, the journalist wrote.

And then Buck's counter-argument followed: 'No fishermen I have ever known have had women on board. And according to their own theory, the landing should have taken place on uninhabited islands – so exactly who became the mother of the Polynesian people?'

This was when I first realised that, in our age of specialisation, the man who knew the most about Polynesia was so ignorant about America that he knew nothing about Pizarro, who had captured a balsa raft on the way from Peru to Panama with both women and men on board – before the Spaniards themselves had reached the Inca Empire. The raft carried thirty tons of cargo, which Pizarro's men stole, and they also captured five women who they trained to be interpreters before their final offensive against Peru. And in addition: would it have been any easier for fishermen to procreate if they had arrived on uninhabited islands that lay upwind, which is what Buck believed?

The joke from New Zealand quickly caught on in the otherwise sombre world of science. Nevertheless the balsa raft continued to float in the imagination of the general public. Many must have thought of this raft as a warship manned by Vikings from the east who were trying to ram their soft balsa logs into the wooden canoes of Sir Peter's Vikings from the west, which were so heavy that they would sink if they shipped water.

I never heard more from Peter Buck, though I was told that he attended the premiere of the *Kon-Tiki* movie in Honolulu.

Opposition to the so-called *Kon-Tiki* theory spread with the speed of modern communications throughout the academic world, eastward to America and westward to Australia, and from Western Europe it swept through the Iron Curtain to the Soviet Union. The daily press became my staunchest ally. They gladly printed all the attacks, but were even happier when I retorted with my replies. Many malicious attacks followed, and the debate became little more than a personal quarrel that rarely rose to an academic level. The replies became so time-consuming that I had to seek refuge in a cabin in the Norwegian mountains to take time to write the story of the *Kon-Tiki* expedition. This would provide income and an opportunity to inspire interest in my weighty scientific manuscript, which no one at the universities would read and no one in the publishing houses would print.

Amongst all the commotion, it was my Norwegian publisher Harald Grieg, of Gyldendal Norwegian Publishers, who first dared to publish my story. He had published the book about my adventures on Fatu-Hiva before the war and had bet five thousand kroner that there would be a new book about the raft journey even before it had started. In the United States the manuscript was rejected by, among others, the New York publisher Doubleday, allegedly because there was no sex on the raft journey and no one drowned.

But then Adam Helms of the small Swedish publishing company Forum got hold of the text and sold a record number of copies in Sweden. And when the Chicago atlas publishers Rand McNally decided to print it, the book jumped to the top of the bestseller list, where it remained for weeks. My British publisher, Sir Stanley Unwin, calculated that if he made a pile from all the books that had been sold about the raft journey, it would have topped Mt. Everest. In due course *Kon-Tiki* was published in sixty-seven languages, including Esperanto, Eskimo, Telugu, Singalese, Gujarati, Marathi, Mongolian and Urdu, as well as several editions in Braille.

It must have been a fantastically good time!

I'd be happy to forget most of it. The more popular the six of us 'raft voyagers' became with the general public, the less popular we became among the scholars, and I still had my serious manuscript about the theory behind the *Kon-Tiki* expedition. No one wanted to read this; its size was discouraging enough, and it had more than a thousand references from various branches of scientific literature.

On the other hand, the travel narrative was written with a

wide audience in mind and contained none of the academic jargon that would associate me with professionals in the field. In those days it was still taboo for a professional to address himself to a large circle of readers. Science was to be cultivated for the sake of science, and one was never to venture outside one's own speciality. I was aware of this, but disregarded it in order to remove the boundaries between Polynesia and America as well as between the academic branches that would have to work together in order to solve the migration puzzle in the Pacific Ocean. I also wanted to keep ordinary people informed, since they often had more insight than the specialists.

As time went on, the opposition from academia made the raft experiment look more like a sporting exercise. I was described as an unknown adventurer, an unschooled daredevil who was stepping into an area where I did not belong. It was paradoxical that I, with my former fear of water, should be celebrated as a seafaring hero, while the fantastic vessel that had carried us to Polynesia like a magic carpet was still seen as no more than a bunch of wooden logs. It was tragicomic that I, who had never hoisted a sail before we stepped aboard the balsa-wood raft, was being invited to yacht clubs and celebrated at cocktail parties with admirals, while doors to academic clubs were closed and university professors shrugged their shoulders.

While I was virtually alone in defending myself and my theories, the Twenty-Ninth International Congress of Americanists convened in New York. For the occasion, an exhibition had been set up at the American Museum of Natural History called 'Across the Pacific'. The title might imply that the *Kon-Tiki* expedition would be discussed, and the well-known Danish anthropologist, Professor Birket-Smith, was interviewed on his return to Copenhagen. The answer to the question of how the experts had appraised the results of my expedition was the following headline: 'THE KON-TIKI EXPEDITION IS TO BE CONSIGNED TO OBLIVION.'

After this, a bomb went off in another corner of the Nordic countries. The Finnish anthropologist Professor Rafael Karsten could not contain himself, and broke his Danish colleague's appeal for silence with a long interview in Helsinki's leading daily newspaper, under the headline: 'THE HUMBUG AROUND KON-TIKI'.

The press described Professor Karsten as a world-renowned authority. I had heard his name mentioned in connection with a planned expedition down the Amazon River. Before we had hoisted sail on *Kon-Tiki*, the professor had said it would be a miracle if we survived in the open seas on a balsa raft. Now he stuck to his words, adding that since miracles rarely occur, the entire journey must have been pure humbug! The raft must have been specially constructed so that it could capsize and still carry us along while overturned. He added that if only half of what I wrote was true, it would have been a miracle.

A few *Kon-Tiki* 'mariners' got together to compose a powerful reply to these accusations, but before we had compiled our answer, the publicity had grown out of all proportions. 'KON-TIKI EXPOSED,' the headlines read in another Finnish paper. 'CAUSE CELEBRE IN THE SCIENTIFIC WORLD: THE KON-TIKI VOYAGE IS HUMBUG, SAYS A FAMOUS FINNISH RESEARCHER', was the Swedish cry. 'IS THE KON-TIKI THEORY A PUBLICITY STUNT?' a Danish paper asked. And the echo resounded from my own country: 'HUMBUG, HUMBUG!'

On the day of the attack from Professor Karsten, I was in Stockholm on a lecture tour with our amateur movie of the *Kon-Tiki* voyage. Never have I felt the earth disappear so completely beneath my feet as when I saw the newspaper. What would my mother think? She, who was an atheist, but one who set great store by the truth. The only time I ever saw her cry was when I lied to her as a boy and told her that I had been playing in the neighbour's garden, when in fact I had been riding my bike on the road to Stavern.

When I went to bed in my hotel room that evening, I felt as if an army of unknown enemies had hit me with a sledge hammer. I was on the verge of wishing I had drowned, as my opponents had expected, instead of having to experience this degradation and shame. At that point I had little faith in any god of justice, and I was unsure that there was any god at all. Though when we hit the reef in Polynesia, and the surf pulled and tore at me, and the whole ocean tried to drag me away from where I was clinging, I had taken a brief glimpse behind the veil of life and experienced a sensation that something was going on there. I had promised myself that if we all survived the towering wall of waves I would never forget that moment. I thought back to the endless gratitude I felt when I waded ashore on the Raroia atoll with all my men alive. I went down on my knees on a calm, golden beach, and dug my fingers into the warm, dry sand. Where had the extra power that I had begged for in the face of death come from? The white birds that flew across the blue sky as we lay and regained our breath on the beach reminded me of the doves of Christianity bringing messages from Heaven. But the help that I felt as a physical force out there in the ocean had not come from above; it came from within. Perhaps Heaven with a capital H of the Bible and the Koran should not be mistaken for heaven with a small h that we can all find within us?

I twisted and turned in my hotel bed, couldn't sleep; thought. How was I to deal with the following morning? How was I to counter those kind of accusations in the press? I had nothing to read, looked at my watch on top of the bedside table, and opened its drawer. A Bible was there, as is often the case in hotel rooms. Black and gloomy, as if it were meant for funerals and sorrow.

That night, as I opened the Bible at random, when everything in my life seemed as black as the cover of the Bible itself, I thumbed through the pages to distract myself and see if I would bump into something that with a bit of imagination could be interpreted as a form of guidance.

I opened it up and placed my finger on the facing page. It was about David and Goliath.

I laughed to myself a little and stopped thinking. Then I pulled the quilt up over my ears and fell asleep.

10

The Scholars

I was still reposing in my world of memory, stretched out on the rocky ledge on Easter Island in the silent company of the stone Goliath, when voices down the hill revealed that the Russian television crew was approaching with Jacqueline. I climbed down amongst all the other unfinished stone giants that were lying scattered about, eyeless with noses pointing skyward. A petrified battlefield of fallen giants.

Symbolic, I thought. I took the Russians to film the island's only kneeling statue. After the battle against the 'short ears', he had literally got back on to his feet, albeit to a kneeling position, and seemed to be begging for mercy. The statue was from the oldest period of the island, and we were the ones who had re-erected it to its current position when we excavated it on my first expedition to Easter Island. All the other statues on the island were busts without legs, cut off horizontally beneath the groin. They had hands with long fingernails resting beneath bulky stomachs. Carved by the first settlers on the island, the kneeling giant was totally unlike all the others, but it was remarkably similar to the kneeling sculptures the pre-Incas had raised in Tiahuanaco by Lake Titicaca in the Andes. All the other statues were of exactly the same type and resembled nothing in the outside world. This entire army of Goliaths appeared to be copies of the same model, either lying legless and blind on the mountain shelves, or buried in landslides with only their heads above ground.

To demonstrate to the Russians the size of the statues, I stood next to the lonely giant who knelt with his hands on his thighs and his head lifted as in a humble prayer to the sky. I felt very small. Sun-worshippers had made this giant, and they had brought the art of sculpture to this lonely island. All the other fallen giants who in later years had been re-erected on their *ahus*, stood there with straight backs and defiantly pursed lips, as if they had no respect for anyone other than themselves. Just as Captain Cook had surmised, they represented the god-like kings of the 'long ears' and the more powerful they had been, the higher their monuments towered over us mortals.

The Russians wanted to continue filming by Anakena Bay in order to secure a few frames of the broad-shouldered giant who was the first *moai* we had restored to his *ahu*. He was the first to have stared at Europeans through his deep, empty eye sockets. When I first saw these meaningless empty eyes, I was reminded of the deep holes I had seen in the heads of stone giants from the Hittite Empire in the Mediterranean. I had also seen them in several stone statues and figures of both stone and wood from the oldest cultures of Mexico and Peru, though in those cases the eye sockets had been inlaid with white eyeballs of bone or shell and life-like pupils of black obsidian. Only when one or both of the eyes had fallen out, did the empty sockets look exactly like the ones on Easter Island.

I told the Russians that a book I wrote in 1975 had presented my conviction that the Easter Island statues had once had inlaid eyes, and that this idea had been rejected by opponents who argued that inlaid eyes on stone statues were not a Polynesian feature. Pointing out that it was an American custom, and that Easter Island was one of the thousands of Pacific islands that lay closest to America made little difference. Two years later, the young Easter Island archaeologist Sonia Haoa found the first huge eye from a classic middle period statue when she was assisting in Sergio Rapu's excavations at King Hotu Matua's *ahu* in Anakena. Later, when she was excavating for us, she also found the first eye to have fallen out of the head of a statue from the earliest period.

But a great deal had happened since then. The discovery in Peru of the inlaid eyes on the mummy mask from Sipan, inspired me to start excavations at the pyramids in Túcume. To obtain blue eyes for the royal mummy mask, in remembrance of the blond god-like people who had visited their forefathers, the seafarers in northern Peru had sailed all the way down to Chile to find South America's only source of blue lapis lazuli. Elsewhere in Peru one had to make do with black obsidian for use as inlays for pupils.

Lazarus and his people had managed to re-erect the broad-shouldered giant without technical help, and the lone statue was now on its former platform in the easternmost part of Anakena Bay. Later, archaeologists using modern cranes, had continued to lift other *moai* back on to their *ahus* all around the island. For those of us who were accustomed to the gaping, empty eye sockets, it was now an almost frightening sight to see the whole row of raised Goliaths standing in rows like soldiers on parade, with straight backs turned to the bay, staring unblinkingly towards us with eyes as large as tin plates.

This was the second time in a thousand years that small two-legged creatures made of perishable flesh and blood had given eyes to the statues. If they had been able to see us and open their pursed lips, they would have been able to tell us how little mankind had changed in the course of a millennium.

While the Russians filmed the statue and there was so much commotion around Kitin Muñoz's reed ship, no one noticed that I had sneaked up the hillside and lain down to enjoy a view over the blue bay, a heavenly mirror partially framed by Anakena's golden sandy beach. It was far from easy to collect my thoughts about the most difficult period of my past when it was so exciting to live in the present, to see the stone giants in place where Hotu Matua had landed and watch a real three-masted reed ship bobbing in the breeze.

Who won? Did David beat Goliath with his sling?

I have never tried to kill anyone. All my battles have been in self-defence. If I have been aggressive, it is because there have been many attacks.

The attacks from Professor Karsten ended abruptly when the Nordenskiøld Society, the Scientific Academy of Finland, invited me to Helsinki to refute his accusations. I turned up for the meeting, but Karsten was not there. He preferred to meet behind closed doors in his home. The secretary-general of the Academy took me to the entrance of an apartment building. We were both let in, but a voice from upstairs insisted that I come up alone. A smiling old lady greeted me, and I loaded my sling with academic arguments in preparation for my defence. The miracle occurred. Goliath dwindled into a peaceful old man sipping a cup of tea in a rocking chair. I was also given a cup, but no chance to discuss my Pacific Ocean theory. He had not called the *Kon-Tiki* expedition humbug. Newspaper editors wrote the headlines. He confirmed this fact later in a newspaper article. I just sat there devouring pieces of cake while the man who had been my greatest opponent told me stories from his travels.

On the surface, it looked as if peace had been declared when Karsten gave up the fight in Northern Europe. But little did I know of the fierce battles going on behind the scenes of Pacific Ocean research. There the war was being waged among big names. I thought of them as a united front, standing shoulder to shoulder, collectively dragging me into the limelight in order to behead me in public.

In the beginning it was obvious that their team effort had been unsuccessful. Denmark's leading anthropologist, Professor Birket-Smith, had suggested to the press that the *Kon-Tiki* expedition should be consigned to oblivion, but his colleague, Professor Karsten in Finland, had started a serious newspaper debate throughout Scandinavia. The vice-president of the Swedish Academy of Science, Professor Carl Skottsberg, also stepped into the debate on a strictly scientific basis.

Skottsberg deserved his position as one of the foremost experts on Pacific research. I had quoted him frequently in my voluminous, unpublished manuscript, but there was no way he could know this. When Skottsberg was exposed as my next opponent in the newspaper controversy, he had one advantage. He had been to Easter Island, and I had not been there yet. For the time being I was more familiar with the islands further to the west, where, according to Skottsberg, I had first spent a year as a savage, and then returned later on a timber raft.

Skottsberg had written botanical works as well as a travel

narrative from Easter Island, and since he was reviewing my travel narrative from the *Kon-Tiki* journey, it was expected that he would choose Easter Island as my Achilles heel. I was praised for being a capable sailor, but not a real scientist. My evaluation of the problem of manoeuvring the statues on Easter Island was faulty, as were their measurements. Before expressing my opinion, I should have read the book about Easter Island by the famous French ethnologist Alfred Métraux.

I answered in the same Gothenburg paper that it was precisely from Métraux's book that I had found the information about the statue transport problems, and the measurements I had given were taken from Skottsberg's own travel narrative.

I never received a proper reply from the professor, just a short note that brushed aside any further discussion by giving the Latin names of three plants, proving that Easter Island was populated by people from Asia and not from America. That was the end of the matter as far as he was concerned.

Skottsberg could not have known that he had now committed himself to a subject I had studied intently before the balsa raft journey. I could quote his colleague, the botanist F. B. H. Brown of Hawaii. Two of the plants that Skottsberg mentioned were species whose seeds could be spread over the ocean without the aid of humans, and the third, *Hibiscus tiliaceus*, was just as common in prehistoric South America as it was in Asia.

Skottsberg did not return to the subject until eight years later. By then, my manuscript *Polynesia and America* had been published under the title *American Indians in the Pacific: The Theory Behind the Kon-Tiki Expedition*. Skottsberg wrote a positive review and now supported the *Kon-Tiki* theory with an important botanical argument: the Easter Island inhabitants built their reed ships with freshwater *totora* reeds. The reeds were only indigenous to South America and therefore must have been brought to the crater lakes of Easter Island by their own forefathers.

Meanwhile, the net was still closing around us; the newspaper duel in Sweden continued for weeks. Sweden had a history of botanical experts ever since Carl von Linné assigned Latin names to all plants and animals, and Erland Nordenskiøld created a school of South American anthropology through his archaeological studies in the border areas of Peru and Bolivia, which provided Gothenburg with rich collections. One of his students was the archaeologist Stig Ryden.

When botanist Skottsberg retired from the controversy about the first settlers of Easter Island, archaeologist Ryden approached the matter from another angle. His speciality was Tiahuanaco near Lake Titicaca, precisely where, according to legend, the white and bearded Kon-Tiki had ruled before he walked down to the coast and disappeared with his followers across the Pacific Ocean. Ryden was the only archaeologist in the Nordic countries who had personally excavated in Tiahuanaco, and now he came forward and claimed that no such legends existed. The Indians of Tiahuanaco were just as beardless and red-skinned as other Indians. The head of the Kon-Tiki statue from Tiahuanaco, the one we had used as a symbol on the sail, had no beard; it was simply some sort of a nose ring.

The genuine archaeologist unravels unwritten, ancient history with an excavating spoon. Reading history is something else. It was easy to provide Ryden with quotes from the numerous Spanish chroniclers who had recorded the Inca legends of the white and bearded *viracochas*, who, the Incas believed, were returning when the Spaniards conquered the land. It was also easy to refer to Ryden's predecessor in Tiahuanaco, American archaeologist W. C. Bennett, the man who had excavated the Kon-Tiki statue and described it as a sculpture of a man with a beard. The head on our sail was a true copy of Bennett's drawing in his scientific report.

I had the last word in the Gothenburg newspaper duel concerning whether or not the pre-Inca artists of Peru depicted their god with a nose ring or a beard. I asked Ryden to go down to the store rooms in his own ethnographic museum to look up a catalogue number that I had found in my own notes. I wish I could have seen his face when he found what I was alluding to: a pre-Incan Mochica jar from the coast of Peru representing a man with a beard large enough to make even Santa Claus envious.

It was no laughing matter to be a Norwegian scientist in Sweden, in spite of full lecture halls and warm applause week after week. It was even less enjoyable as a Norwegian on home ground, accused of everything from dishonesty to ignorance, in the daily press of all the neighbouring countries. There was little help when my former zoology professors praised my academic achievements, and invited me to lecture about my theories at the university. Although my one-time geography professor, Werner Werenskiold, supported me wholeheartedly in the press, I was still on my own. None of those professionals were specialists on the migration in the Pacific Ocean.

I was ready with my sling and waiting for the next Goliath to appear, when a wondrous event occurred in Stockholm. One evening in the lecture hall Sven Hedin, one of the real giants of the Swedish Academy of Science, sat and joined in the applause at the end of the amateur movie of the raft journey to Polynesia. As unpopular as Hedin was for his political views during the war, he was both popular and with good reason world famous for his adventurous explorations in Central

Asia. A few days after the lecture I received a card in the post from Hedin, reminding me that where great feats were performed the wolves will always howl and the claws of the ravens strike, but that this was part of the game.

In the late autumn of 1949 I received an unexpected call from the secretary-general of the Royal Swedish Society for Anthropology and Geography, Associate Professor Calle Mannerfelt. He was an elegant and sporty-looking young geographer, about my age, who communicated the message that Sven Hedin had suggested I be invited to the Society to defend my theory before the leading experts of Sweden. At the same time, Mannerfelt invited me to dinner at his home in order to meet Sweden's youngest professor, Dr Olof Selling, who had returned from Polynesia the previous day. It was obvious that I was to be tested against this young scientist, before the major confrontation that Hedin had organised. Selling already had a brilliant career behind him, despite the fact that he was three years younger than me. He had received a doctorate in botany as the first person to introduce the technique of pollen analysis in Polynesia. And he was the only twentieth-century botanist to have discovered a completely new order in the plant kingdom; fifteen new plant species were named after him. In competition with far older colleagues, he had just been appointed director of the paleo-botanical department of the National Museum in Stockholm.

My private life had taken a totally new direction when I met Yvonne. Now my life as a scientist took a turn that was just as unexpected when Yvonne and I dined with Calle and Ebba Mannerfelt and guest Olof Selling in their beautiful home outside Stockholm. The somewhat retiring and stuffy professor of botany had a contagious smile that bore witness to his special sense of humour. His replies and penetrating eyes also revealed an unusually acute mind. It was easy to understand that with his memory and insight, he was ahead of his age and our time.

Our introductions were formal and full of anticipation, but Ebba and Yvonne took to each other immediately. And when we sank into our deep chairs with a cocktail, not much time passed before the three of us, who had been meeting for a preliminary joust, quickly understood that we had a common background in geography and biology and that we spoke the same language.

Any final uncertainties melted around the dinner table as quickly as the ice disappeared in the white wine cooler. Following Swedish custom, the host suggested we refrain from using titles, and I, who had no title, was more than willing to comply. The basis for a lasting friendship was established that evening.

I opened the conversation by asking Olof if he knew the botanist F. B. H. Brown.

Forest Brown? Olof called him Forest. My F. B. H. Brown, the author of three volumes on the flora of the Marquesas Islands, the man whose solid genetic evidence had given me the faith and courage to experiment by bringing sweet potatoes, bottle pumpkins and coconuts from Peru to Polynesia by raft, turned out to be Olof's personal friend. My personal friend, Tei Tetua, son of the cannibal Uta on Fatu-Hiva, had affirmed that Olof's friend Forest was right. This was going to be fun.

The geographer Calle was no less interested. To him the earth was round, and therefore the distance along the equator from Asia to South America was just as long as the distance from the equator all the way north to the Bering Strait and south again to the equator on the opposite side of the Pacific, even though it seemed like a detour. Calle understood that the oceans were crossed by invisible currents that would drag everything afloat westward from South America to Polynesia in the southern hemisphere, and eastward from Asia via the northwestern American archipelago to Polynesia in the northern hemisphere.

Then the great day arrived, 23 September 1949. Not a single seat was empty as the secretary-general opened the meeting in the Royal Swedish Society of Anthropology and Geography. When I stepped up to the podium I caught an encouraging look from the famous Sven Hedin, who was sitting directly in front of me in the first row. That helped. The other faces melted into a many-headed creature whose eyes reflected everything from curiosity to friendly expectation and demonstrative contempt.

It went well, almost too well. Where were my opponents? It was so surprising that no one protested. I was almost more confused than comforted.

The unexpected outcome was my first scientific award: the silver Retzius Medal, for organising and carrying out the *Kon-Tiki* expedition with scientific objectives. No scientific award that I received later in life has pleased me more and meant more to my ongoing uphill battle than this first official recognition by the academic world.

But the battle against a growing band of specialists was far from over. In the months that followed there were never enough hours in the day. Olof's extensive Pacific library included an up-to-date and comprehensive filing index which touched on subjects which could be added to my already voluminous manuscript, with regards to new knowledge and alternative thinking about the Pacific.

We were lent a summer house on the outskirts of Stockholm and Yvonne went to and fro to the Royal Library with index cards from Olof's library, and returned with more books than she could carry. She then sat down and hammered away on the typewriter with her sister, while I cut and glued pages of manuscript that were sometimes more than a metre long.

But I was a hair's breadth away from losing Olof as a colleague. A senior botanist, who had been passed over when the Academy of Science installed Selling as director of the National Museum's paleo-botanical department, tried to unseat Selling by announcing that he was insane. Olof had changed the locks to his department after his old rival had locked himself in at night with his own key, and borrowed herbariums and documents without informing the new director. The papers were full of protests. Could the Royal Swedish Academy of Science do something as barbaric as to declare a colleague insane when he was not? I was given access to some of the documents in the case and saw that my own statements had been manipulated. One of the accusations against Selling was that he had written two favourable articles in Svenska Dagbladet about the *Kon-Tiki* theory.

The so-called 'battle of the keys' raged so violently that the Academy did not dare fire him. The newspapers started an appeal that raised 150,000 Swedish crowns in order to engage independent doctors for a second psychological examination. The popular Swedish author Vilhelm Moberg, who in 1996 was named Sweden's greatest all-time author by the general public, wrote a play about Olof Selling's battle which was translated into several languages and performed on stage in Moscow.

Professor Olof Selling was declared completely normal, and the insanity charges were annulled. A few years later he received the Academy's highest award, the Order of Knight of the Swedish North Star.

Attacks against me in the Swedish press waned, and this

had some influence in my own country, where the Norwegian Geographical Society invited me to lecture on the *Kon-Tiki* expedition. I was subsequently made an honorary member, and as a result invited to the Royal Norwegian Academy of Science, where my excited aging mother sat in the first row with King Haakon, anticipating the barrage of attacks from Norwegian research scientists. Our two leading language researchers had threatened to refute my migration theory. After the lecture, they both remained seated in silence. The king looked at them until one of them got to his feet and said in a friendly tone that since the lecturer agreed that the Polynesian language had distant roots in Southeast Asia, he had no objections to my suggestions of migration routes across the ocean.

'Do you agree, professor?' he asked, turning to his long-time colleague who was a specialist in Asian languages.

He rose rapidly, said 'I agree,' and sat down.

My mother left with pride, having made a solid contribution to the applause. The Norwegian publisher, Harald Grieg, who had been the first to publish an edition of *Kon-Tiki*, had to reset the type and run a second edition. My initial relief at being accepted on the academic front would have been considerably less if I had been aware of the new storm that was brewing behind the scenes and across international borders.

The movie about the *Kon-Tiki* journey took me to Paris, where French ethnologist Dr Alfred Métraux was the director of UNESCO. The book's tremendous sales had awakened the movie industry's interest in the film from the journey. With this, public interest increased, as did the academic opposition's indignation about a researcher who appealed to the masses without having published any scientific work. However, my scientific work was by this time on the point of being published, consisting of an enormous pile of loose manuscript pages with my Swedish publisher Adam Helms.

However, the film from the *Kon-Tiki* journey was a fiasco when it was shown in its unedited version in New York. President Truman's enthusiasm for the voyage had been reflected in the American press, where the *New York Times*, *Life Magazine*, and other leading newspapers and illustrated publications had given the expedition tremendous exposure. The film producers were pushing relentlessly, and the Norwegian Embassy organised a screening of 800 feet of unedited 16mm film for the country's most interested buyers.

It turned out to be a veritable nightmare. I had been given twenty minutes instruction when I bought the small wind-up camera with a loading magazine and three changeable lenses in a photography store in Oslo before I left. We were now gathered for the screening and realised that over half the film was completely damaged by water, and the other half was projected in slow motion. It looked as though it had been filmed by someone swinging in a hammock on a train at slow speed, moving in and out of tunnels. The film was interspersed by blinding periods of light when one could just make out the mouth of a shark, a bearded head, a naked foot or a squirming fish.

One after the other, the onlookers silently tiptoed from the room, and the hours passed. In the end I was left alone with a single buyer from the RKO company, who offered two hundred dollars for the lot, in the hope of being able to splice the usable parts into a ten-minute news reel. No deal was made.

I had no choice but to swallow the first bitter disappointment. With a friend who had a small splicing machine, I went to work in my small hotel room in New York, splicing together whatever film frames could be used for a silent movie. Without being able to see the result, we just managed to glue the last parts together before hailing a cab and driving to the renowned Explorer's Club. Ever since my time on Fatu-Hiva, I had been the club's youngest member. I have never been more surprised. After sitting in a packed but totally silent hall, suffering from the realisation that the most dramatic parts of the film had ended up in the bin, the applause broke loose. I was still burdened with all the expedition debt, so I signed a contract with an experienced lecture-tour agent who gave me a high percentage of the lecture fees on condition that I paid hotel and travelling expenses. He then accepted all requests for lectures, and for three months I criss-crossed the United States, giving over a hundred 'movie lectures'. I slept on planes and trains as often as in beds, from New York to San Francisco, from Washington DC, to Los Angeles. Once, when Toronto, Canada was followed by Chattanooga, Tennessee, I made a profit of seven dollars, in spite of the minimum lecture fee being two hundred dollars.

Europe was next in line, and the performances were sold out in Stockholm when former Prince Lennart Bernadotte had the idea of offering a movie version to Hollywood. He was not discouraged by my pitiful story about the highest bid being two hundred dollars. While my friends from the raft took turns lecturing to packed audiences in Sweden, the former prince followed me to Copenhagen, where Queen Ingrid, the princesses and a few others were placed so close to the screen in the first row that some of us became seasick from the motion of the waves. At one embarrassing moment we heard a splash, and when the usher came running in with a bucket of sawdust, the queen enquired whether this was part of the show.

Lennart Bernadotte wanted to correct the raft's violent dance across the screen and increase the speed of the film which I had filmed in slow motion. He bought Europe's very first optical printing machine, which could make a 35mm copy of a 16mm film by rephotographing every third frame and replacing the duplicates in order to achieve the speed of a standard movie projector. The next morning, I went on to Vienna and he returned to Stockholm, but first we drew up a handwritten contract, half in Norwegian, half in Swedish, about dividing the profits equally. We lost the one-page contract, but in the meantime a small new company, Artfilm, which consisted of Lennart and his friend Olle Nordemar, had stabilised and enlarged the 16mm film to 35mm. They sold the final version for a fifty-fifty share to the Tarzan movie producer Sol Lesser in Hollywood, who then sold it further for a fifty-fifty share to the distributing company RKO. RKO and I would both have enjoyed greater profits had we made a direct fifty-fifty deal from the very beginning.

The contracts rolled in, in as many languages as the book, and we ended up with two documentary film Oscars, one for the producer and one for the cameraman. Since I was caught up in the middle of scientific arguments, I refused to show up in Hollywood, and received my Oscar from the hand of Tarzan's producer aboard the raft at the *Kon-Tiki* Museum in Oslo.

Later on I did visit Hollywood and Sol Lesser offered to hold a cocktail party in my honour. He asked who I wanted to meet in this movie metropolis, but my ignorance in this area was all too obvious. After a little hesitation I blurted out 'Walt Disney'. He came and proved to be an extremely humble and gentle person who kept his sense of humour to himself. He greeted me very seriously and thanked me for the publicity I had given him in the *Kon-Tiki* book. Publicity? I asked. I couldn't remember having mentioned him at all. Oh yes, he said, on three different occasions you mention me by name when you describe the most fantastic and imaginative creatures in the ocean as beasts that not even Walt Disney could have come up with.

There was a world premiere in Stockholm on 13 January 1950, with the Swedish royal family, Sven Hedin and Olof Selling among the invited guests. I only attended a few opening nights, but the French were so interested in the film that an innovative company had been allowed to truck the raft around country roads while we were constructing a home for it in Oslo. The raft arrived home with apples wedged between its logs after it had passed by a fruit orchard and ended its final triumphant journey in the Champs Elysées.

Despite the reception at the airport, my own arrival in Paris the day preceding the movie première was not among the happiest of occasions. Alfred Métraux had set in motion a powerful offensive in his home country. Once again, I was portrayed in a professional French journal as an adventurer devoid of scientific competence. One of the journalists showed me a copy of the day's *Carrefour*, where Métraux, commenting on the movie premiere, labelled me a '*mauvais savant*', an inept scientist. I was asked to comment, and I promised to do so in the company of Métraux if they could arrange a meeting.

The next morning I was taken to Métraux's office at UNESCO. He was there with Dr Walter Lehman, the leading specialist in South American archaeology at the Musée de l'Homme in Paris. The *Carrefour* journalist was there too, pad and pencil poised.

Following the introductions, I opened my briefcase and pulled out an advance copy of my forthcoming work, *American Indians in the Pacific* – 821 pages long and with a list of more than a thousand quoted sources and a great many illustrations. My two opponents grew silent and confused, and after they had asked complicated questions and been given answers, it was my turn to take the floor. I had brought a large stack of pictures of different stone statues from the Marquesas Islands and Easter Island, and from the entire Andes area from San Agustin in Columbia to Tiahuanaco in Bolivia. Métraux had claimed that there was no similarity between the stone statues in the two areas. I placed the stack of pictures on the desk and asked them to separate the Polynesian ones from the South American ones.

Dr Lehman grabbed the stack immediately and wanted to start sorting them. Then he hesitated and pushed the whole stack over to Métraux. This was, after all, his speciality. Métraux took the stack with a smile.

'This is from Polynesia,' he said, placing the first picture on the table.

'No!' I said triumphantly. 'It is from San Agustin!'

'This is also from San Agustin,' Métraux said, unaffected, placing the next picture on the table.

'No!' I countered again. 'I took this one myself on the Marquesas Islands!' I then added that if two of the world's foremost authorities in the field saw no difference, might they be willing to admit that there was a similarity?

They agreed. Métraux looked at his watch and suggested pleasantly that the four of us should go down to the UNESCO bar and have a drink. We did. What a delicious drink!

That same evening the cinema was filled to capacity and the atmosphere was one of expectancy. There was a large gathering of French explorers and mountaineers, including the polar explorer Paul Emil Victor and the Anapurna climber Maurice Herzog. Paul Emil introduced the movie, and I made two new lifelong friends.

The next morning *Carrefour* was slipped silently under my

hotel room door. David and Goliath, I thought, when I saw the story of the confrontation at UNESCO. A large picture of Métraux on the upper left, lifting a large glass to a toast. A small picture of myself on the bottom right, returning his toast with a small glass. 'A Métraux half convinced by Thor Heyerdahl,' the headline ran. And then the journalist reported that when the two experts were asked to distinguish between South American and Polynesian statues, they failed as often as not. Furthermore, Métraux had retracted his earlier statement and admitted that his opponent was a true scientist.

When Adam Helms and his small Swedish publishing house, Forum, gambled on publishing the voluminous scientific tome on the theory behind the *Kon-Tiki* journey, the book was very amicably reviewed by Métraux in the same Swedish paper where his attacks had first appeared. He pointed out that had he not been informed, he would have thought it inconceivable that such a young man could have managed to collect, between two covers, so much important scientific material from different branches of science.

His partner from the Easter Island expedition, the Belgian archaeologist Dr Henri Lavacheri, never joined in the controversy, and he visited me in Oslo after my own expedition to Easter Island to study the material I had brought back. He later wrote the introduction to my work on the art of Easter Island in 1975.

But the ceasefire in France did not bring an end to the conflict. The more attention the book and the movie received around the world, the more fiery the opposition became among a growing number of experts who felt they had become the object of public ridicule. In their eyes the public was delighted that I had dared step on the toes of the learned. Professor Birket-Smith's suggestion at the Twenty-Ninth International

Congress of Americanists to consign the *Kon-Tiki* expedition to oblivion had not succeeded, and when the Thirtieth Congress was planned in Cambridge in August 1952, the organisers decided to try a far more effective method. I was invited to participate as a lecturer at the Congress, where all the foremost experts in the world would be present. My *American Indians in the Pacific* had finally been published, though only the week before, so hardly any of the participants would have been aware of its existence.

The invitation provided an unexpected challenge. In the guidelines it said that every active participant would be entitled to deliver three lectures. I signed up for all three.

When the next circular arrived from the Congress, including the printed programme, I noticed that they had chosen, of all people, Professor Birket-Smith as moderator for the section where I would present my lectures.

If I ever felt humble in the past, then I felt even more so on my way to Cambridge to speak in front of the collected world anthropology elite. Two hundred participants from thirty countries would be present, and when Yvonne and I arrived most of them were already standing around in groups in the university corridors speaking like old friends. The manuscripts for three controversial lectures were in my bag. Curious glances revealed that a few people recognised me, some with a cold smile or an empathetic twist to the corner of the mouth.

No one knew Yvonne. She waited in the corridor while I found a place to leave my bag and my slides. As I returned, she suddenly heard a voice say, 'Let's turn our backs. Here comes Heyerdahl.' Shortly after this, Yvonne was drawn into a conversation with the friendly Swedish anthropology professor Sigvald Linné. While they were talking, an elderly participant approached Linné and said, 'I'm sorry that I didn't say hello, I thought you were Thor Heyerdahl.'

I was not feeling very confident while I waited my turn on the podium. I had three lectures to deliver, while the others mostly had no more than one. The atmosphere was clearly one of expectancy: someone was about to be held up to ridicule. There was an unusually large group of journalists with cameras, a rare sight at these events. This increased both the hostility towards the adventurer and the hope that he would be slain on stage before their very eyes.

Two other lecturers were due to speak before it was my turn, but their topics were so specialised that only a handful of listeners had come in to hear them. The rest of the participants remained in the corridors, obviously waiting to experience something of a circus. When the first lecturer had finished after half an hour, Yvonne and I were among the few remaining listeners who faithfully waited for the second lecturer, who for some unknown reason never turned up. Normally this would have resulted in a half-hour break before it was my turn to stand in the line of fire, but Birket-Smith went up to the podium and, as he looked out over an almost empty auditorium, asked me to come up and begin.

I made my way up to the lectern and started reading to Yvonne and half a dozen uninterested listeners. It was as though I were reading to myself. I had worked hard to prepare the lectures, and the people who were supposed to listen were still out in the corridor.

I may have been reading for about five minutes with the same lack of interest as the listeners when I saw Yvonne sneak out. A moment later the huge entry door was opened wide, and people literally poured in behind Yvonne. There was such a clamour of feet and chairs that I had to wait until silence settled in the crowded room, with people lined up against the walls and elbowing their way through the doorway. When I tried to continue, there were cries from the hall that I should start from the beginning, and Birket-Smith asked me to start all over again.

I saw many puzzled faces in the auditorium. Rather than the bearded savage they had expected, there on the podium was a freshly shaven young man in a blue suit. According to the papers, he looked more like a well-dressed bank clerk than a seafaring explorer. Whether the audience or the lecturer was most surprised is difficult to say, but I was bewildered by the total silence after the first lecture. Not one malicious comment, and only a few careful, friendly questions that were easy to answer.

The next day, after the second and third lectures, the audience and I had both had time to warm up. These last ones were given without a break, and they were an in-depth consideration of the possibility of American contribution to the aboriginal population of Polynesia. No one raised any counter-arguments. On the contrary, the first response came from the renowned Canadian researcher on race, Professor Ruggles Gates, who admitted that the latest blood analyses provided sound support for the speaker's conclusions. Hugely relieved and totally exhausted, I made my way out of the room with Yvonne. The reporter from Oslo telegraphed the news of my survival back to Norway, noting the fact that my opponent, Professor Birket-Smith, had thanked me for unusually important scientific work. Without exception, the Finnish newspapers that had spread the accusations of humbug published positive reviews of the scientific work and emphasised that the critics had been silenced.

Later I learned that the little old man who had refused to acknowledge Linné, thinking Linné was me, was the famous French ethnologist Paul Rivet. I never did meet him; he had overtly avoided all my three lectures. I was informed that he later proposed a resolution that the Congress declare

Heyerdahl's theories unacceptable. The proposal was turned down on the grounds that the Congress could not consider resolutions from someone who had not attended the lectures in question.

Nevertheless, I was not yet home and dry. A few days after the Congress in Cambridge had ended, the Fourth International Congress of Anthropologists and Ethnologists opened in Vienna.

Like many others who had been at Cambridge, Yvonne and I bought rail tickets direct to Vienna. Before boarding the train, we heard from a friendly scientist from Vienna that one of my keenest opponents, Professor Robert von Heine-Geldern, had been appointed vice-president of the Congress in Vienna. He had printed a circular containing violent criticism of my theories and they would be distributed at no cost to all Congress participants.

I immediately cancelled our tickets, and Yvonne and I flew to Vienna instead.

After landing, I dropped Yvonne off at the hotel and continued in the taxi straight to Heine-Geldern's office. I was received by a stooped but active elderly professor with alert bespectacled eyes, who immediately gave me a copy of the circular which was ready for distribution. When I asked for time to refute the attack, he answered negatively, triumphantly. If I had wanted to speak at the Congress, I should have requested this when I was invited. It was now too late.

Two students, who had been waiting impatiently outside the door, were shocked when they overheard that I was refused the opportunity to defend myself. A delegation of students went to the professor and suggested scheduling an open debate during the Congress. They were turned down.

That evening the students took me to a secret meeting with

their favourite professor, Dominik Wölfel, in an abandoned wine cellar. The students were nervous of being seen in public with Professor Wölfel because he was no friend of their own professor, Heine-Geldern. Wölfel was known as one of the old-timers with the sharpest eye for realistic cultural contacts. I had quoted him on the culture of the aboriginal inhabitants of the Canary Islands, whose island he thought of as a possible stopover point between the old and new world in antiquity. As we sat and made plans with muffled voices in the dim glow of a lantern, I was reminded of groups hiding in the catacombs during the Christian persecutions. I learned that the Museum of Ethnography in Vienna was ready to distribute its yearbook to all the participants in the Congress. Neither the museum director nor the yearbook's editor were particularly close to the vice-president of the Congress, Heine-Geldern.

I visited the museum director the next morning and received permission to submit an article for the yearbook. He was probably unaware that it had already been printed, and sent me to the co-editor, Dr Etta Becker-Donner, a friendly and well-known specialist on South American Indian cultures. She pointed to the stacks of yearbooks in her office, but agreed to insert a separate response to Heine-Geldern before the books were distributed in the Congress halls.

This was Friday evening, and the Congress was due to open on Monday morning.

Luckily my German publishers, the Ullstein family, were in Vienna, and we were on very good terms with them after the tremendous success of the German edition of *Kon-Tiki*. After meeting the publisher and the production manager I was promised that my off-print would be printed by Sunday evening if they could have it by Sunday morning.

I went to bed early on Friday evening to ensure a good night's sleep. Heine-Geldern had written his attack before having read my recently published scientific work, which I had brought along to Vienna. On Saturday I effortlessly drew on quotes from my own text as adequate answers to all Heine-Geldern's arguments; I had already dealt with them. The professor's only new contribution was an admirable list from sources all around the world, giving examples of days when the wind blew in the opposite direction to the trade winds that carried the *Kon-Tiki* raft to Polynesia. To this new and unexpected argument I simply commented that if one used a method of research rather than a personal visit to the Pacific Ocean, then it would also be possible to compile a list of hurricanes, sufficient to prove that the Pacific was uninhabitable.

Yvonne and I were among the first to arrive in the flag-decorated auditorium on Monday morning. We were cordially received by the Congress president and vice-president, who expressed their slightly confused appreciation for the printed article I pushed into their hands.

Heine-Geldern was extremely pale when he walked up to the lectern and declared the Congress open. He did not respond to my off-print because he had expended all his ammunition and realised that he had run out of credible arguments in his final attempt at turning the winds in the Pacific Ocean.

Heine-Geldern's great chance for revenge finally came eight years later. In 1960, the Thirty-Fourth International Congress of Americanists was held in Vienna, and this time Heine-Geldern had been appointed Congress president. When the invitation came in the mail, I considered the pros and cons and decided to attend, and to deliver a lecture. This time I chose a topic within the field of biology, where I knew I had the upper hand over Heine-Geldern and his disciples.

I have often wondered whether Heine-Geldern had intentionally marshalled all his disciples in the front row. When I stepped on to the podium I felt more openly unpopular and hated than ever before. If looks could kill, I was on the verge of thinking this might come true, as I leafed through my manuscript and looked out over the audience. I read as if in a trance, convinced that these people, who were staring at me intensely with cold eyes, would not be listening to a word I said. And then the incredible happened. I had just about read the final sentence when I looked up and saw Heine-Geldern rapidly approaching the lectern. He grabbed me by the hand as if I were a long-lost friend, and gave my lecture such overwhelming praise, the likes of which I would never hear again. His disciples in the front row must have been just as surprised and confused as I was. I had not realised that my lecture on the ethno-botanical proof of contact between South America and Polynesia, had killed the isolation theories of Heine-Geldern's worst enemy, the super-isolationist E. D. Merril. So delighted was he that I had refuted this American botanist, that he completely forgot that I had sailed across the Pacific Ocean in the wrong direction. On this occasion the wind was blowing so favourably my way that it felt like I was being hugged to death up on the podium, even though I am assured it was only a handshake.

Skottsberg, the botanist who had the support of the ethnologist Métraux, also capitulated. He re-evaluated his own studies of the Easter Island flora, and was the first to point out that the island's only two freshwater plants, the *totora* reed and the medicinal plant *tavari*, were South American species that could only have been brought by pre-European seafarers. The *totora* reed was the most important cultivated plant on this unforested island, and along the desert coast of Peru the reed was used for houses and boat-building. Attempts to claim that freshwater plants could have arrived on the Easter Island crater lakes as pollen stuck to the legs of birds failed, because no seabird could have reached this island from South America. Furthermore, without the aid of humans, the pollen from freshwater plants would have drowned en route to Easter Island, together with such plants as sweet potatoes, cassava, pumpkins and chilli peppers, all of which were already cultivated on the island when the Europeans arrived.

The battle with the great Goliaths finally ebbed out in Europe. But the web I had been caught up in during the years of battle had also spread across the Atlantic Ocean and gone straight through the Berlin Wall and behind the Iron Curtain.

In the United States the book and the movie of the *Kon-Tiki* expedition were received with just as much enthusiasm as they were in Europe. The expedition participants were invited to the White House, where President Truman welcomed us to the Oval Office. He gave a speech where he praised our courage and our seamanship, and he showed us his book of news clippings from our journey.

However, the enthusiasm amongst American scientists was slightly more subdued, while their attacks were more moderate than they had been in Europe. This country had originated the dogma that the South American balsa raft could not stay afloat all the way to Polynesia. The world's leading authority on navigation in prehistoric Peru, Dr S. K. Lothrop at Harvard University, had written a special dissertation on the balsa raft and concluded that it would sink after two weeks on the ocean, therefore it could not have transported Peru's original inhabitants all the way to Polynesia. Lothrop was quoted by all scientists engaged in Pacific Ocean research, and Sir Peter Buck and all the others based themselves upon his theories. Among them was the friendly, aging Professor Herbert Spinden, whom I stayed with in New York, when I tried unsuccessfully to get him and his colleagues to read my comprehensive, but as yet, unpublished manuscript. When I claimed that Polynesia's oldest inhabitants had come from South America, he only smiled and said, 'Well, you could try to sail a balsa raft from Peru to Polynesia.'

I had accepted his challenge.

My greatest surprise during the academic battle that raged after the journey, was that Professor Lothrop and his wife invited my wife and me for cocktails in their apartment in New York. There he showed me an exact model of the *Kon-Tiki* raft, sitting on the piano. He had built it himself. This friendly and gentle scientist was the first to admit that I, with the raft journey, had convinced him that my theories were correct.

When we were building the balsa raft in Callao, the famous American archaeologist Dr Richard P. Schaedel was excavating ancient Inca ruins in Peru. When asked by the press if he thought we would survive the raft experiment, his answer was as negative as that of everyone else. After the journey had been safely completed, Schaedel was asked what the *Kon-Tiki* expedition had proven. He answered, 'Nothing. Except that Norwegians are capable sailors.'

We met many years later in Peru, and by then he was so convinced that there had been early seafaring in this country that he suggested that we should work together on archaeological projects on the islands off the coast. In the 1990s, Schaedel's colleague and my good friend and co-worker, Dr Daniel Sandweiss from the United States, uncovered archaeological proof of a Peruvian coastal maritime culture, dating as far back as 10000–9000 BC. These coastal people subsisted almost entirely on fish from the ocean.

Did you find a little time to satisfy your adventurous spirit in the midst of all the scientific controversy?

When involved in researching prehistoric civilisations, adventure adds spice to the sober world of science. After the breakthrough at the Thirtieth Congress of Americanists in Cambridge, I was invited to act as honorary vice-president to the Thirty-First Congress in São Paulo in Brazil in 1954. There I presented amongst other things the material from my first archaeological expedition to the Galapagos Islands in 1952. A journey to the interior of Brazil had been planned for all the Congress participants, and Yvonne and I were among those who had signed up for the trip. To our great disappointment, the journey was cancelled owing to the suicide of President Getulio Vargas.

To make up for this, I managed to charter a small single-engine plane to fly us and our guide to Santa Isabel, a small Indian village by the Araguaia River in the southwestern Amazon basin. The trip did not quite work out as planned.

Provisions and equipment that had been bought for the occasion had to be left behind at the airport. Not wanting to overload the plane, the pilot refused to allow us to bring anything but a fishing rod and a rifle. After a while, when the green jungle canopy lay far beneath us, the plane made a complete 180-degree turn and the engine went silent.

'Don't be afraid,' said the pilot. 'I've made twelve emergency landings before.'

Back at the airport he changed all the spark-plugs, and we headed off again. The pilot navigated by means of an old school map with villages marked as red rings on a green background. After some hours the plane touched down in the middle of the rain forest, in a clearing that resembled a potato field. In the immediate vicinity there was a bar with a local beauty behind the counter, and for some unknown reason the pilot told us that it was impossible to get the plane back in the air.

A long, carved log canoe lay by the riverbank, and I saw this as our only chance of getting out of the jungle. Two Caraja Indians were willing to paddle us in the direction of the Amazon. We crawled aboard with rifle and fishing rod, and moved rapidly down the river. For several days we saw nothing but green jungle, brown water, colourful parrots and screaming monkeys. At night-time we slept on the bank, either on the sand or on mattresses of branches. Staying close to the edge of the river in case of unwanted visitors, we found it hard to fall asleep with the unusual sight of pairs of shining eyes staring at us like bright marbles on the water's surface. They were caymans, the alligators of the Amazon, slipping silently through the water without taking their eyes off us. The daytime heat was suffocating and we had no drinking water but the chocolate-brown river water that we were floating on. The first day we used handkerchiefs to filter out the mud, but after a while we were so thirsty and tired that we drank straight from the river.

During the next few weeks, imprisoned in the Amazon's amazing virgin forest, we experienced an incredible world. The first person we saw was a stark naked man who stood staring at us from a sandbank in the river. When he caught sight of us he ran into a hut and came out again just as naked as before, but with a belt around his stomach. There were more huts in the forest and we were welcomed with a large meal of fried fish, turtle eggs and cassava roots. We fell asleep on hammocks in the great outdoors, but were woken up in the moonlight and witnessed a strange drama. At regular intervals, two naked young girls ran like frightened gazelles past our hammocks, and the forest was filled with an eerie, mumbling song. On the sandbank, four swaying figures, wearing towering headdresses and flowing capes of straw, danced. We were never given any explanation for this peculiar night-time performance.

However we did learn a lot about the art of survival in close contact with such overwhelming surroundings – searching for roots and turtle eggs, hunting crocodile with an axe at night and experiencing almost supernatural meetings with dolphins and flying fish in a lake that had been cut off from the river during a period of drought.

Our days as guests of the jungle Indians were an extreme contrast to the glitzy business areas of the skyscraper city São Paulo that we had just left – not to mention the sober world of science that we soon encountered.

The international breakthrough came at the important Tenth Scientific Congress on the Pacific, in Hawaii in 1961. Olof Selling was the representative of the Swedish Academy of Science and we flew over together. Today some of his best friends are members of this Academy, while Forest Brown did not live to see the triumph of his botanical theories, nor was Buck present. Olof had long since been adopted by the *Kon-Tiki* group as a sort of honorary member, and now he was credited with the drilling for pollen on Easter Island. Together with three American archaeologists from the Easter Island expedition I submitted the results from our excavations there and elsewhere in Polynesia and on Galapagos.

The result was that the three thousand delegates of the Pacific Ocean Congress unanimously agreed to a resolution tabled by archaeologists, that South America and Southeast Asia represented the most important sources of culture and peoples of the inhabitants of the Pacific Islands.

11

Behind the Iron Curtain

You're finally going to do something sensible again.

The old familiar voice had returned after several weeks of silence.

Sensible?

I was on all fours, making my way among the lava boulders on the Teide volcano in Tenerife. Jacqueline was on my heels. What we were doing was really rather crazy; it was Sunday and we could have slept in and relaxed in our garden hammocks down in the pyramid valley.

I keep Sundays sacred. It is a principle. I put aside whatever I am working on. This may be a combination of respect for the symbolic seventh day, and purely practical reasons. It allows me to feel the call of the wild, to recharge my body and soul, so that I can attend to the work of the coming week with renewed energy.

I had no desire for any more talk at the moment. I had

enough to do breathing in the thin air and finding a foothold
so that loose rocks would not fall down on Jacqueline's head.
Odd that my *aku-aku* should spring back to life right here.
My schedule had been so busy, with travel and appointments,
that I had forgotten the *aku-aku* ever since I climbed down
the statue-strewn slopes of the Easter Island crater. Maybe it
was this crater wall that had us thinking about one another
again.

But now it was Christmas and the end of a memorable
anniversary year. A new year was on its way and I might have
enough time to get back to work again.

What a wonderfully beautiful view. Even the black lava
boulders around us that had been moulded into so many
shapes in their wild dance down the mountain wall, gave life
and colour to the emptiness high up here beneath the blue
vault of the sky. We had left a world of almost tropical lush-
ness down in the Güimar valley. Further up the hill, on the
outside of this enormous witches' cauldron, a dense pine
forest grew to about 2,000 metres above sea level, petering
out just below the rim of the crater. The crater's interior was
a gigantic bowl, twelve kilometres in diameter, half-filled with
dried lava. Teide's highest peak soared to 3,700 metres and
was the highest point on Spanish territory. We were climbing
away from the witches' cauldron, from what looked like both
black and brown burnt porridge, with a sprinkling of ashes
coloured like sugar and cinnamon. The only sign of any
organic growth in the bowl were some dense, perfectly round
bushes that occasionally stuck out of the porridge like
unkempt trolls' heads on their way up from the centre of the
earth, captured in dried lava before they had time to sniff the
fresh air.

Ocean, mountain, forest or desert – I like to see something
of humanity's birthday gift from the creative powers. A lover

of nature is someone who shares Our Lord's taste. Enter a synagogue, a church, or a mosque, and you will hear that Our Lord created everything that is in nature, and then declared a day of rest, proud of His work.

My invisible twin was in quite a chatty mood during our ascent of the rock-strewn slope. The *aku-aku* was as frivolous as my own thoughts, while I myself was wheezing in the thin mountain air and relieved whenever I could sit down without losing face because Jacqueline was falling behind. She certainly was tough, and had more willpower than muscle.

Why always higher and higher?

I had to admit I thought that climbing a mountain and being rewarded with such a panoramic view was a special treat. As in science, although the narrow valley is also very beautiful, in the long run there is a danger of becoming narrow-minded.

We reached the ledge of a high lava peak and the view opened up in every direction. I pulled Jacqueline up beside me and we sat down to catch our breath and enjoy the sight of the world beneath us.

'It makes you feel safe to sit on top of an island and see the ocean all around you,' she said.

As usual, I agreed with most of what she said. Maybe I had an atavistic feeling that no one could come out of the dark forest and take us by surprise. Perhaps we have hidden memories in our inherited genes, from the time when our biological ancestors emerged from the depths of the ocean and drew their first breath. One thing was certain: the great ocean was the source of life, and as long as there was life in the ocean, there would also be conditions for life on land. But if the ocean died, the plankton near the water's surface withered in the sunlight and stopped helping the trees pump oxygen into the air, then it would be of no consolation to future generations that Our Lord had equipped us with lungs instead of gills.

We were both stretched out on our backs on the lava boulders, staring at the blue sky and the blue ocean. The curtains of our eyes gradually closed, and Jacqueline fell asleep.

You were in the Soviet Union in the middle of the Cold War. How do you really feel about communism?

I have seen communism from the inside as well as in countries where the line of demarcation between communism or capitalism is razor-sharp. Having seen frightening poverty and inhumane conditions in places where a tiny upper class refuses to acknowledge that people are starving on the streets and simply steps over them, I have realised that a society where people die on the street or a country road from hunger, or a society that cannot provide food and shelter for everyone, is a sick society. When a person is ill, he needs medicine. In my view, communism is a strong medicine. When this medicine has been taken long enough for everyone to have food and a roof over his head, then it is time to stop taking it. A healthy society does not need that kind of medicine.

Other than that, I really have no political conviction. I have yet to find a political party that stands for everything I am for and is against everything I am against. They are all a mixture of good and bad. I remember sitting with my Russian interpreter, Lev Zjdanov, and his aging mother, a little withered woman. She told us that she had taken part in the Revolution and that she had grabbed a red flag and waved it enthusiastically, believing that now they were finally going to live in humane conditions. Her enthusiasm made me think of Joan of Arc, and I imagine that I would have grabbed a flag myself under similar circumstances.

*

The *Kon-Tiki* book was banned in the Soviet Union, and I was an unknown entity during Stalin's lifetime. When Nikita Khrushchev came to power and allowed the book to be translated, it went to the top of the bestseller lists in all the East European countries. The Russian edition was the first to sell more than a million copies in any one language. With this, my peaceful days ended and controversy started among the literati of the Soviet Academy of Science.

It was launched by the literati in the deepest sense of the word, because they specialised in letters that they themselves were unable to read. In the whole Pacific area, which covers exactly half the world's surface, any form of writing was totally unknown until the arrival of the Europeans. The only exception was Easter Island, where around twenty wooden hieroglyphic plaques have been found; not even Easter Island inhabitants could decipher these. A team of language researchers and cryptologists in Moscow had attempted to understand this *rongo-rongo* writing, but no one paid any attention to them until the hostile review of a book, that had passed through the Iron Curtain from the West, hit the newspapers. My brave translator Lev Zjdanov sent, by censored mail from Moscow, copies of the attacks translated into Norwegian, and the controversy started all over again.

At that time, no Russian researcher had been free to travel outside the Soviet Union, least of all to Easter Island. The mail was slow and the attacks from the Soviet researchers increased and became more aggressive as I started answering them. There were always a few weeks' delay, since the censors thought that everything I wrote was written in code.

Then something totally unexpected happened. The supreme director of the Soviet Academy of Science, Mstislav Vsevoldovich Keldysh, the man who had launched the first

Sputnik into space, entered the arena. He invited me to Moscow to meet Soviet academics face to face.

I accepted. The year was 1962, the height of the Cold War. I had not met any Russians or communists since the battles in Finnmark, so it was a new experience to arrive with my Russian translator as interpreter, in a hall filled with Soviet scientists, presided over by President Keldysh himself.

Keldysh opened the meeting by giving the floor to a comrade who was head of the anthropological division, and a powerful hulk of a man rose to his feet. With a muscular physique and an impressive Stalin moustache, he was the stereotype of the Western image of a communist. With a voice as deep as a sailor's in a storm, and his fist clenched to emphasise his point, I grasped quickly that these introductory words to his comrades were far from flattering. There was a deadly silence when he finished and returned to his seat. As my interpreter quietly translated into Norwegian, a totally new argument against an early migration from America was revealed to me.

My theories of migration routes in the Pacific Ocean were not in accord with the teachings of Lenin. According to Lenin, all emigration began with pressures caused by overpopulation or enemy invasion.

An expectant silence filled the room. What could I answer? The interpreter looked unhappy. The discussion was doomed before it had begun.

I surprised myself and everyone else by saying out loud: 'I had no idea that Lenin was an anthropologist.'

Still there was total silence until the interpreter, in a low voice, repeated my words in Russian. Then I saw some of the audience put their hands to their mouths, to hide smiles. A feeling of unease began to grow, and Keldysh immediately invited me to take the stand. I had summed up the situation.

Academics were present. The Stalin lookalike who had opened the debate was not a scientist but a faithful party member, who had been rewarded by the party and made manager of this department of the Academy. Each and every professional field within the arts, culture and sciences had a leader who resembled Stalin, if not physically then mentally. The man with the giant moustache had done his duty – he had referred to the teachings of Lenin – and had no more to say.

Nor did anyone else object when, without wavering from Lenin's line, I used Peru as an example of how, since time immemorial, overpopulation and pressures from the country's interior had caused problems for the fisher population in the narrow river valleys along the desert coast of the Andes. Cultures replaced one another in succession, until the Spaniards came to power in the Inca Empire in the 1530s. The Spaniards learned that the Incas' history was preserved in the sun temple in Cuzco, on wooden boards that the Spanish subsequently burnt. But the *amauta*, the Inca Empire's scholars, could refer to frequent migrations in the country. The last had taken place only three generations before the arrival of the Spaniards. Inca Tupac Yupanqi, the grandfather of the two Inca brothers who were the first to welcome the Spaniards, left his own empire in the mountains and found his way to the coast. He conquered the Chimu Empire and all the settlements along the coast from the equator and four thousand miles to the south. When the coastal population told him there were populated islands out in the Pacific Ocean, he ordered them to build hundreds of balsa rafts, and he set sail with a flotilla that carried half his army, returning after nine months with dark-skinned prisoners.

I had no idea whether my Russian listeners knew any of this. They were a docile assembly. They sat in silence and let me continue. I added that every so often Peru still suffered dreadful natural catastrophes along its coastline, when floods from the mountains and the El Niño current from the ocean inundated the valleys and drove the whole population away from their homes and on to their rafts. In the so-called El Niño years, the mighty ocean current ran swiftly from Peru to Easter Island. I added that we must not think people in ancient times and foreign countries had less courage, curiosity, greed or need for adventure than we had today. Moreover, in those days there was no one to stop them if they had wanderlust.

No one protested. Keldysh demanded to hear the arguments from those who had most keenly opposed my theory on the origin of the Polynesians. Several got to their feet, but there were no new attacks; those who had something to add were satisfied with the answers they received.

Soberly and calmly, the man who had sent the first manned capsule into space, chaired the debate about who had sent the first vessels out into the Pacific Ocean. He refrained from making any personal comments during the discussion that followed, and waited until everyone had spoken before giving his. At that point there was no doubt about his personal opinion. He unconditionally reprimanded the anthropologists in his own Academy, pointing out that they were poorly prepared for the debate and lacked any basis for their earlier criticism. Speaking directly to me, he said smilingly that the next time I set off on an expedition he hoped I would include a Russian in the team.

This ended my small, private cold war with opponents in the Soviet Union. It was definitively over, and final proof of the fortunate outcome was the Lomonosov Medal from the State University in Moscow. In the meantime I had become a Fellow of the New York Academy of Sciences, and it must have been President Keldysh who saw to it that I also received an honorary doctorate from the Soviet Academy of Science while the Iron Curtain was still in place.

A few years later, whilst planning the *Ra* expedition – crossing the Atlantic in a papyrus boat with a multinational crew – I recalled President Keldysh's words. I wrote and reminded him of his suggestion to include a Russian in the team, and I asked him to choose a medical doctor who spoke English and had a sense of humour. And thus Dr Yuri Aleksandrovich Senkevich, smelling faintly of vodka and slightly intoxicated, stepped off the plane in Cairo, to meet me for the first time. Keldysh had won the political tug-of-war against the highest political leadership, and Yuri became the first Russian to be let out of the Soviet Union on his own, to participate in a private capitalist-funded raft journey. I had asked for a Russian with a sense of humour to avoid getting a fanatical party politician, and because a good laugh takes up little space and counts for a great deal on any expedition. Yuri later told me that he had doused himself generously aboard Aeroflot, afraid of not being considered amusing enough.

Yuri was later appointed chief doctor to the Russian civilian astronauts, and after our three multinational reed-boat journeys, he was invited to the United States by American space researchers to discuss future long-term co-operation, to promote peaceful co-existence, amongst individuals of different nationalities, living under stress and in overpopulated areas.

The learned *rongo-rongo* experts who had been my most bitter opponents in the Soviet Union became important collaborators in the labour of deciphering the Easter Island hieroglyphics.

At the Thirty-Second International Congress of Americanists in Copenhagen in 1956, a completely unknown name in science turned up with a sensation. A German wartime deciphering expert, Thomas Barthel, claimed to have deciphered the mystical *rongo-rongo* alphabet. The story grew, and the world press smelled a scoop, when he revealed that one of the boards related that the forefathers of the Easter Island population had come from Raiatea in Polynesia, in 1400 AD. In other words, from the opposite direction and much later than I myself claimed.

Even the celebrated Musée de l'Homme in Paris mounted Barthel's deciphering of the hieroglyphs on a board in its Easter Island exhibit. The fuss died down when Russian language researchers went to work on the *rongo-rongo* hieroglyphs with the help of computers. They discovered that the texts were written in an unknown language, unlike that now spoken in Polynesia, and without knowing which language they were written in it would be impossible to decipher the hieroglyphs.

Barthel's fantasy had intrigued a whole world; but even his own students have dismissed his translations and are fighting among themselves with suggestions that are equally fanciful. The *rongo-rongo* writing of Easter Island remains a mystery.

When I was invited to travel around the Soviet Union after the *Kon-Tiki* movie, I did so on condition that I could travel freely and that the programme would be of my own choosing. I learned a lot by experiencing the world on both sides of the Iron Curtain, during both the Second World War and the Cold War. There are no sensible national borders between friends and enemies.

My first loyal friend at the Academy of Science was the ethnologist Genrikh Anochin, a war veteran and a specialist in Nordic languages and culture. He was responsible for my meeting not only scientists but, to an even greater degree, members of the authors' guild and the artists' union. Vodka and caviar were plentiful, as was the general atmosphere of tolerance, but the rooms were small in the crowded workers' dwellings and isolated dachas in the forests around the capital. They accepted that I was both a Fellow of the New York Academy of Science and an honorary doctor of their own Academy of Science, but no one cared to talk about science or politics.

On the endless Russian plains, and on distant journeys by plane or train to other republics in the Soviet Union, the Russian translator of my books came along as interpreter. We were guests of the *kolkhose* peasants, and visited small orthodox village churches, which, to my amazement, were filled with people and the pleasant aroma of incense. The lighted candles were so plentiful that the walls shone like gold, and the colourful icons in these simple peasant churches would be the envy of museums all over the world. Inside the heavy church doors there was a tangible atmosphere of past memories and hope for better times to come.

We travelled westward with the night train to Leningrad to study art from the islands in the Pacific that had been brought to the Tsar's museums in the previous century. And we rode eastwards on the Trans-Siberian railway through the entire length of Siberia, passing endless forests and wooden fences, the locomotive letting off steam every time we stopped at the frost-bound new settlements along the line to let fur-clad passengers on or off. We rode all the way to Vladivostok, to the point where the Soviet Union and China meet, in the northeastern corner of the Pacific Ocean. There, Japan, the Kuril Islands and the Aleutians form a bridge over to the American coastal archipelago of British Columbia, my pre-war home where I had become acquainted with the natural sea route from Asia to America and Polynesia. To my amazement I saw that the Soviet regime, notorious in the West for its total contempt of environmental considerations, was building a lumber-processing plant, where environmental concerns had been given top priority.

It was too cold up there on the coast of Siberia to suit me. I would have much preferred to drift by on the warm Japan current, just off the coast, than to wade over land to North America in snow and ice.

My fondest memories from the Soviet republic are of Georgia, when Lev and I went on a fishing trip along a crystal-clear brook in the Caucasus Mountains with actors and musicians from Tblisi. We lay in the grass and ate fresh trout that we caught as fast as we could fry them. Like Vikings we drank Georgian wine out of cowhorns that had a habit of tipping over, so we had to empty them immediately, before breaking off chunks of bread or eating the fish. According to local custom, we had to drink a toast to each of the guests, to the women, to peace, to friendship between our people, to King Olav and President Khrushchev, to our forefathers and our descendants, to love of all kind, to the fruits of the soil, and to a long and happy life. It turned into a long and enjoyable out-door lunch. Even my dutiful companion Lev forgot the time. Speeding across fields and around house corners back to the railway station in Tblisi, we arrived just as the night train to Moscow was departing. I quickly thanked everyone for their hospitality, and while Lev jumped on to the nearest moving railway carriage, I ran after the next one with my suitcase as the train increased its speed. I was due to give a lecture in Moscow the next day and managed to throw the suitcase on board, but by the time I finally managed to grab the railing by the wagon door the train was going so fast that I ended up hanging on, with my feet in the air. It was impossible to get a foothold on the step. I hung horizontally by my hands, as if I were on the *Kon-Tiki* in a strong wind, my body streaming behind like a burgee. I thought my final hour had come, but the conductor, with the help of other passengers, managed to haul me on board.

I escaped with a few bad bruises, although a nurse came to attend to one leg, which was bleeding right through my trousers. She put a large bandage around it and I was still wearing it under a clean pair of trousers the next day when I appeared in a blue suit to present my lecture in Moscow. A dark suit and tie was still the proper attire at such occasions, east of the Iron Curtain. Cap and overalls were not in favour.

As the evening's guest of honour and his interpreter, Lev and I were placed in comfortable, adjacent chairs in front of the first row. Just before I was asked to speak, I noticed that Lev was carefully leaning over, staring intently at my left trouser leg. It looked as if he were about to remove a piece of lint from my black sock. In fact it was only a white piece of thread, but it was not a short one, and when he started pulling, it grew longer and longer. He had not realised that the thread was part of the bandage. Calmly and silently he kept pulling and rolling the thread into a ball. We were both calm, but I tried to yank my leg away so he would figure out that he was about to unravel the whole bandage. Finally he bent over and quietly shoved the ball of thread up my trouser-leg. I was not looking forward to the walk up to the podium, in case the bandage would fall down and drag along the floor.

As I recalled this, I could still almost feel that bundle in the leg of my trousers, but now I was the one to fall asleep. Jacqueline woke me up for the climb back down. Still stiff from the ascent and having fallen asleep sitting up with our legs resting on the lava boulders, we stumbled down just in time to meet the shadow of the crater's edge creeping upward as we reached the marked trail. And then we experienced the awesome splash of colour as the sun set beyond the edge of the crater to the west. We said goodnight to the silhouettes of an army of coal-black trolls which we had not seen in the daylight. We knew that when the sun's rays started to play on the cone-shaped walls of Teide next morning, we would recognise the silhouettes as some of nature's most bizarre sculptures, in the form of statues and monoliths of dark and light brown lava.

The next day, without any particular goal or route in mind, we set off across the bottom of the crater to enjoy close contact with nature. The world around us soon disappeared behind lava protrusions and piles of yellow sand and black boulders.

We had brought a picnic, and worked up a healthy appetite. It was the penultimate day of the year, but the sun up here in the clear air was still so strong that we sought the shade of a large bush. Jacqueline fell asleep on a soft mattress of dry branches, without seeing the two small, happy birds sitting on a branch of the bush. One of them almost sat on the tip of her nose, not realising it was *her* beak.

I met President Nikita Khrushchev at the Kon-Tiki Museum. He was visiting Norway with his loyal Foreign Minister Gromyko. Khrushchev had permitted the publication of the *Kon-Tiki* book in Russian and now he wanted to see the raft, as he felt he had been responsible for record sales. Gromyko always walked behind him, without saying a word, but when we went down into the basement to see the Easter Island sculptures he leaned over and whispered that the interpreter with them was the one who had translated my book *Aku-Aku* from the Norwegian. The interpreter was kept busy because the jovial Soviet communist boss asked and queried and broke all rules of etiquette and his own timetable. He obviously would have enjoyed himself more if he had been barefoot with us on the raft, rather than in a political meeting, where he would remove his shoe with the sole purpose of thumping the rostrum to express disapproval.

When we were about thirty minutes behind schedule, Khrushchev stopped and asked if he could come on the next raft journey. Interpreters and journalists craned their necks, and long poles brought microphones right down to the tip of my nose. What could I answer to a question like that from the world's leading proponent of Soviet communism?

'What could you do aboard a raft?' I asked.

'I could cook,' came the answer. Well then, Khrushchev could cook.

'What could you do as a cook aboard?'

'I can cook on a Primus.'

'Don't worry about the cooking as long as you bring along enough Russian caviar,' I jested.

We shook hands on that and, as an initial first proof that he hadn't forgotten the agreement, later that day a whole bucket of caviar and a case of celebration vodka arrived from the Soviet embassy in Oslo. As if that wasn't enough, later that same day, he proved that he could satisfy my condition for a Russian to have a sense of humour before being invited on a raft journey.

A totally unexpected invitation arrived from the Department of Foreign Affairs later that day. It was for an informal but exclusive reception for the Soviet head of state in the Folk Museum park, just a few hours after our visit to the Kon-Tiki Museum. The whole park had been closed to tourists for the occasion. Khrushchev was in high spirits and enjoyed himself royally when we all gathered on the lawn after the meal to watch a 'Halling', a folk dance performed by two Norwegians in traditional national costume, accompanied by a fiddler.

There was no doubt about who had invited me. There were

no other outsiders and no press, just a small group of politicians from Norway and the Soviet Union, and myself, standing in the background and peering over the heads of the other guests.

When the couple had finished leaping around and performing the acrobatics involved in the folk dance, the Soviet head of state went out on the lawn, signalled for the fiddler to start playing, and then went over and asked Foreign Minister Gromyko to partner him in a 'Halling' dance. Gromyko despaired; he hardly looked the athletic type. After Gromyko declined, Khrushchev calmly walked over to the Norwegian Foreign Minister Hallvard Lange and bowed deeply. I knew Lange as an experienced world citizen, who was accustomed to difficult situations, but this was too much even for him. He blushed and remained rooted to the ground, while the fiddler played gutsy folk songs on the lawn.

There followed one of the funniest things I have seen since my boyhood days in Larvik, when we sat in the front row of the movies and ate peanuts and laughed until we cried at Charlie Chaplin in one of his silent films, as music issued forth from a piano in the corner.

Little chubby Khrushchev would not give up. This time he went over and bowed low to our tall, skinny Prime Minister Gerhardsen. Khrushchev barely reached up to Gerhardsen's stomach. When Gerhardsen accepted, I couldn't help myself. I doubled over in laughter, and stomped my feet on the ground like a little boy, while our Norwegian hosts struggled to smile politely and the Russian guests stood seriously watching their own head of state skip around like a ball in the embrace of the tall Norwegian.

Later, I met Khrushchev's daughter and son-in-law in Moscow. She was the editor of an ecological journal and he was the head of the communist paper *Izvestia*, and the only person ever to give me a political classification. I was invited up to the editorial offices and he took me out on to the balcony overlooking Moscow's rows of houses and the main street, almost traffic-free.

'All this we have managed since the Revolution,' he said.

'You saw Karl Johan's Gate in Oslo with your father-in-law,' I said, and he had to admit that he had been impressed.

'We managed that without a revolution,' I said.

Then he laughed and turned to his colleagues. 'Heyerdahl is an incorrigible social democrat,' he explained.

The relationship between East and West was still frosty when I visited the Soviet Republic of Azerbaijan by the Caspian Sea for the first time, meeting the republic's president, Heydar Aliyev, one of the non-Russian members of the Supreme Soviet. Without being aware of the family relationship, I drove around this fascinating republic for a week with his brother, Hassan Aliyev. He was the president of the country's Academy of Science, which had invited me to come and see the world's oldest datable rock carvings of ships. In Gobustan, just a few kilometres south of the capital Baku, the vast Caspian Sea had receded over the millennia, exposing cliffs. Humans had settled above the cliffs, and it was thus possible to carbon-date the rock carvings. Some were more than five thousand years old, and were reminiscent of the oldest rock carvings of reed ships by the Red Sea, in Egypt, whose ships carried a symbol of the sun in the bow. Others could be mistaken for our Nordic Viking ships. Seafarers must have been in this area for a good many generations.

Travelling with Hassan Aliyev, I became acquainted with the people and landscape of a fascinating country. He was an agronomist and even then, in the 1960s, he was one of the leading environmentalists of the Eastern Bloc. The only thing that made me suspect that his personal connections went higher than the Academy of Science, was that every time he saw a column of smoke on the horizon he immediately whipped out his notepad and made a note of the location. If the factory pollution could not be halted it would be shut down. I was faced with the fact that we Westerners had not always been a good example. This was where Alfred Nobel had started early oil explorations, and great stretches of land were black and barren.

The day that I was leaving, Hassan asked hesitantly whether I had anything against meeting his brother. I then realised something was awry, and my suspicion was confirmed when we ended up at the presidential palace. It was a very formal meeting, featuring strict rules of etiquette. The president and I each entered an enormous hall through separate doors and then walked to the centre, having measured one another carefully, to exchange powerful handshakes. Then we sat down simultaneously at opposite sides of a long table, politicians arrayed on his side, scientists on mine.

After speeches and toasts and an ever increasing pile of empty bottles appearing between the sandwich platters, people started to circulate and it was impossible to tell who was a scientist or who a communist politician. Brought up in a conservative home in the West, as I was, where communists were regarded as a different species of humanity, it was in itself a frightening experience to shake hands with a real bona fide communist leader, and to sit at his table and talk to him in the same way that I would to anyone else. In fact I was very impressed with him. He was very much a leader, both physically and mentally.

Later, after the fall of the Soviet Union, Heydar Aliyev became the first elected president of a free Azerbaijan. He was so popular abroad that England and Norway competed to curry favour with him. The West wanted to continue oil explorations where the founder of the Nobel Prize had started them. An English delegation sent to negotiate with Aliyev was headed by Margaret Thatcher, and the Norwegian delegation was informed that they were also welcome if I came along. Aliyev remembered the meeting at the presidential palace as the only visit from the West during the Cold War.

Thus I returned to Azerbaijan and found myself sitting next to President Aliyev again, at the same long table, but this time as the spokesman for an official Norwegian delegation and with Jacqueline at my side. It was in late November 1994 and Aliyev's favourite older brother was no longer alive. Nevertheless, our previous conversations about the environment were still alive in the president's memory. The Norwegian delegation hoped to be granted a licence to exploit oil from the rich wells at the bottom of the Caspian Sea. We scored heavily with regards to our long experience and conscious and honest desire for environmentally clean drilling.

Aliyev and all the ministers demanded that I opened all meetings with the words 'Dear Azers'. Azerbaijan was the home of the Azers.

I repeated the word 'Azers' so often that it sounded like 'Asers', the people who lived in the homeland of the Vikings, the land of the Asers. And I remembered the rock carvings that resembled our Nordic Viking ships. And then at the museum in Baku Jacqueline discovered that the models of Azers hunting during the Stone Age were depicted with blond hair, and the museum director explained that the Azers were of Nordic descent. At the same time, I learned from our own delegation that the easiest way for Statoil to transport drilling equipment from Norway was via the old Viking route from the Baltic Sea, down the Volga through Russia, and on to the Caspian Sea.

I sent a fax from Baku home to Norway, and asked that the first six pages of Snorre's *Sagas of the Kings* be faxed back to me. Before he died in 1241, the Icelander Snorre had written in his history of Norway, that to the east of the Black Sea, on the border to the Turkish Empire, the chieftain Odin had ruled. The forefather of Harald Hairfair and the Norwegian royal line had been threatened by the Romans and fled northward with his people, through Russia, Saxony and Denmark, up to the Scandinavian peninsula.

Everyone knows where Vikings went to, but no one asks where they came from. They did not simply emerge from the ice at the end of the Ice Age. Could they have originated from the area around the Caspian Sea? Could this have been the point of dispersion whence long-distance travellers, with light skin and blond hair, now being excavated by the Chinese from the frozen tundra in central China, appeared in prehistoric times as Berbers along the north coast of Africa and out to the Canary Islands?

I have often felt that leaders of the communist world have worn an official iron mask when they have received press and politicians from the West. I've had the opportunity to meet several of them in less formal circumstances, and got to know them as individuals. A few of them became extremely popular in the capitalist world after the fall of communism. Heydar Aliyev was one of them; Mikhail Gorbachev another.

During the Conference on the Environment in Rio de Janeiro in 1992, Gorbachev was appointed to lead the foundation of a worldwide organisation for the environment. Shortly thereafter I received a letter from him, inviting me to act as his personal advisor at the inaugural meeting of the Green Cross International in Kyoto. To me this was a strange meeting. I had seen his face so many times on television and in so many newspapers, that it was like a reunion with an old friend. I could hardly resist throwing my arms around him, but it was not necessary. He had read all my books and seen all the movies from my expeditions, so he also felt that we were old acquaintances, and we met in a warm embrace.

Gorbachev's warm personality and his honest smiling eyes did not seem to belong in the world of politics. He proved this by setting greater store by human beings than on artificial boundaries and the arms race. When those of us who had been invited to participate at the meeting were in his company, it became obvious that here was a leader who fought on the side of all humanity, against an enemy that threatened all of us, regardless of nationality or politics. He was aware of the fact that, with the rapid development of modern technology and the population explosion, our generation was in the process of putting the essential conditions of human life at risk.

I had been an active member of other environmental groups, ever since Prince Bernhard of The Netherlands invited me to become an international advisor to the World Wildlife Fund, about twenty-five years ago. At that time Neil Armstrong and I took part in a meeting in London where all the European royal families were encouraged to increase public awareness of the WWF. There was so much blue blood present, that when Bob Hope walked on to the stage and scanned the audience, he quipped that it was like seeing a live deck of cards.

This meeting had been organised by Prince Philip. In all my years as an active member of the WWF, he was the driving force behind the organisation. He had the wisdom and foresight to change the definition and goals of ecology, away from the narrow desire to protect large game from hunters

toward a full understanding of taking care of the planet's ecological systems, and thereby protecting humans.

Prince Philip also played a key role in the days when the
Kon-Tiki raft lay forgotten in a shed outside the Maritime
Museum in Oslo. After having visited it, he later returned
with the Queen and with King Haakon, and caused such a stir
of publicity that the income from ticket sales made it possible
for Knut Haugland, the curator, to build the Kon-Tiki
Museum.

Now, in Kyoto, we saw that even a former arch-communist
had the foresight to understand that the nations of the world
had to join forces and take care of the environment. During
the meeting, Gorbachev obviously agreed with my own main
point, namely that other environmental organisations were
already working to save threatened animals and plants, rivers
and forests. The greatest threat to humanity lay in the fact that
the winds and the currents of the oceans paid no attention to
national boundaries. The wind that blew in Asia one day,
swept across Europe the next day, and from experience I knew
that the current along the coast of Africa ran into American
waters as rapidly as a raft can move. On the *Tigris* journey we
had noticed a change in the direction of the monsoon. This
meant that our planet could experience rapid climatic changes,
with unknown dangers to islands and continental coastal areas.
In practical terms, however, it turned out to be necessary to
start the work of Green Cross International on a national level,
before achieving global agreement.

Mikhail Gorbachev held a deep, spiritual belief in the
necessity of protecting nature. He told me that this began
when he experienced the wonders of nature in the small
garden around his childhood home. Once, we were in a synagogue in The Hague during a Green Cross International

conference and saw the Jewish worshippers performing their religious rituals. When we emerged from the synagogue, we stood beneath a large tree. I have a weakness for big trees, and the bigger they are, the more I feel for them. I couldn't help myself, and with a glance up at the tree I turned to Gorbachev and said, 'This is my temple.'

He quickly gave me his hand and answered, 'Mine too.'

At that instance I realised that the rabbi was standing close by, and I hurried to add, 'But we still have to admit that there must be something behind this, something that has created this temple.'

Then all three of us shook hands, in full agreement.

As an advisor to the Green Cross, I was asked by Gorbachev to help him persuade the world leaders who I knew to join the organisation. I mentioned his one-time comrade Fidel Castro, who I knew to be just as intensely interested in protecting nature as Gorbachev himself. Gorbachev liked the idea, also because he regretted the break between Cuba and Russia. He very much wanted to meet Castro, anywhere and at any time. I promised to try to arrange a meeting. The last time I saw Gorbachev during the conference, he was on an open-air platform, giving a final speech to a large gathering. When he stepped down and marched out with his official delegation, he happened to pass by me in the crowd of people. He gave me the thumbs up and mumbled, 'Remember your promise!'

This would be the first and last time I attempted to get involved in international politics. It was not a success.

Fidel Castro was fervently interested in the goals of the Green Cross, but he said immediately that Gorbachev was not very popular in Cuba after the recent period of political turmoil. Instead he suggested that I give an interview about the Green Cross in his country's political newspaper, *Granma*.

When I came right out and asked whether he was willing to meet Gorbachev, he answered, 'Well, one has to like a man with eyes like his, but he has caused Cuba so much hardship.'

I've rarely met two people who had so much in common, not least a strong appreciation of nature and a conviction that it must be preserved. But I never did manage to bring them together.

12

A Red Island on
a Blue Planet

When we stopped to take a breather, during our walking
excursions in Tenerife, we took it easy, and I had plenty of
opportunity to talk to both Jacqueline and my *aku-aku*. The
trade-wind clouds passed silently over head, like small cotton-
wool balls, evoking many associations. I recognised them from
my year on Fatu-Hiva, and from the voyages in prehistoric
vessels that followed the sun and the endless tropical clouds;
from Africa, over the Canary Islands and west to America, and
further on across the Pacific Ocean, to Easter Island, Tahiti,
Fatu-Hiva. Below, where the waves broke against the coast, I
knew that the surface of the ocean itself beckoned in the same
direction, with the Canary current to Barbados, where we
landed with *Ra*, and to Cuba, where Columbus landed.

Cuba. Could you have landed there with Ra?
    Actually, I could have, but the funny thing is that it was the

Kon-Tiki journey across the Pacific Ocean that brought me to Cuba. When the Revolution of 1959 was over, the first book published in Cuba was the *Kon-Tiki*, published by Fidel Castro, in a pirate edition, of course, as he himself laughingly admitted when we met.

Whilst still living in Colla Micheri, I kept on getting dinner invitations from the Cuban embassy in Rome, but it was a long trip from my little village in northern Italy to the capital, so I had every reason to turn down these invitations. I didn't really understand the embassy's interest in me, and suspected that it was based on political motives. Little did I know that Fidel was behind it. One of his main interests in life was the ocean, and he had built a well-equipped ocean research ship.

One day the Cuban ambassador visited a small town on the peninsula where I lived. Could I meet him for dinner? As it was only four minutes away, I could hardly refuse. He was waiting at the restaurant table with a senior member of the Cuban Foreign Office, who was visiting Europe. During the aperitifs they placed a tape recorder on the table between us, and on behalf of Fidel Castro they invited me to visit Cuba. The microphone was switched on, and I answered that I had been to Cuba during the Batista era, the year before the *Kon-Tiki* expedition. En route for New York, I had been a passenger on a cargo ship that was re-routed to Cuba, and I was put ashore in Santiago de Cuba. The owner of the shipping line, my good friend Thomas Olsen, got his agents to provide me with train tickets across the country to Havana, and put me up at a first-class hotel while I waited for the first available seat on a plane to New York.

I had never seen worse poverty or misery or greater contrasts than when I entered the luxury hotel. Even in the lobby I was run down by a countless number of uniformed piccolos, all wanting to carry my solitary suitcase and openly competing to show me photo albums of beautiful ladies. When I tried to slip away, they sidled up to me, wanting to know if I preferred young seven- or eight-year-old girls.

Still speaking into the microphone, I accepted the invitation, hoping to see a changed Cuba.

Yvonne was a typical Oslo girl, and she had friends and relations there. She looked upon our property in Italy as a holiday home, but I insisted that it was our permanent base. In the years following the *Kon-Tiki* expedition, I had travelled alone, as Yvonne could not join me on the numerous sea voyages. This left her in Colla Micheri with our daughters, Anette, Marian and Bettina, wonderful children who kept us together, even when we started to slip apart. My long and frequent absences were probably the main reason that the marriage to Yvonne came to an end. She was a model of patience, but in the long run it was difficult to live with a man who was rarely at home and who was often risking his life. Disagreements on how to bring up our children also played their part, as in so many marriages. I played the strict guardian of morality, but played the role poorly as an absentee. I must take the entire blame for our separation.

For Yvonne, Colla Micheri turned into a wonderful holiday home, while I once again travelled out into the world.

At this time, the bond between Yvonne and myself severed, I met Liliana, who would be part of my life for several years, until I finally left Europe and settled permanently in Peru. With her raven-black hair and her warm, southern eyes, there could not have been a greater contrast to Liv and Yvonne. Her background was exotic. Her great-grandfather had been an Indian trader who ran a caravan route between Calicut in India and Carthage in Tunisia. His son married the daughter of a Berber chieftain, and Liliana's mother was their child. She ran away when her father, a rabbi, refused her permission to marry an Italian Catholic. Liliana was born on Italian soil, and when I met her looked like a fantasy figure from *A Thousand and One Nights*. I was not alone in my opinion. Princess Caroline of Monaco, who later became her friend, said: 'You're like the real princess in a fairy tale. I only have the title.'

Liliana was with me when I went to Cuba for my first visit to Fidel Castro.

After arriving, we were driven to a house in the outskirts of old Havana, near a lake and in the middle of beautiful gardens. It was in a wealthy residential area, the houses having belonged to old families who chose to leave when Castro came to power. We lived in one of the residences that had been fitted out for official guests to the country. I was to meet Fidel Castro in his office the next morning.

As we entered the house, the wind picked up outside, growing ever stronger, scattering twigs and branches and whipping them into the air. Then came the rain. It was a terrible storm. People came in and taped the windows – a hurricane was expected. Liliana went into the bedroom, climbed into bed, and drew the quilt over her head. Suddenly the door flew open, and a huge man, wearing a sou'wester and full rain gear appeared. He greeted us and introduced himself as Chomi. El Commandante wondered if we would like to see the hurricane from a car. I asked myself who this Commandante might be, thinking of course that it might be Castro. So I replied that if El Commandante thought it was safe – surely he would not have invited me if it wasn't – then I would be pleased to come. We drove off.

Cuba had been hit by hurricane Kate. Whole trees lay across the streets and we constantly had to turn around to find new routes. Finally we arrived at the mole in the old city, where the waves usually break against the promenade. But now it was impossible to tell where the ocean ended and land began; everything was flooded. Again and again the car got bogged down in the mud, and we had to get out and push, in the sea-spray and pouring rain. Chomi said we would have to give up, we couldn't get any further. He wondered if I wanted to come home with him for a cup of coffee. I thought it would be interesting to see how a Cuban driver lived, and accepted the offer.

All the high-tension wires and masts were down, and there were no lights in any windows. We parked in front of a brick wall by a low house, where we rang the bell and knocked on the door. An old lady appeared with a candle and invited us to come in. First a small hallway, then through a small room with all sorts of strange things on the walls, then through a large room, and here there was no end to all the strange objects, huge pictures, photographs of Fidel, curiosities from around the world dedicated to Fidel, and pottery from different pre-European periods from Peru and Mexico. As I was shown into another room, I suggested that this was the home of a well-travelled intellectual.

'No, I'm not an intellectual. I'm a doctor. I'm El Commandante's private doctor and accompany him on all his travels. He keeps his souvenirs here.'

We finally came into a cosy living room with big, comfortable chairs and a pleasant atmosphere. The sweet woman, who turned out to be Chomi's wife, asked me to sit down.

'I'm sorry,' I answered, 'but I can't sit, I'm soaked through.'

'Maybe you want to borrow a pair of dry trousers from my husband?'

And then I was guided back into the hallway and shown into a little toilet with the aid of a flashlight. I was handed the dry clothing, and closed the door. Off with my own soaked trousers and on with the dry ones. However Chomi was somewhat of a giant, so it was impossible to keep them above my hips and I had no belt. I clutched them with one hand, and went back out with a smile. As I entered the hallway, the front door was opened by the lady of the house and in strode Fidel Castro, wearing a uniform and cap and with a full beard, just as he looked in his pictures. We stood there, face to face, and then Fidel opened his arms to embrace me. I couldn't let go, but tried to embrace him with one arm.

That was my first meeting with Fidel.

Castro asked immediately if Chomi knew how the botanical garden had fared. Chomi had nothing to report because all Cuba's telephones were dead. He was ordered to go out and take a look; I could go with him if I wanted. Then Castro disappeared.

The storm had died down and we drove on and on until we were miles outside Havana. We came to an enormous complex, a mixture of a nature park and the most marvellous botanical garden I had ever seen. The amazing complex was totally undamaged, as it had not been in the direct path of the hurricane.

'This will please him,' Chomi said. 'Next to the ocean research vessel, this botanical garden is his great hobby.'

When we had checked that everything was in good order, I was driven back to the guest house. The next morning Chomi reappeared in our doorway. The whole country was in chaos. The meeting at the office was cancelled. El Commandante was to inspect the damage after the hurricane, and wondered if I wanted to come along. 'Bring your toothbrush and clean underwear and come immediately.'

I ran in to Liliana and said that I would be back soon.

With Chomi at the wheel we raced away. We were part of a four-car escort: police or military in the first car, Fidel in the second, ourselves in the third and another escort car at the rear. For three continuous days I was as close to El Commandante Fidel Castro as anyone could be. The destruction was awesome. The hurricane had raged along the entire southern coast of Cuba and hardly a dwelling or an industrial complex had escaped damage or destruction.

The first night we slept in a Nissen hut belonging to the army. Early next morning, Fidel was waiting outside the shack where we were supposed to eat. He refused to enter before his guests. When we sat down I saw that five glasses had been placed in front of Fidel's place. The rest of us had only one glass each. I asked if he was planning to use all five. We were going to drink goat's milk from an agricultural college, Fidel explained, and he wanted to judge which type of goat gave the best milk. I told him that as a child I was raised on nothing but goat's milk.

'Then you shall also judge,' he said, and I was given five glasses. The two of us sat there like wine connoisseurs, tasting the goat's milk. The difference was small, but I made my choice, which happened to be the same as his. All that was left was to finish breakfast and race on.

I will always remember visiting the fishing village where all the small wooden houses had been destroyed. People ran back and forth in all directions, calling 'El Commandante, El Commandante'. There was no end to the enthusiasm. We jumped out of our cars and went to see where the destruction was worst. An old woman was clutching her small radio. It was broken, and Fidel gave her a big, comforting hug. Her face lit up and she said: 'Now it doesn't matter that I've lost everything. I've met El Commandante.'

We stopped at a brick house, and Fidel gathered the local leaders in the attic to discuss matters in the light of a guttering candle. The ground floor was one big chaotic mess. It was like being back at the front in Finnmark, the same spirit of co-operation in times of catastrophe. Fidel worked through the night organising his countrymen.

'How many trucks can you get over there, and there? Where is the closest cement supply? How many bags?'

And so it went on. He had an ability to organise and to give orders that made people flock around him, eager to fight for a common cause.

In the evening of the third day we reached a small airstrip, and he, Chomi and I flew back to Havana.

During my first visit I discovered that, owing to the country's scientific isolation, little was known of Cuba's archaeology. This led me to work with local archaeologists, and it resulted in many visits and meetings with Castro.

I came to look upon Fidel as a rather unusual dictator. He lived in extreme simplicity; no one knew exactly where, but I assumed it was in the area where we ourselves were staying. I have dined with him and his closest friends countless times, but never with a politician or military person as a fellow guest. His circle of friends consisted of artists, authors and scientists. His private parties were always held at Chomi's, where I'd first met El Commandante, as I struggled to keep my trousers from falling down.

We often had to wait for dinner until ten or eleven, because he worked virtually around the clock. Every once in a rare while a message would arrive at around midnight, telling us to start without him, while cold food was sent to his office.

Even Castro's keenest opponents recognised his great contribution to the country's schools and health-care system. Once when I was in Cuba, long before the Pope's visit, I was amazed to learn that this communist had made it possible for Catholic nuns to work in hospitals. When I asked him about this, he answered quietly: 'Many old people in the hospitals feel a sense of comfort when they are visited by the nuns.'

I failed to persuade Castro to receive his former colleague, ex-communist Mikhail Gorbachev, but he did agree to meet Norway's arch capitalist, Knut Kloster. Kloster had bought the giant ship *France* shortly before this meeting, and now he planned to build the largest passenger ship in the world, *The World*. He dreamed of routing it between Miami and Havana, in order to build a bridge between the United States and Cuba.

Fidel's favourite meal was spaghetti with tomato sauce and parmesan, and Liliana always brought a rich supply when we came from Italy. It was over a spaghetti dinner in his own guest house that Castro first met the Norwegian shipping magnate. After the meal, when Kloster unfolded the drawings for this incredible ship, Castro was clearly just as impressed as I was. When the two of them started discussing whether profits from arrivals and docking should be distributed to Cuba's hotels or the local port authority, I had trouble figuring who was the capitalist and who was the communist. The two ended up lost in a conversation about religious mysteries, but when they started on the question of the origin of life, galaxies and the Big Bang, I suggested with a smile that they return to earth.

Kloster continued with his giant ship-building plans, but the bridge across the Florida Straits remained a dream.

My small attempt to build a bridge between scientists on both sides of the same strait was more concrete. In spite of the blockade, I brought two American archaeologists to Cuba for a meeting with El Commandante, and this led to a five-year contract for archaeological co-operation between the Carnegie Institute and the University of Havana. The first result of this co-operation was the book *Art and Archaeology of Pre-Columbian Cuba*, written in partnership between two American and two Cuban archaeologists, with an introduction by myself.

In the 1980s I kept travelling back and forth between my research studies in Cuba and excavations on Easter Island. One day, while waiting for a ride to the airport with my packed suitcase, the door suddenly opened and revealed the towering, well-known character with a beard and a green uniform. He sat down and asked for a cup of coffee.

'Where are you going now?' he asked when he saw the suitcase.

'To Easter Island,' I answered.

'Hmm,' he said and stroked his beard. 'Then you mustn't tell them you have come from Cuba. Easter Island belongs to Chile and the governor is married to Pinochet's daughter.'

'No,' I answered. 'The governor is a friend of Pinochet's daughter, but he is in fact married to an American woman. He is, by the way, an archaeologist himself and my closest associate on the island. He knows very well that I'm coming from Cuba.'

Fidel was pleasantly surprised and asked if I thought the governor would appreciate a case of Havana cigars, but I wasn't certain that Sergio smoked. Then he asked, 'Does he drink?'

'Yes, of course.'

At that, Fidel sent for a bottle of Havana Club from the kitchen. The driver who was responsible for getting me to the airport on time grew visibly nervous. When the bottle arrived, Castro grabbed his fountain pen and wrote on the label:

'Best regards to the governor of Easter Island from Fidel Castro.'

I barely managed to get the bottle into my hand luggage

before we raced off to the airport, a stopover in Panama and then on to Santiago de Chile.

I got all the way to Easter Island without anyone examining my hand luggage. The governor had arranged a reception with hula dancers and a party at the hotel, and I only just had time to deposit my luggage before he approached me with a whisky glass in his hand. I remembered the gift and asked him to come into the room, where I gave him the bottle and told him to read the label. Before I realised what was happening, I heard a crash and saw pieces of glass and liquid flying in all directions. That was the end of the gift from Fidel, I thought. But it was the whisky glass that the governor had dropped. He held the bottle of rum from Castro with both hands.

'When you return to Cuba,' he said in jest, 'you'll have to take a case of Chilean red wine from Pinochet to Castro.'

I reminded him of that when I was leaving, but he smiled and said that he doubted if Pinochet's sense of humour was as sophisticated as Fidel's.

13

In the Garden of Eden

We were up in the mountains in Tenerife and could see the blue ocean curve like a giant circle in all directions, and we realised that neither the planet nor we who live on it had changed dimensions over the ages. We think we have made our world smaller because we travel fast to save time. But in former times people could afford to travel slowly. They were rich in time.

Around the year 1200, when Iceland's Snorre Sturlason wrote the *Sagas of the Kings* using a quill pen and parchment, three centuries were yet to pass before the vast royal empires of the Aztecs and the Incas were known to Europeans. But the horizons of Snorre's geography were not limited to the coast of Iceland. He recorded the geography of his time in detail, from the Norse colony in Greenland and its discovery of Vinland in the far northwest of the Atlantic Ocean, to the coasts of Africa in the south, and the Black Sea and the Caucasus mountains bordering Asia. While he was in Iceland and recording his own historical and geographical knowledge, his forefathers' descendants in Norway were still engaged in trading expeditions, Viking raids and pilgrimages throughout this enormous area. The ocean was unobstructed by borders and limitations. Thousands of years earlier, the same ocean had enticed others to take a look at the world. From the day humans learned to build means of transportation that could float, the continental coastlines became points of departure, and navigable rivers led inland through virgin forest and wilderness. Humans learned to paddle and sail before they learned to saddle a horse or discovered the wheel.

In 1977, once again I tempted fate on the ocean, on a fourth raft journey, and this was the longest journey of them all; five months and eleven men aboard a reed boat, from Iraq to the mouth of the Indus, and across the Indian Ocean from Asia to Africa.

Seven years earlier, with an untrained crew recruited from around the world, we had sailed from Africa to America aboard the papyrus reed boat *Ra II* without losing as much as a single reed. We arrived however, with a vessel so waterlogged that barnacles grew on deck and sharks could virtually swim aboard. During the last week we spent most of our time on the roof of the bamboo hut, consoling ourselves with the thought that the papyrus bundles might be saturated, but they were still capable of carrying us. We could have kept afloat for weeks, with the deck at the same level as the surface of the water, but we pulled the waterlogged raft ashore when we arrived in Barbados and freighted it off to Oslo, where it joined the *Kon-Tiki* balsa raft.

Something must have been wrong with *Ra II*. The ingenious pyramid builders from antiquity would not have persisted in building reed vessels for hundreds of years if they hadn't succeeded in keeping the cargo dry on deck. Mythological motifs of god-like forefathers navigating reed ships at sea are depicted on the oldest temple walls in Mesopotamia, Egypt and Peru, on insignia seals from the oldest seafaring cultures of the Indus valley, and on ceremonial bronze drums from the oldest known dynasty in China. In the Middle East these reed ships are so large that there are one or two cabins on deck in addition to horned cattle and a large crew. In China they are also depicted with royalty and crew on board, and all the details are as realistic as in Egypt. The pre-Inca culture in Peru often shows these motifs with the king and his court on the upper deck, and on the lower deck a line of prisoners and water mugs lashed down with rope.

But what did they do to prevent the reed bundles from becoming waterlogged?

That is what I wanted to find out when I built my third reed ship, *Tigris*.

I found all the papyrus I needed to build my first two reed ships near the source of the Nile in Ethiopia, and I found experienced reed-boat builders from Lake Chad in Central Africa and Lake Titicaca in South America. But reed boats on Lake Chad and Lake Titicaca were pulled into the shallows or on to dry land after a fishing trip. No one had any idea of how long a reed boat would float. In the academic world, the floating limit of the reed ship was estimated at about two weeks, like that of a balsa raft. From our own experience we knew that in both cases the theoreticians had been mistaken. Both balsa raft and reed ship can transport people across the ocean, but no one could tell us what the reed-boat builders of old had done to improve the buoyancy of the reed.

Is it possible for people to forget something they have known for thousands of years?

I had to ask the Marsh Arabs in Iraq for an answer. I went to the Madan people who still lived undisturbed in the land of their forefathers, the land the Greeks called Mesopotamia, the land between the rivers. While the rest of Iraq had become desert, these people lived on floating reed islands at the confluence of the Euphrates and the Tigris, where the river flows into the Persian Gulf. The generals ruled the country with a firm hand from Baghdad, but in the infinite marshes, where the two rivers meet, and where, according to both the Bible and the Koran, the Garden of Eden was situated, life was as peaceful as it had been at the time of the Sumerians. There were no roads into the reed marshes and no television antennae to announce the presence of people. Only along the bank of the river was there evidence of life. Hidden from the world at large and concealed in a swamp of about 15,000 square kilometres, the Marsh Arabs had managed to preserve the culture of their forefathers for five thousand years, undisturbed by the upheavals of history in the rest of the planet.

Two British explorers, Thesiger and Young, had recently come out of the marsh area with reports of almost Biblical conditions. Neither rock nor clay were available in the swamps, so the Madan people built their beautiful dwellings with artistically woven bundles of reed, according to models depicted in art from the age of the Sumerians. In antiquity, the whole of Iraq was criss-crossed by large and small channels for navigation and irrigation. The Sumerians' first king arrived in these plains accompanied by his followers on board large reed ships, and according to their own written history, built the first capital, Ur. According to archaeological datings this was around 3100 BC. There are many indications that this was also the birth of civilisation in Egypt.

In spite of the fact that there has been human life on earth for two million or maybe three million years, civilisations sprang up, simultaneously and apparently suddenly, and in a fully developed form, along the riverbanks in Egypt and in Mesopotamia, on either side of the Arabian peninsula. And in the nearest neighbouring valley to the east, along the banks of the Indus River, the Indus civilisation developed at the same time. The three oldest known civilisations first saw light simultaneously and bore striking resemblances: worship of the sun, pyramid-building, city-planning and adobe dwellings, complex forms of metallurgy, writing, and everything that characterises civilisation on an impressive technical and cultural level. And they all depicted their first kings as seafarers who arrived from mythical homelands on large reed ships.

Initially, the three fertile river valleys enjoyed a period of power in early antiquity, but then the large navigable channels disappeared in Mesopotamia, the landscape dried up and was eventually buried in sand dunes, and the influence of the Sumerians, the Babylonians and the Assyrians waned. As memorials to the transience of culture, ruins of the palaces and temples from the golden era protrude from an endless desert surrounding the green marshes and the clusters of date palms and gardens around the cities and along the riverbanks.

When I first arrived in this area in the early 1970s to seek permission to travel into the marshes, a revolution had just taken place in Iraq after the fall of royalty and the cessation of British influence. Two generals had established a dictatorship as leaders of the pan-Arab Bath party, and the borders were closed to tourists. I received a visa at the Iraqi embassy in Rome owing to my status as a researcher and because on my first visit I had brought along an entrepreneur from Mexico who imported machines from communist China. In the eyes of the Iraqi ambassador, China was then the real paradise.

We were warmly received by the archaeologists at the museum in Baghdad, where we had a great deal to learn both from them and from the rich collection of Sumerian reed-boat models, as well as descriptions and pictures on clay tablets and Sumerian cylinder seals. We were invited to lunch with the two generals who enthusiastically welcomed the idea that I build a new reed boat and set sail from their country. They made strict conditions with regards to the nationalities I could bring into the country to join the voyage, but withdrew these when I implied that I actually had a choice of starting point; either in Iraq, or in Iran, which was on the opposite bank and further down the same Tigris River. They settled the matter by suspending passport and customs regulations, and granted me permission to travel into the marshes to meet the inhabitants and find help to build the reed ship.

I have never met people quite like the Marsh Arabs. I got on with other Arabs in the country, but my friendship with one of the generals, Saddam Hussein, who later assumed complete power, was to come to an abrupt end. I was grateful that he had made it possible for me to meet a people who had lived untroubled lives in harmony with nature and their neighbours for thousands of years. Little did I know that this very same general would later brutally order the draining of the marshes, thereby destroying the basis of life for the Madan people. In addition, when I later burned the *Tigris* and pleaded with the United Nations to restore peace in the region, his fury knew no limit. *Tigris'* crew of eleven, who had lived together peacefully for five months, claimed that if the arms shipments to the Middle East were stopped, people around the Gulf and the Red Sea would be forced to fight with clubs and swords as in the olden days. This did not please the general.

When I met Saddam Hussein, I was unbiased. I only knew that he wielded tremendous power. I must admit that when we first had lunch together, he made such a small impression on me – as a person – that I only recall that the food was good and he supported my project.

As an assembly point for the construction crew and the large amount of reed needed, we were allowed to stay in an abandoned inn called the Garden of Eden, which lay on dry ground on the banks of the Tigris, immediately before it joins the Euphrates and the marsh area begins. A stone's throw from the house was a cluster of date palms and a few leafy green trees arched over the river. Between them a huge moss-covered tree stump was fenced in as if it were a holy site. It was covered with candle drippings. According to ancient records, this was the spot identified by Jews, Christians and Muslims as the birthplace of Adam and Eve. A sign with a text in Arabic and English left no doubt that this tree-stump was the remains of the Tree of Knowledge, and Abraham himself had come here to pray. We were treading on historical ground, biblical as well Islamic.

The trip down the quiet river, from the wooden tree-stump by the Garden of Eden to the confluence of the rivers by Qurna and the marsh area, was not a long one. We immediately realised why the people who lived in the compact brush of tall berdi-reeds had been allowed to live in peace, without border signs or defensive weapons. No one could enter the area without a knowledge of the labyrinth of canals that were often completely invisible. The water level was so shallow that not even a raft could float; if one tried to wade, one sank through the peat-filled bed of the marsh. This would also be the case for horses' hooves and camels, as well as tanks. Neither the Assyrians' war fleet, Alexander the Great's army nor the mechanised troops of the world wars had managed to disturb the peace of the Madan people. It would be the general in Baghdad who outmanoeuvred the marsh people by pulling the reed carpet from under their feet.

Travelling in the marshes took me back to the time before the invention of the wheel, before street noise and antennas numbed the mind, and streetlight blocked out the stars.

With an interpreter from the museum in Baghdad, I was picked up from the riverbank just south of Qurna, where the deep water came to an end. Two Marsh Arabs in long, white robes stood upright in a slender canoe and punted their way forwards with long poles with slow, calm strokes. After the simple greeting, which consisted of placing a hand on the heart, the interpreter and I were seated in the bottom of the narrow *mashuf* to keep it stable, while the two barefoot men in their wingless angel outfits punted us away from our world and into theirs. The reeds closed behind us in the wake of the canoe, higher than a standing man could see. Further into the marsh, the canals were sometimes both wider and deeper, and surprisingly the water was crystal clear, not muddy or brown as it was in the rivers. Green plants grew on the bottom, and in the clear, shallow water fish swam, while long garlands of crow's-foot snaked along the surface. We glided silently forward between dense walls of reed and cat's-tail, and for every slow push of the punt we felt that we were further on our way into the past; not towards barbarism and insecurity, but towards a culture just as removed from the age of the apes as our own, only safer and less complicated. When we reached the first settlement, my Arabian interpreter was just as moved as I was.

Initially only a few thin, scattered columns of smoke indicated that people lived in the marshes. We saw no trace of human litter, and not a single roof to reveal where the inhabited area began. There were no mounds or stones to stand on, to provide a view beyond the reeds, and the mud bottom gave way like a mattress. We saw geese and duck and wildfowl of all colours and sizes paddling fearlessly around as if guns had not yet been invented. A solitary eagle circled over us from the lifeless desert, and an ice bird, on its migration, perched and swayed in the reeds in company with countless smaller, wonderfully multicoloured birds. Tall, snow-white cranes and red-beaked storks stood like sentinels, motionless among the stalks, and fat pelicans scooped up fish with their large beaks. Once we saw a bushy, coal-black wild boar push its way through in heavy leaps between the swaying stalks. And when we closed in on the settlement, mighty water buffaloes met us, wading lazily, their broad, black backs glistening like wet seal fur in the sun. They stopped to stare at us, waved their wide ears and thin tails patiently to chase away the flies, and continued uninterrupted to chew the green watergrass that hung from their mouths.

Then suddenly the first houses appeared, a revelation in total harmony with nature. They blended into the surroundings as naturally as a bird's nest in the reeds. With no other building material to hand, everything was built from reeds. The only solid ground that gave anchorage to a few date palms was on the outskirts of the marshes. House-building in the marshes called for large amounts of reed for the foundation. The canals often debouched into small open lakes where reed houses were built on floating islands, artificially constructed of thick layers of reed that had to be replenished from above as the lower layers rotted and sank. Walls and roofs of large and small houses curved in harmonious arches from side to side. Compact bundles of reed were bent elegantly into rows of rib-like curves and covered with thick mats of reed. Not one piece of wood, not one nail; everything was tied together with reed fibres. All the houses had the same shape, whether small overnight shelters, spacious homes, or huge assembly halls resembling hangars, with ceilings so high that one could barely reach them with a punting pole.

This enchantingly beautiful architecture had survived in the marshes from the time of the Sumerians, each abode built as a small temple to honour the past, afloat in its own golden-grey reflection on blue water and an eternal blue sky. The surprisingly transparent water flowed slowly towards the Gulf and, to keep the building foundations from moving, they were fenced in with palisades of bamboo-like reeds stuck into the silt. The islands and the reed houses rose and sank within the palisades as the water level changed with the seasons. The slender *mashuf* punts created a Venetian landscape.

Some of the floating islands were so small that with the main house and the water buffalo barn, they looked like houseboats, or Noah's Ark, with just enough room left to walk around the perimeter. A Marsh Arab cannot take many steps before he has to get into a canoe. Deep in the marshes, in the open lakes, floating Madan families gently swayed on reed mattresses together with their buffalo, duck and hens, and when the owners opened the gates of the hangar-shaped barns, the buffalo rolled into the water with the duck to swim to their grazing grounds, while the shepherd paddled his canoe.

I spent the night in the home of a sheik, where a gravel road ran out, leading to the Madina ferry landing. He had organised the journey into the marshes, but first he served me a breakfast I will never forget. Coffee, tea, fresh buffalo milk, yogurt, egg, lamb, chicken, dates, Arabian bread, cakes and jam. I barely managed to stumble down to the riverbank and squeeze into the narrow *mashuf* that would take me to Om-el-Shuekh, deep in the marshes. This was the home of Hagi, the oldest man the sheik knew. According to the sheik, if anyone could remember the vessels of the past it was Hagi, because he was more than one hundred years old.

As we glided out of the reed and crossed open water toward this old chieftain's abode, I was not expecting much from the memory of such an old man. And my optimism did not increase when I saw that he looked like Methuselah, wearing a white robe and with a long white beard, sitting in front of his huge floating residence. When I jumped ashore with the interpreter from Baghdad, his island rocked beneath our feet. It was like standing on a hammock, and we swayed and grabbed for support while the man rose and walked briskly toward us.

As he greeted me with both hands, touched his heart and wished me peace, I looked into eyes that were so wise and friendly that time and place disappeared. He obviously deserved the great respect he was shown by the men who eventually arrived and sat down on the floor with us, in two rows along the side of the huge hall. With legs crossed, we sat and listened to the wisdom and wit of old Hagi, while the embers were stoked and tea was served. There was no electric wiring here, but the stars in the sky winked at us through the archway opening and the flickering fire caused shadows to dance on the walls.

Large fish were sliced open, folded out like huge butterflies, and placed on end on the flames. The fish was brown and crispy on the outside but white and juicy inside, and it was rolled into oven-heated Arabian bread as thin as pancakes. It was so delicious that I ate as if the sheik in Madina had starved me. The wise old man paid attention to everything and made certain that the man at my side served me the best pieces of fish and fed me like a five-year-old prince. True to custom, a man came around with soap and a towel after the meal and poured a stream of warm water over a basin so each of us could wash our hands.

Hagi made excuses for the simple meal, as if he had not noticed my appetite, and spoke of an even better meal in the future if I promised to return. I promised, and I did return, knowing that I had to. Good meals are one of the highlights of life, and not least of expeditions.

This was not the only reason I enjoyed life with the people of the reed marshes. I had lived with so-called primitive people in Polynesia, America and Africa, but these Marsh Arabs were not primitive in any sense of the word. They were civilised, though in a different way to us. As people, we were totally alike, both physically and spiritually. The road back to our mutual ancestors in the wilderness was equally long. It was our way of living that had changed, the daily existence of traffic jams and computers that earned us our daily bread. In our form of civilisation there was no one who, like Hagi and his people, lived in the midst of their food supply. The more we remove ourselves from nature, the more complicated our existence, and the more difficult to bring fish and potatoes from rivers and fields to the dining table. We have managed to complicate everything that was once simple in our existence, and we try to mend our ways with traffic rules and computer programs, with doctors who get paid for repairing damage caused by a poor diet and lack of exercise, with lawyers to lead us through the jungle of laws and regulations. We race on with beating hearts and screeching wheels, finding vicarious thrills through sex and excitement on television, experiencing life through watching the lives of others. We believe we are rich when we have money in the bank.

'We're not poor,' old Hagi said, who owned no more than the mat he sat on. 'Our pride is our wealth. And no one in the marshes starves.'

These people had an inner wealth. They envied no one. This is why their culture had survived, while the Assyrian,

Persian, Greek and Roman civilisations that had flourished around them had disappeared. These centuries of stability bear witness to qualities that we lack: a respect for our forefathers and confidence in the future. We think that we have created the first lasting civilisation, but we cannot stop to think, we just go on and on. We build without plans, and in so doing, new problems arise. Stress, juvenile delinquency, unemployment, the arms race, terrorist activity, overpopulation, climatic changes, decreasing resources and increasing pollution of air, water and earth.

In fact, we might be happiest when on holiday, when we can escape stress and the trivialities of daily life. This is when *we* turn to God's great outdoors, and go fishing and hunting. Then we pity people we call primitive because they have to live in this way all the year round.

Hagi sat there nursing his hundred years, dignified, safe and satisfied, poking the cinders from the reed fire that had flamed up on the clay hearth in the middle of the floor. No one here was missing anything they didn't know existed. The old man entertained us with tales of his experiences and his sense of humour. The fire shone on the faces of rows of silent Arabs, clad in kaftans and capes, sitting attentively between columns of reed along the wall. An elegant Arab teapot was passed in front of me, and when the tea was poured into small glasses edged in silver, the aromatic fragrance titillated my nostrils.

I looked around the large and airy building that was the old man's guest house. The ceiling was high, in every sense of the word, and seven strong reed bundles, thicker than a human body, arched elegantly from floor to ceiling and back down on the other side. Like parallel ribs they bore a tight covering of braided reed mats. I felt as if I were sharing Jonah's experiences in the whale's stomach, but this whale opened at both ends and had a gilt-edged view to a twinkling night sky. I wondered what the Marsh Arabs thought about the world out there.

As if Hagi had been reading my thoughts, he said that he had once been to Baghdad, and that when he was there he deeply missed the peace and safety of Allah's marshes. In his opinion the city bred greed, envy and dishonesty. In the marshes no one steals, he said. Everyone has what they need, and no one has more than necessary. Praise Allah. The buffalo had enough fodder, there were masses of fish to spear, and chickens, duck and wildfowl; boats filled with watermelons, braided reed mats and baskets from the marshes were exchanged for supplies of flour and tea.

In addition – and the old, wise man lifted his hand in a blessing – there were beautiful women here. He himself had four wives. Along the walls there was merry whispering, acknowledging his zest for life. The old man with the long white beard knew what he was talking about.

As we all know, we should not succumb to temptations in the Garden of Eden, but on one occasion I was with the expedition's Mexican mechanic on a bridge by the outskirts of the marshes. He shared my sense of all that is beautiful and well formed, and when a beautiful woman came paddling past in a canoe he got out his camera. What he did not see, but I did, was a man with a raised spear running toward us as fast as he could with his long robe flowing behind him. I had to tear the camera away from the photographer, who only had eyes for the woman. We ran for our lives and left the beauty to her guardian.

The women were quite well guarded in the marshes. They were not allowed to eat with us, not even to serve tea. As if to protect those of Adam's gender from falling for a severely punishable temptation, they were robed in black. Only their faces and beautiful feet were visible when one from time to time caught glimpses of shadows gliding between the reed curtains or when they fed the chickens, sat in a canoe or baked bread. In the marshes the flat bread was baked with a dough that the women flattened against the inner walls of the round clay ovens, which were open at the top like a jar. If one was attracted by the fine aromas issuing from the ovens, one had to be quick to catch a glimpse of more than two sparkling eyes and teeth that shone like virgin snow in the sun before the woman managed to turn her head away or pull the black cloth over her nose. The women had the same fine, clean-cut profiles that characterised most of the Marsh Arabs. They were just as skilled as the men in paddling and punting large boats loaded with reed or reed mats, but they were only allowed to assemble together with the men, or to laugh and wave as we paddled past their dwellings, when they were either very young or very old.

The idea of whiling away the time or indulging in light entertainment had not reached them from the outside world, but smiles and laughter revealed that they got along well without it. Hagi was aware that we city-dwellers could not get by without earning money for a car and electricity. But he was not at all certain that his people would be any happier now that the government in Baghdad planned to bring electrical wiring and bricks for construction of houses into the marshes. When people are happy, they smile, he said. No one had smiled at him in the streets of Baghdad.

'There are too many people on the city streets,' I explained. 'One can't smile at everyone there.'

But Hagi had walked in streets where there were almost no people, and no one had smiled there either.

The arched reed bundles that held the roof and walls together in the chief's dwelling were exactly like those tied side by side to form the shape of *Ra II*. I had found people here who could make the necessary constructions to build a solid reed ship, but they had only used them to build houses on their floating islands. They themselves punted around in the shallows with the *mashuf* made of planks treated with asphalt. But if they could teach us the art of maintaining the buoyancy of the reed, then we could help the Marsh Arabs regain the lost art of their forefathers' forgotten boat construction from the Titicaca Indians.

When I first entered the marshes, I wondered if Hagi and his people would understand my plans. He was willing to listen. With his appearance and mien, he could have been a wealthy oil sheik, a former diplomat or a retired scientist. In his long white robe he looked more like a Biblical prophet or a patriarch, as timeless as the Sumerian reed house we were in. I felt as if I were with Moses or Abraham. Of course old Hagi must have experienced real reed boats.

And he had. Three types were in use when he was young. Two were hollow, like baskets, and stayed afloat because they were treated with asphalt both inside and out. One was the *guffa*, as round as a hide coracle from Ireland, and the other the *jillabie* with an extended structure, which was the forerunner of the plank-built *mashuf* they used today. Both had survived from ancient times, and I had seen models of these five-thousand-year-old boats in the museum in Baghdad and been aboard the last ones still in use on the river above Babylon. The third type was the *elep-urbati* and this one was not treated with asphalt because it was made of tight bundles of reeds without cavities, and stayed afloat by itself.

This was the reason I had come! But didn't the reed get waterlogged?

'Not if you cut it in the month of August,' Hagi assured us, and everyone around the walls nodded. It was a matter of general knowledge. Everyone in the marshes knew, but we who had cut papyrus reed by Lake Tana in Ethiopia in December for *Ra* and *Ra II* had not known. In August, during a full moon, a special sap in the reed prevented water saturation. There was nothing written about this in the textbooks, but then they are not always the best place to find answers.

14

In the Wake of Noah

I continued to relive Biblical history when, with ten companions from different countries, I made my way to the ocean from the Garden of Eden. From the legendary birthplace of Adam and Eve at the confluence of the Euphrates and Tigris rivers, we sailed out to sea where Noah had contributed a completely new chapter to the Christian and Muslim religious history. The story of Noah and the animals in the Ark who survived the Deluge had thrilled me as a child. The same fairy-tale atmosphere surrounded me when I saw the Marsh Arabs on the bank of the Tigris tying the enormous bundles of reed for our ark, which we had named after the river that would carry us to sea. Noah symbolised the world's oldest known boat-builder. In the dawn of seafaring, no ships were built with boards; Sumerian art shows both people and cattle on large reed boats.

There are no limits to the size of a ship that can be built

with bundles of reed, and there were unlimited amounts of reed in the marshes. We had crossed the Atlantic Ocean on *Ra II*, which was twelve metres long and had one cabin. The *Tigris* was eighteen metres long and had two cabins. In comparison to the pyramids and reed ships that were built for the most powerful Sumerian kings, we were launching a modest vessel in Noah's wake.

I will always think of the aging Hagi as the rightful successor to the Sumerian throne and the direct heir to the Garden of Eden. His dignity reflected an inner wealth and a time-honoured culture. Saddam, with his imported tanks in Baghdad, was protected by an arsenal of weapons as if he were a foreign soldier in a conquered country. His Arab fore-fathers had arrived in Mesopotamia victoriously with the teachings of the Koran, and taken possession of the ancient cultural centres of the Sumerians, the Babylonians and the Assyrians in order to redeem a promise from Our Lord to Abraham. When Abraham and his people came to the Mediterranean coast and the land of the Pharaohs on their journeys, according to the Bible and the Koran, he claimed that God had promised his family all the land between the Tigris and the Nile. Ostensibly this was the promise that the prophet Mohammed wanted to redeem many generations later; he even managed to extend the limits of the area to include the land both west of the Nile and east of the Tigris. However, when Abraham revealed God's promise to his descendants, he could not have foreseen that both Jews and Arabs would count him as their progenitor.

At the time when Abraham visited the tree-stump where the Arabs had built the inn called the Garden of Eden, it was easy to construct and equip a reed boat on the river bank. Reeds were as plentiful then as now, and they could build on centuries-old traditions in binding hundreds of reed bundles to achieve the same elegant shapes and lines as boats made of wood. From grave excavations, we knew that they had been expert in twining and braiding rope from fibres taken from the tough outer covering of the reeds. Farming, fishing and a lively trade up and down the rivers and into the Gulf had made it possible to load all the necessities on to a vessel at short notice, to hoist sail and cast off for a long voyage.

In modern times it was not that simple. As a result of the oil boom in Iraq the demand for consumer goods exceeded supply. The borders of the enemy country Iran ran down the centre of the river, and despite changing water levels and unpredictable sand banks, the line could not be crossed. Merchant ships were moored like sardines outside the river delta, waiting for weeks to move up the river and discharge their cargo. Merchandise that was unloaded in the ports along the Euphrates and Tigris was grabbed by local traders before it had time to reach the stores. No one could make rope anymore; rope-makers were as out-of-date as reed-boat builders, and the only people who had heard of the large Sumerian merchant ships, the *magurs,* were the scientists in the museum. Our shopping trips to Baghdad ended with empty baskets.

The art of building a sickle-shaped ship robust enough to maintain its shape in the open ocean, prepared the way for the development of seafaring in both the Middle East and South America. This art lives on at Lake Titicaca. When *Ra II* dried out in the Kon-Tiki Museum in Oslo, it became as flat as a pancake, and we had to cross the Atlantic again to find the same South American mountain Indians who had built it for us. The Indians from Lake Titicaca were the only ones who could put it back to its original shape, because neither scientist nor boat-builder today have any idea of the technique they used.

So the ancient barbarians possessed knowledge we don't have?

The Aymara Indians from Lake Titicaca were by no means primitive barbarians. Their ancestors in Bolivia had founded the outstanding Tiahuanaco civilisation, and built the Akapana pyramid that loomed over the plain by Lake Titicaca, just as impressively and in the same style as the pyramids in Mesopotamia and the oldest pyramid in Egypt.

The Aymara Indians had also made a statue of the bearded Kon-Tiki that we painted on the sail of our *Kon-Tiki*. The Incas gave him the symbolic name *Viracocha*, which means 'Foam on the Ocean', because he was a seafarer. After conquering all the ancient kingdoms in Peru and the neighbouring countries, they enlarged the name to *Con-Tiki-Viracocha*, because they found that the coastal Indians called the same legendary god-king Con while the Indians at Lake Titicaca called him Tici or Ticci. When the Spaniards arrived, the Aymara Indians in the Tiahuanaco area told them that this god had come to their ancestors with his retinue of white, bearded men and crossed the ocean in the same kind of reed boats that they themselves had learned to make. He claimed to be the son of the sun, and after arriving at Tiahuanaco, he built the large pyramid. He left just as he came. And throughout the whole Inca Empire, the Spaniards heard the same story that the Aymara Indians told me on the shore of Lake Titicaca four hundred years later. In the end, the divine priest-king moved on with his retinue to the north, all the way to what is today the republic of Ecuador. He then disappeared across the ocean, sailing westward from the coast by Manta.

It was easier said than done to invite the descendants of the god-kings to Iraq. August is the hottest month in the marshes, and the Aymara Indians live in cold mountain air on an island in Lake Titicaca, four thousand metres above sea level in the Andes. First, four of them had to be fetched by reed boat from their island. Then we had to find a place for them to live for two weeks in Bolivia's jungle in order to accustom them to the difference in air pressure and temperature. The next hurdle was to fly them to Baghdad in a plane that landed at night, in order that the car ride through the desert to the inn by the Garden of Eden would be over before the heat of the scorching sun proved too much. Only three of the four men could build reed boats, and they only spoke their native language. The fourth man was a Bolivian interpreter who would translate the mountain Indians' Aymara language into Spanish for me, so that I in turn could translate it further into English for my interpreter from Baghdad, who spoke Arabic to the leader of the Marsh Arabs, who then in turn translated it into their own Madan language.

It was an irony of destiny, I thought, that I should have to deal with these language problems on this very spot, not far from the ruins of the legendary Tower of Babel. When I visited the ruins, I found no more than a pathetic pile of sand, a few scattered clay bricks and a sign reading 'The Tower of Babel', erected by Iraqi archaeologists. It had probably been some sort of a step pyramid. I had now assembled a crew representing eleven different languages, and in addition I had twenty Marsh Arabs who only spoke Madan and who were to learn how to build a reed boat from three Indians who could only speak Aymara.

The Aymara Indians were allowed a long lie-in on the morning after their journey. I got a shock when I peeped into their room and found it empty.

They were already sitting outside with a group of Marsh Arabs in the shade of some date palms by Adam and Eve's tree-stump. They were still wearing their warm woollen hats and thick, colourful ponchos in contrast to the Arabs in their snow-white linen robes. They were nodding and pointing while they talked, and everyone had a handful of reeds. The interpreters simply stared at them. 'These señores are very wise,' the interpreter from Bolivia assured me when I walked over to him. 'They understand everything we tell them without understanding a word of what we're saying!'

'*Totora*,' he said to the ones dressed in white, holding up a reed.

'*Berdi*,' they answered, raising another one.

We never had to resort to the interpreters. The world's foremost experts on reeds had met one another. They were just as smart as the rest of us, but when it came to skills, life had made us experts in different areas.

The worst thing was that I needed experts in areas other than reed-boat building. Not a single sail-maker could be found in modern Iraq!

Modern Iraq had no sailcloth either; it was being trucked in from Europe. In the meantime I searched in vain for someone who could sew us a normal dhow sail, the typical sail for local vessels. No one had heard of anyone who could sew a sail in modern times. Sailing ships were just as outdated on rivers as camels were on highways. We were about a generation too late in Iraq.

I searched along the riverbanks all the way down to the Gulf and even crossed the border into Kuwait in the hope of finding an old-fashioned dhow with sails. The dhow had been a typical sailing vessel in these waters since time immemorial. The sail was most likely the transition between the first square sails of antiquity and the modern lateen sail. It looked like an old Egyptian sail hanging askew. When I first came to Iraq all the Arabs in the area had sawn off the masts of their dhows and installed outboards. Fuel was as cheap as the wind in the Gulf countries. However, I had seen white sails on Indian dhows that came all the way up to Basra to transport dates back to Bombay. This traffic had now ceased owing to smuggling, and I had to turn to the Indian consul in Basra and ask him to find three dhow sailors through the seamen's employment office in Bombay to help us sew a sail and then escort us out of the Persian Gulf, which was currently a nightmare of oil platforms and shipping.

The three dhow sailors were not on the plane we met in Baghdad, and a telegram from India confirmed that contact had been lost with them in New Delhi where they had gone to get Iraqi visas.

Two weeks later our local assistant Ali turned up at the breakfast table and reported that he had finally found the men. They were outside the door with their sacks, and one of them was called Saleman.

We tried all the European languages, as well as Arabic. Toru tried Japanese, and Yuri Russian, but only Saleman understood enough English to enable all three to sit down happily and enjoy a hearty meal.

After the meal their eyes filled with wonder when they saw the reed boat, with its impressive hull, glistening like gold in the morning sun. The shock came when Saleman wanted to know where the engine casing was to be built. No one at the seamen's office had said anything other than that the three of them would be sailing on a newly constructed dhow. They had never worked on a dhow with sails, and they had never been in the Gulf.

After a good deal of linguistic confusion, it became clear that co-operation with our new friends was confined to clearing the table after breakfast. We appointed Norman as our navigator and sail maker and he had the bright idea of taking the three new arrivals down to the harbour in Basra. There they could help him as interpreters and glean information about dhow sails from some of the Indian sailors who were anchored in the river. Yuri had managed to borrow a wonderful new Russian car from the Soviet consulate-general in Baghdad, and Norman drove happily off with the Indians on a main road crowded with trucks.

The next time we saw Norman he was standing in the doorway with his head wrapped in bandages. All that was visible was one ear and his nose, which was red and bruised.

'Where are the Indians?'

'They're being treated at the hospital.'

'What happened?' I asked horrified.

'The car turned over three times.'

'And the Arabian interpreter?'

'At the police station. He was driving.'

'And the Soviets' new car?'

'Upside down; a total wreck.'

When the three dhow men finally came limping back, one with an aching foot, the other with an aching head and the third with an aching back, they were not in the least bit hungry. They simply pleaded with me to send them back to India on the first available plane.

After this we were ready for our next surprise: this came in the form of a message that a man in European clothes was at the back of the house throwing sausages into the river.

I found a sunburnt man with a beetroot face looking totally disoriented. He was standing there in the heat throwing salami sausages into the river. I interrupted him carefully just as he heaved a huge chunk of ham into the water in the style of a hammer-thrower. He wiped his face and I had to nod in agreement, yes, this was a tough job in the midday heat. And then I heard his terrible story, which would affect us greatly. He was the truck driver who had come all the way from Hamburg with the wood for the mast and everything else we had ordered.

'Eine Katastrofe,' the man assured me in German. And I was in total agreement when I realised that it was our food supply that he was offering to the fish in the Tigris. While he was speaking I heard sharp noises coming from his truck. He calmed me down by saying it was the bamboo splitting in the heat. And then I saw an open case filled with tins of food that had grown to the size of cannon balls.

'Customs!' the German explained. Ali had to run and find a cold beer in the refrigerator before we could get another word out of him.

He was a special envoy from an excellent shipping company in Hamburg, sent with two drivers to make certain the cargo arrived at its destination quickly and safely. The truck was not refrigerated, so they drove continuously, taking turns in order to arrive within the fourteen-day limit. Everything went smoothly until they were in southern Turkey. Kurdish snipers along the country road had started shooting at them. Then they really stepped on the accelerator.

There were already bullet holes in the truck when they caught up with a large transport convoy that, like them, drove as fast as it could to reach the border with Iraq. In the confusion they had forgotten to obtain clearance from the customs officers at the Iraqi border, who were waiting for them with a special order from Baghdad requiring them simply to break open the seals. Instead they had just sped southward, into constantly warmer temperatures. They passed Baghdad, passed the detour to the Garden of Eden, and arrived at the crowded seaport of Basra. A friendly policeman gave them directions through the harbour area where all the ships were moored waiting to unload and clear customs, and suddenly they found themselves outside the customs and excise building without a shady place to park. The man claimed it was 45°C outside the truck and probably 70°C inside, and he assured us that both he and his two drivers almost died inside the truck on the third day in the customs yard. A friendly soul who spoke English had finally helped them to contact the ministry in Baghdad, who rescued them from their involuntary stay in Basra. The two drivers had disappeared straight back to Europe, and left him to deliver the cargo – which he did, in this peculiar manner.

'All the food is spoiled,' he assured us furiously. Before anyone could stop him, the last salami sailed out over the river.

At a bound our youngest crew member was over the terrace railing and in the river. He returned with a huge salami, cradling it like a baby in his arms, the only one. The rest had been swept away by the current.

The Garden of Eden was far from the ocean. In both Peru and Morocco, with the east winds behind us, we had been able to steer straight out to sea. This time our challenge was to manoeuvre the reed ship with the current along the border between Iraq and Iran and all the way to the Persian Gulf. Then we had to make it through the long, heavily congested Gulf and the Straits of Hormuz before reaching open sea.

Our first problem after the launch on the river was the heavily polluted water, which was even more polluted as we approached the delta. Large patches of white foam floated like loose ice on the surface, effluents from paper factories. Chemicals had transformed enormous amounts of reed into wood pulp. I had once been on board a giant reed raft on this same river, on my way down to a paper factory. A friendly Arab had invited me to tea in the reed hut on deck, where everything was made of reed except for an area of clay for burning dried stubs. The giant raft consisted of reeds placed loosely in layers criss-crossing one another, and I measured it: thirty-four metres long, five metres wide and drawing three

metres. It rode high on the water because the owner had cut
the reeds in August and he lived on board for two months,
waiting to deliver his reeds to the cellulose factory. On our current trip, the major fear was that our ark would dissolve and
end up as pulp before we reached the Gulf.

The fact that the fertile gardens of Eden and Babylon now
lie buried under desert sand is interpreted by some as the punishment of Our Lord and by others as a result of the Sumerian
over-cropping. But it is our own generation that has travelled
further down the Biblical rivers and smeared black oil on
golden sand and on every green blade of grass beside the river
delta. It looked more like a sewage outlet or the inside of a factory smokestack. Here Iran and Iraq were eyeing one another
like Cain and Abel across the river, competing how best to sac-
rifice virgin terrain to the oil pumps. Ships from east and west
were lined up at their moorings, either pumping oil or waiting
to move up the river with their cargo. Our aim was to sail
with the wind, through the chaos, and out into clean open sea.

In tropical waters there is an interplay between air currents
and ocean currents. Equatorial currents and trade winds keep
one another company from east to west all year round across
the Atlantic and the Pacific Oceans. The Indian Ocean differs
because the monsoons dominate, and the ocean current is
influenced by winds that blow from south to north in the six
summer months and from north to south in the six winter
months. This is the only ocean area in the world where currents change direction with the seasons. Arab and Indian
dhows took advantage of those varying tailwinds when they
sailed back and forth with their merchandise, in and out of the
Persian Gulf. The changes in the monsoon were part of
nature's clockwork, and just as reliable as the sun and the
moon.

But it seemed that the gods had deserted the Gulf area,

Allah as well as the weather gods. They cared little about maintaining old traditions and acted as though the age of the sailing ship had passed. The rainy season surprised us by appearing a month early in the Garden of Eden, and the Arabs in the area told us that the wind had been totally unpredictable for the past two years. In the Persian Gulf we thought we were in the doldrums, and that was not supposed to happen in November, when the north wind should have blown us straight out of the Gulf.

We had to make do with a few small gusts of wind. While sand had conquered the Sumerian fields and cities, sludge had transformed the whole coastline by forming endless banks of silt outside the harbours. They stretched out, invisible just beneath the water's surface, for many hundreds of square kilometres, all the way to Failaka Island off the coast of Kuwait. We ended up here, against our will, because we were trying to avoid the dangerous super-tankers that dominated the Gulf and could not navigate around us. Sudden and extreme gusts of wind from the south threatened to send us back towards Iraq and the shipping lane, and they drove us closer to the dangerous rocky coast of Failaka than we wanted to be.

One night the helmsman woke us up because he heard the sound of the surf. First we heard a deeper rhythmical undertone beneath the sizzling orchestra of regular ocean waves breaking around us. The sound increased and became a constant roar that came out of the night somewhere ahead of us; land; cliffs or reefs. We dropped anchor in the hope that it would take hold in the mud, but the rope and both anchors disappeared overboard simultaneously. We threw out another rope with a dredge – an open bag that was towed astern and reduced our speed. Luck was on our side; the water was so shallow that the anchor settled into the mire and stayed there until sunrise, by which time we were able to steer free of the reef that rose from the endless banks of mud. But we were even closer to the shallows along the coast of Failaka. No ship could navigate here, but we could have waded up to our knees if the bottom hadn't been a quagmire of soft mud.

We were in the innermost nook of the gulf; charts warned against pirates and the steep coasts of Failaka which were completely inaccessible, blocked by reefs and shallows. The only harbour on the huge island was on the other side.

And then the pirates really did appear, just like a fairy tale, as they must have appeared since the time of Sinbad and the Sumerians. They did not climb on to the reed ship brandishing swords; they did nothing, they just waited.

First we saw the lights of their kerosene lamps swaying between the cliffs on land, and we waved our own lanterns in response in the naive hope of being saved from the breakers that were thundering against the reef. With daylight we saw one small boat, and then another, dancing across the breakers between the reefs. Soon they both closed in, but never within bullet range. They hovered around us, and as far as we could see they did nothing but stare, knowing that we were drifting slowly toward the thundering breakers. It occurred to us that we were in bad company.

On our radio transmitter Norman made contact with a Russian voice from a Soviet ship that was anchored further up the Gulf. Yuri explained our precarious situation to the captain in his own language, and not many hours later we saw the outline of *Slavsk* anchored on the horizon, as close to the renowned Failaka banks as they dared. The captain himself and a full rescue crew with lifejackets came in over the shallows in a huge lifeboat.

After welcoming hugs, one of the Russians was able to haul our sea anchor out of the mud, but the increasing wind took such a hold on the reed-boat's light hull that we dragged the

Soviets with us toward the reef; the Russians were trying to pull us out toward *Slavsk* with their motorised lifeboat.

One of my crew who spoke Arabic, Rashad from Iraq, volunteered to row over to one of the threatening boats and explain that we had no propeller and would soon be wrecked against the reef.

Rashad returned and relayed the message that they wanted a substantial ransom in Kuwait currency. Otherwise they had time enough to wait for the inevitable.

I was ready to negotiate, but Captain Igor from *Slavsk* was furious and would not let me make a deal. He offered the pirates six bottles of vodka and two cases of wine. Rashad rowed over again, and came back with the message that the men were Muslims, and Allah forbade them to drink alcohol. With this, they moved a little further away, and stopped, ostensibly to fish. The other boat came within hailing distance, and Rashad explained that they had now doubled the price. Then they disappeared. The Russians refused to give up trying to tow us off, and both boats drifted further toward the reef. Then a third and larger boat appeared, seemingly from around the headland from the Kuwait side. It came close, and turned out to be a dhow with a sawn-off mast. The other men had looked like fishermen, but these looked like pure and simple bandits.

A fat gangster type with a big turban and fair skin sat with his legs crossed over pillows and studied us with calculated contempt. His fat hands had never touched a fishing line. He was the archetypal crook. The others were a mixed gang under his command. They demanded outright a ransom, and the alternative was to beach the boat in the dark of night. The best-case scenario would be to survive and end up naked on the reef. The Russians had set their own anchor and ours was down in the mud again, but nothing held. I took over and ordered Rashad to negotiate. The sun would set in one hour. No coastguard would ever show up in these infinite, unnavigable shallows. We had heard that organised gangs smuggled human labour from Pakistan to work in rich Kuwait. Failaka was part of the sheikdom of Kuwait, and we had landed at the back door, normally closed to legitimate travellers.

The bandits would not reduce the price. It had obviously been agreed upon in advance. We had no Kuwaiti currency, but the robbers accepted Iraqi bills, which was hard currency in these parts. They demanded that Rashad transfer to the dhow as a hostage. The boat came alongside and I placed the money, bill by bill, into someone's hand, who then passed it on to the fat person on the pillows. After a wave from him, Rashad was set free and joined us.

Then the Soviets threw a towing line over to the dhow, and we hung on while the dhow, helped by the Russians' propeller, slowly pulled us out into open water next to *Slavsk*. There was no time for farewells; when we reached deep water the dhow was already moving at full speed on its way back to the shallows.

Igor set a course for the sheikdom of Bahrain without permission from Moscow, and did not leave us until we reached the island's territorial waters, where *Slavsk* was refused entry owing to its Russian crew, in spite of having saved our lives.

We had arrived where written history began. Never has anything given me such a sense of reliving a dramatic period in the history of man, as when we reached Bahrain in the reed boat. Inscriptions on Sumerian clay tablets report that after the Deluge their first king took his people and their livestock to Dilmun. The Assyrians confirm this in *Gilgamesh*, the world's oldest example of epic literature. Danish archaeologists, first P. V. Glob and now Geoffrey Bibby, had started extensive excavations in Bahrain and found that the legendary Dilmun was identical to this highly modern Arab sultanate. We had barely moored our boat before Bibby arrived on the first plane from Aarhus to see a reed ship, as it had looked thousands of years ago, on the coast of Dilmun.

It was quite an anachronism that the reed ship *Tigris* should have inaugurated what was then the world's largest dry dock. It was built to handle oil tankers of up to 450,000 tons, and we arrived two days before the official opening. Bibby landed at the ultra-modern Concorde airport, and we drove over to the other side of the island where it seemed the clock and the calendar had been turned back five thousand years. Humble fishermen still paddled out into the Gulf with boats made up of bundles of palm-leaf stems.

We were struck by how frivolously today's people cut their roots to the past in the blind faith that what they have now will last forever. Wherever we went we saw that large palms had been razed to the ground. Only the stumps remained, and the landscape looked like a man's unshaven face. One could buy dates in the stores. One could buy everything in the stores, flown in fresh from the whole world, and there was money enough as oil flowed in through huge pipes from the mainland. Dilmun had become an important stopover for the shipment of oil from the pumps on the Arabian peninsula.

But in the centre of the island we were filled with a feeling of reverence. Here springs of clean fresh water literally sprang from the ground and ran like streams through the remains of ancient irrigation channels. 'This water comes from the high mountains in the interior of the Arabian desert,' Bibby explained. When it rains there, the water percolates through the rock and follows underground water arteries that run beneath the desert before resurfacing here on the island, like fresh water pumped by hydraulic power.

I drank some and sat down on a tree-stump to think. Was it faith or superstition when the old Sumerians thanked the god of heaven for gifts? I had made a note of the text on a Sumerian clay tablet, which relates that the seafaring god Enki had asked the highest god of heaven to bless Dilmun with fresh water:

> Let the sun god Utu who lives in heaven
> bring you fresh water from the earth,
> from the earth's water springs.
> Let him bring water to your large pools,
> let him give your city an abundance of drinking water,
> let him give Dilmun an abundance of drinking water

Before we humans built our own world, we were grateful for all the miraculous god-like gifts nature had given us, regardless of what name we gave the god of heaven. In the briny Gulf, where desert and wilderness dominate the coasts, the inexplicable law of gravity made it possible to pump drinking water up to the aboriginal inhabitants of Dilmun. And from the springs in Dilmun the fresh water still pours out of the ground on its way to the sea.

In the impressive ruins of Dilmun's port I felt that the ancient texts on seafaring that dominated the Sumerian clay tablets had come to life. Bibby showed us that at high tide large vessels could be moored right beside the warehouses near Dilmun's city gate, while at low tide a keel boat had to leave the harbour to avoid being grounded, tipping over and losing its cargo. Now it was our turn to demonstrate how a reed boat consisting of two huge bundles of reeds side by side can float higher over the shallows than a boat with a hull and a keel, and when the tide is out it can rest on the bottom with its cargo intact.

It was hardly necessary to close our eyes to picture the traffic in the harbour, when Bibby took us through the remains of the ancient warehouses, and pointed to the places where he had found trademarks and other identification, proving merchant contacts with both Sumerians and the distant Indus valley, our destination on *Tigris*. I felt I was part of the scene when I stood on the edge of the dock and looked out over the waves that united the people of the world's oldest cultures. Before leaving Iraq I had delved into translations of the ancient texts in the library in Baghdad. If I had not already been convinced, then I certainly was now.

Modern people are so strongly influenced by Darwin's theory of evolution that we believe that five thousand years ago people were five thousand years closer to the apes. In the interest of truth we must revise our understanding. If we are to use a timescale for the development of human beings, we have to go much further back than we can by reading ancient texts. And if we talk about culture, then we cannot use a general timescale at all. Civilisation was far more developed in parts of Asia, Africa and America in antiquity than it was in Europe in the Middle Ages. And it was seafaring that made it possible.

What struck me most on reading the ancient Sumerian texts was that, deep within themselves, they could not have been as different from us as we like to believe. In his essay, 'The Seafaring Merchants from Ur', the Sumerian expert Oppenheimer maintains that the most interesting information on the clay tablets from Ur is about the role that seafaring played in the city's life as a trading port in the earliest prehistoric era. Both the harbours and the inland canals were dredged and maintained, and they were inspected by high-ranking officials who reported to the king. The port authorities taxed all imports, and the captains had sealed documents describing their ships and cargo.

The largest reed ships at the time of the Sumerians had a cargo capacity expressed in *gur*, which when converted was about thirty or forty tons or more, and by comparison, this made our *Tigris* seem like a tiny boat. The Finnish language researcher Salonen described the largest reed ships as *magur*, and they were also called 'god ships', 'the sea-going ship', or 'the ship with the tall stems'. We had named our vessel after the river that was our starting point. The Sumerians had romantic names for their ships such as *The Protectoress of Life, Morning* or *The Heart's Delight*. The texts refer to passenger ships, ferries, fishing boats, warships, troop transport ships and private and chartered merchant ships. The cargo could be anything from timber, copper, ivory, bricks, hides or textiles, to corn, flour, bread, fish, dairy products, wine or livestock.

I was totally engrossed in harbour life when we left to visit something that made a permanent impression on my personal view of both the past and the future: the world's largest prehistoric graveyard, an endless field of sand covered with grave mounds as far as the eye could see. Archaeologists had estimated the number of graves at about one hundred thousand. Most of them only rose like tightly packed mounds in the terrain, but many were of impressive dimensions. The largest were grouped together in a place of honour by the sea, and they were obviously the oldest graves, built while there was still plenty of room. The others were scattered in all directions and looked like giant turtle eggs. All had been plundered by grave robbers.

I was aware that Dilmun was as holy to the Sumerians in ancient times as Jerusalem became to the Christians, and Mecca to the Muslims. Even the Assyrians made pilgrimages here, according to their most important written tablets. Perhaps they wanted to be buried in the native country of the first god-kings, because it was here that the progenitor of the family of kings had come ashore after the Deluge.

Today no one showed any respect for this plundered field of graves. Those who had earned enough money from the oil boom flew to Mecca. My attention was immediately caught by the largest of the grave mounds, which lay close to a modern Arab settlement. Bibby took me round the back and showed me how the locals had started an industry by breaking off limestone from the pyramid-like structure that lay within the huge mound, and used for burning lime. This kind of limestone did not exist in Bahrain. Just like the Sumerian empire on the mainland, the architects of this colossus used *magur* to transport the beautifully carved stone blocks to the island's coast. I recognised the ingeniously fitted limestone blocks that I had seen in Iraq's famous Nippur pyramid, where they lay hidden beneath a layer of sun-dried clay blocks.

One day, when I returned alone to Dilmun's abandoned field of graves, I crawled up on to the giant mound where I could look down over the roofs of two- and three-storey white-washed houses and across the whole dead, cupola-covered landscape. I lay down to think.

Do you remember what you thought?

I thought that five thousand years ago mankind's written history began on this island, and I wondered what would be written about this same island five thousand years hence, when the pipelines from Arabian oil reserves, now lying on the bottom of the sea, were empty.

I thought how Europeans smile at oral traditions, and claim that history began with the written word. But unless we write it ourselves, with letters learned from the Phoenicians, we don't take it seriously. I had the oldest known written version of the Sumerian history fresh in my mind, from the library in Baghdad. And lying on the giant mound, with a view of one hundred thousand forgotten graves, I decided that I would do my best to ensure that these texts would never be forgotten. They were, after all, the oldest known version of the birth of world history.

I thought how Jews, Christians and Muslims in their common heritage of faith have all incorporated into their traditions the story of Noah's Ark and the Deluge; an oral tradition that Abraham brought with him from Ur in Mesopotamia. As a child, nothing had captivated me more than the story of Noah saving all the animals, but I never thought that I would speculate how this story became part of religious teaching. The Bible gives prominence to this story by placing it after the account of the Creation, while the Koran often mentions Noah and the Deluge as Allah's punishment. If we go back to Ur, where the original version of the Deluge had been buried on Sumerian clay tablets for more than two thousand years even before Abraham left Mesopotamia, we find that something happened that relates to all of us.

No one knew that the Sumerians had existed until an expedition from the University of Pennsylvania began excavations of the Nippur pyramid and found a library of thirty-five thousand clay tablets, among them the original edition of the Deluge.

To the Sumerians this was not legend but their own recorded history. We know all the essential parts from the Bible, but the original version is more realistic. In the Sumerian original the name of the god-fearing king who saved us from the flood is given as Ziusudra; there were no elephants or giraffes on board, just his own livestock. And the Ark did not land on a mountain top, but on the blessed island of gods, Dilmun, in the Persian Gulf. From there the king's descendants later moved to Ur, which then was a port on the river delta in the Gulf.

When the British started archaeological excavations in Ur at the end of the 1920s, Leonard Wooley found that the holy city of the Sumerians lay on top of a three-metre layer of a particular type of river silt. Beneath this layer, the British found the ruins of an even older settlement that had been buried in silt, caused by an enormous tidal wave. This tidal wave covered the entire lower half of Mesopotamia with an estimated eight metres of water before retreating. The silt was the same type that we had been stuck in on the very same coastline when we were towed off by the Russians and the pirates from Failaka.

The Danish archaeologist Glob, who had supervised the first fifteen years of excavations in Dilmun, was also the first one to take the Sumerian record of the flood catastrophe seriously. He related it directly to the three-metre layer of dried silt on which Sumerians had settled about five thousand years ago.

And then many other strange things happened on this planet of ours.

About five thousand years ago, or around 3100–3000 BC, the oldest civilisations in the world were developing rapidly. Not only did the Sumerians sail from Bahrain to establish their first kingdom in the area at the mouth of Mesopotamia's rivers, but the ancestors of the Pharaohs came sailing up the Nile and settled in Egypt. For a short time these people continued to tax the mighty kingdoms that suddenly appeared on Crete and Cyprus. Immediately thereafter, if not simultaneously, other seafarers travelled up the lower part of the Indus River and established the third great civilisation in Mohenjo Daro. They all appeared from unknown origins with fully developed civilisations, but each possessed a distinct system of writing and used the motif of god-kings aboard reed ships in their religious art.

I doubt whether I have ever puzzled so much about any-thing as I did about what happened on our planet at that time. Something happened, we know that.

In the Atlantic Ocean something happened to cause Iceland to split in two across a fault line that continued across the bottom of the sea and beyond the Atlantic Ocean mountain chain. When the Vikings went there a few thousand years later, they founded Europe's first parliament in that very fault line. When I visited Iceland, I learned that a tree-trunk which had been petrified in the lava that had poured out of the fault line could be carbon dated to around 3000 BC.

Something happened to the climate at that time too. Through pollen analysis, botanists have found that this was the time when rivers and lakes in North Africa started to dry up and both the Sahara and Mesopotamia turned into desert landscapes.

Something also happened in the Pacific Ocean. Today the whole world talks about the El Niño current, which appears at regular intervals off the coast of South America and causes storms resulting in flooding and periods of drought over the whole world. It raged terribly in the village of Túcume a few years before I arrived to start excavations in the area of the pyramids. When we stopped our digging, Daniel Sandweiss continued excavating further back through time on the coast of Peru. He and his American colleagues found remains of a hitherto unknown fishing population that had subsisted on shellfish and ocean fishing along the coast for more than ten thousand years. By studying the presence of tropical shells in deep refuse mounds, they could reconstruct the occurrence of definite El Niño years through the last five thousand years, as far back as about 3000 BC. Prior to that there was no El Niño current. For totally unknown reasons it was at that time that masses of tropical water first started to pour down along the coast of Peru, and this influenced the climate of the whole planet.

Modern researchers talk about approximate datings when referring to the millennia before Christ, because our own accounting of time does not go back any further. Christians count year 0 from the birth of Christ, while Muslims count year 0 from Mohammed's flight to Mecca, which in the Western calendar would be the year 622 AD. Buddhists start their time with the death of Buddha, which in the West is 544 BC. But on both sides of the globe, the ancestors of the Indians and Mayans had a calendar system based on astronomical observations so accurate that it forces us to wonder and reconsider history. Both systems seem to have started independently of one another in the same century, 3,100 years before Christ in terms of the Western calendar.

Then what happened?

The main interest of the Mayans was astronomy and history. The Europeans managed to burn the books of hieroglyphics that were written on paper, but the Mayans had also carved countless astronomical observations and mathematical calculations in stone on their temple walls and monuments. And they had calculated that one year consisted of 365.2329 days. This figure is one day short in every five thousand years, and it is 8.64 seconds closer to the truth than our present calendar. It is therefore interesting to note that the Mayans started their account of time with 4 Ahau 2 Cumhu, which corresponds to 12 August 3113 BC.

The Hindus, who are the rightful heirs to the civilisation of the Indus valley, also kept meticulous records of time. The historian A. Z. Chandra writes: 'Arybhatta, the greatest astronomer of his time, lived and worked around the year 499 according to our calendar, and his calculation of the beginning of the Kali era was midnight after Ujjain, which ends after 17

February, 3102 years before Christ.' That is only eleven years after the Mayans started to count days, months and years.

The Hindus also have another tradition with regards to time immemorial. Converted to our time, it has Brhaspatrikaka start in the year 3116 BC. And that is only three years after the start of the Mayan calendar.

The Sumerians are not alone in starting their history by recording a natural catastrophe. Accounts of a flood that destroyed most of humanity are found in the introductions to the histories of both the Aztecs and the Incas. It is also repeated in the same version on every island throughout Polynesia. The only written text about the discovery of America that escaped the fire is the Quiche-Mayan's sacred history book *Popul Vuh*, which was copied in Guatemala before the original disappeared. To me it is like a small piece of lost world history in fairytale form. The god of heaven, Huracán, was not satisfied with the first people he created, for they were like wooden dolls, without hearts. He rued the deed and sent a horrible flood as punishment: 'a flood was called forth by the Heart of Heaven; a large flood he created, that fell down over the heads of the wooden figures . . . This was to punish them because they had not thought about their mother or their father who was the Heart of Heaven, Huracán. And for that reason the face of the earth darkened, and a black rain started falling, day and night.'

The list of royal dynasties in Guatemalan culture starts with the leader of the group stepping ashore after the flood, on the Atlantic coast, and making his way through the country in search of new residence.

Now we're back to the Atlantic Ocean; now you can't get away without relating the legend of Atlantis.

It has been abused so much that it frightens scientists. But it would be as unwise to discard it, without analysing its origins, as it would to accept without question all the versions that have appeared in the wake of Plato. In typical Hellenic style, in 400 BC, Plato spoke for historical figures such as his countrymen, Solon and Socrates. And Solon described his visit to Egypt, where the priests at the temple library in Sais mocked the Greeks for their historical ignorance. They excused the Greeks, as they had lost their scholars when a terrible tidal wave raced in over the Mediterranean, and they and their neighbours suffered more than most. The only people who escaped were the shepherds in the mountains, and the Greeks had to rebuild their culture from scratch. And then Solon learned that there had been an island in the Atlantic Ocean, outside the entrance to the Mediterranean. The priests told him that they had learned from their papyrus scrolls that the city of Athens once repulsed a mighty army from the island that had entered the Mediterranean to attack the cities of Europe. And then we get the Egyptian version of the flood, in Solon's words: 'In a later time there came earthquakes and tidal waves of unusual violence, and during one horrible day and night all their warriors were swallowed up by the earth, and the island of Atlantis was in the same way swallowed up by the ocean and disappeared. That is the reason that the ocean in those parts even today is unnavigable, with mud banks just below the surface, remnants of the sunken island.'

No one knows exactly what happened about five thousand years ago to cause civilisations the world over to use it as a starting point for history and the accounting of time. As a contribution to this riddle, the first project to be financed with FERCO funds from the pyramids on Tenerife, will be an international conference with participants from all fields at the University of Maine. The subject will be 'Climatic and cultural changes around 3000 BC'.

Maybe in the future science will discover more about the past and we shall stop running about like wooden dolls, and think more about remaining on terms of friendship with our mother and father, who is the Heart of Heaven.

15

The Ocean and the Sky

I was sitting on a spot in the Northwest of America looking out across the Pacific Ocean, where Asia and America curve towards each other, and Siberia and Alaska almost meet. Waves from the Japanese current rolled gently over the broad, white, sandy beach and over my shoes, where I was perched on a huge piece of driftwood, ruminating about life.

The circle is complete, I thought, almost sadly, the second circle. The first circle was completed when we celebrated the *Kon-Tiki* expedition's fiftieth anniversary in Peru. But now a year had passed and I was back with the Northwest Indians, the island people off the coast of British Columbia, where I had started looking for the closest relatives of the Polynesians. Then I was interrupted by the war that engulfed Europe.

In my opinion, it was here that the last immigrants to Polynesia had cut timber for their enormous double canoes and started their journey propelled by the currents and wind en route for Hawaii. From Hawaii they conquered all the Pacific islands that had already been settled by raft voyagers from Peru.

Fifty years ago I had been accused of creating a storm in a teacup. At my feet, waves were still rippling, nature's own creation. The Pacific Ocean could be compared to a hemisphere of its own, occupying as much space on the surface of the earth as all the other oceans and continents together. Unaffected by all theories, the ocean currents in this hemisphere rotated according to the laws of nature in two enormous circles that almost touched on either side of the equator. South of the equator, the ocean ran anticlockwise, guiding seafarers en route from Peru to Polynesia. Up here the ocean rotated with the clock, carrying everything that floated with the Japanese current on a return trip back to the same islands. I thought of the two glass balls that I had just seen in the home of one of the Indians up here, floats from fishing nets from Japan's coast that the son of the house had found on the beach.

With Jacqueline and my American colleague, the archaeologist Donald Ryan, I had come to British Columbia to tidy up the loose ends from my first visit to British Columbia. The reception in scientific circles in Victoria and the university city of Vancouver was as sincere as it had been the previous time, not least at the Royal British Colombian Museum, where the present director was an anthropologist, not a zoologist. He invited my small group out to dinner after having shown us around the impressive exhibition halls in the new building. It was odd to recognise many of the artefacts that had been stored in the basement the last time I was here. This museum had not forgotten that, in 1939, I sat in the director's office with books and stone axes and concluded that the Polynesians had stopped off here.

On our journey further up the coast of Vancouver Island, into the heart of the Kwakiutl Indians' island kingdom, two of Canada's foremost experts on the original coastal population came with us, anthropologist Jerome Cybulski and archaeologist Bjørn Simonsen. In addition, we were accompanied by the Kwakiutl Indian, Stan Wallas. Jerome was employed at the National Museum in Quebec, and had such a good relationship with the original coastal population – who now called themselves 'First Nation' – that they even let him examine the skeletons of their forefathers. Bjørn was the archaeology inspector for the authorities and the museum in Victoria, because, better than anyone else, he knew all the tribes and every island and cove along the coast. Stan was an enthusiastic amateur archaeologist and Jerome's invaluable assistant.

Jacqueline and I were so tired during the long car trip up Vancouver Island that we could barely open our eyes to look at a bear on the road or at rock carvings or a magnificent view. Following our arrival from Europe the week had been incredibly hectic. I had squeezed in visits to four universities in the United States. First, in cap and gown, as the main speaker and honorary doctor at the annual graduation for six thousand students at the University of Maine; then in another cap and gown for yet another honorary title received in pouring rain in front of thousands of umbrellas at Hartford University. The following day I gave a lecture at the Peabody Museum at Yale University about the role of the ocean in the development of civilisation.

The day after the Yale lecture Don Ryan picked us up at Seattle airport to drive us to the Kwakiutl Indians. He came from the Pacific Lutheran University in Tacoma, where I was going to give the annual graduation speech on my way back. All we wanted to do today was cross the border and get to the Indians who were the goal of the journey.

The great forest crowded in on all sides, enveloping us completely, as we crept to bed in the tiny Pioneer Inn at the northern tip of Vancouver Island. This was old Kwakiutl territory, and Stan would assume the lead here. He was staying with his own family in the new Kwakiutl reservation, Quatsino, nearby, but the next morning he met us before sunrise to take us to old Quatsino, where he had been born. He helped us on board a powerful, fast motor boat, and we took off at full speed.

It is hard to imagine that Norway might have more fjords and islands along its coast than British Columbia. On the chart Quatsino Sound, with all its tributaries, looked like a rock carving of a man with long, extended arms. We started with an early breakfast in the former coal-mining port of Coal Harbor. After that, during our whole trip, we saw no traces of human habitation, apart from shell middens from earlier settlements and a few abandoned buildings.

One of these was the former schoolhouse, a forlorn reminder of the original Indian village of Quatsino, where Stan had grown up, the son of the chief. Not a trace remained of the other dwellings. I felt a lump in my throat as we fought our way through the bushes and arrived at the burial ground at the edge of the woods. Most of the area was covered by rotten old timber and fresh bear droppings. But it was thrilling to see a more recent group of well-preserved grave monuments shaped like huge fish or whales. They were carved in wood and painted like figures on totem poles, though placed individually on top of poles stuck in the ground. Only one of them was of a wolf, with its head lifted high and seemingly howling at the moon. On the mainland the motifs carved on the totem poles were mostly animals of the forest, bear and beaver and eagle. Here animals of the ocean dominated. All of them bore fresh garlands of flowers.

I asked no questions. This was the resting place of relatives who had not yet been forgotten.

'These are not reproductions of idols,' Stan said calmly. 'People who come from the outside think that totem poles were worshipped, or meant to scare enemies away, but we believe in the same invisible god as you do. These animals are the symbols of our families. The tall totem poles relate the history of a family.'

We ate a picnic lunch on the beach and walked over to another spit of land. We found a rotten plank roof, and when we peeped underneath we saw a well-preserved skull gaping up at us. We touched nothing, since Jerome would have to request the permission of the Indian Council before we could take any samples for DNA analysis. Later we landed at a wonderful little island, and in the distance Bjørn caught sight of a shining white pile of shells left behind by a prehistoric settlement. Even Stan had never been here before. The tiny island was covered with forest and undergrowth, and as we were making our way under branches and over huge rocks we heard a cry from Bjørn. He had found an open grave containing three skeletons and the remains of old timber under an outcrop on a small hill. One of the skulls was as white as chalk and well preserved, but of an unnatural shape. These coastal Indians were masters of many arts, and the quality of their work would go down well in our modern society. As in many other ancient cultures, the skulls of the newborn infants were sometimes artificially enlarged, but in no museum have I ever seen a skull this long and slim; it could almost have been wearing a stocking over its head. I didn't like the thought of leaving an artefact like this behind, without the care of relatives or museum curators.

Later, Stan took us to his home, a spacious wooden house in the new Quatsino reservation. The sight of some of the beautiful women in the family deflected my attention away from

the surrounding pine forest and to the palm-studded islands
further south in the same ocean. On the wall there were pictures of the older generation. The grandfather, Jimmy Jumbo,
and his wife, were both Kwakiutl from Quatsino, and a great-
uncle dressed in a bark cape could easily have been a Maori
chief.

We flew further north in the Kwakiutl Indian archipelago in
a small chartered plane, and when we parted company, Stan
inscribed a small book and presented it to me – *Kwakiutl
Legends*, as told to P. Whitaker by Stan's own father, Chief
James Wallas. I thought I had finished with the legend of the
Deluge, but here it turned up again in an even more realistic
guise.

Up here, farthest away from the Sumerian Empire, it was
not a king but the whole population who had sensed an
approaching flood. They tied all their canoes together with
cross-poles and filled them with dried meat, fish, shells,
berries and plenty of water in wooden containers. When the
warning cry came from the lookout and they saw the flood
approaching, like a wall, they quickly manned their canoes.
The flood lifted them up to the level of the hillside, and in the
ensuing chaos they had to fight their way clear of uprooted
trees and parts of their own wooden houses that were crashing
into the canoes. When the ocean receded, they ran about on all
the hilltops, calling out in the hope of finding survivors. Some
canoes were swept away from the main body and either disappeared in the storm or ended up in other places where new
tribes were founded.

I may have paid more attention than most researchers when
listening to what so-called primitive peoples are trying to tell
us in their own way. I have never really met any who are much
more primitive than we are. After the old man on Fatu-Hiva
told me how the god-king Tiki got to his island, and I learned

that the Aymara people of Lake Titicaca had told the Spaniards that he originated from there, I have listened carefully to the stories that have been passed down by people with no written records.

Ever since I suspected that the archipelago along the coast of British Columbia had been a point of stopover for Asians who went on to conquer Polynesia, I have had a suspicion that the coastal Indians might also have something important to relate. When my new friend Stan gave me the book about his ancestors' oral traditions, and having read only one page, I felt that he had given me the key to a gold mine.

I had always suspected that the Kwakiutl Indians were visited by a representative of the same wandering god who played a leading role in spreading culture from Mexico to Peru and in the Pacific Ocean. The Kwakiutl Indians remembered him as *Kane-akeluh* or *Kane-akwea*; Stan pronounced the name Kane-kelak. The book was filled with stories about this god and his creations, and how he enchanted the Quatsino tribe when he and his brother landed on the beach in Sand Neck about two thousand years ago. He performed miracles with a two-headed snake that he wore as a belt around his waist and sometimes used as a sling.

Folk tales? Myths? Certainly. But this sling has only been found in certain areas, and it is this weapon that accompanied the spreader of culture from Mexico to Peru. In pre-Incan art along the coast of Peru he was depicted as a seafarer and always wore a two-headed snake as a belt around his waist.

I also concluded that the Kwakiutl tribe's wandering *Kane-akwea*, whose representative was the sun, was the Polynesian *Kane-akea*, god of light. *Akea* or *Atea* was the highest deity and the word for 'light' in all Polynesia. In addition, I knew that Kane was remembered as an extremely important human god in all Polynesia, but especially in Hawaii, where he was so influential that the sun was called 'the resting place of Kane'. And the sun, known as *ra* in large parts of Polynesia, was called *La* in Hawaii while it was called *na-la* by Dawson's Kwakiutl tribe.

I had all this stored in my mind, like scientific folk tales, when we said farewell to Stan, and Jacqueline and I crept into the small plane with Don and the two Canadian archaeologists.

We took an alternative route, flying just above the treetops. We were on our way further up the coast, over the uninhabited Hakai Straits which was the final destination of our journey, over the Bella Coola valley where I had lived when war broke out in Europe, then skimmed the tops of the waves and landed in calm waters in the fjord outside Bella Bella, the centre of the surviving Kwakiutl tribes.

We were expected, and a group of representatives of the Elders welcomed us on the quay and took us to the traditional long-house in the middle of the village, where we attended a meeting and were served refreshments. The outside of the huge wooden building was decorated with totem poles and gigantic wall paintings of the tribe's animal symbols in typical Kwakiutl style, but just inside the door there were rows of fax machines and computers. The rest of the wall space in the large hall was lined with men and women, councillors from the Kwakiutl reservation.

It was an unforgettable meeting, with one foot in the past and the other firmly placed on contemporary soil. At least half the faces that were studying me, while I studied them, reminded me of Polynesia. They too were aware of what I had observed in 1940 and what Captains Cook and Vancouver had surmised as soon as they arrived here from Polynesia: there was a striking physical resemblance between the 'First Nation' people and those who had greeted the Europeans on the other islands further south in the same ocean. Everyone talked about it, and since my last visit, tourism and communication systems had had a visible effect. By now many of the local population had visited Hawaii, and they themselves had welcomed visitors from Hawaii, Samoa and New Zealand. Guests were received as relatives, and they felt that they were amongst their own.

The dialogue in the long-house was proof that the Kwakiutl people still possessed the gift of speech. Their ancestors did not have a written language, but they were renowned for powerful oratory, far superior to most other nations, and professional speakers were highly respected in their society. The participants sat along the walls and listened to the reason for my visit with composure and dignity. Their well-placed comments were made in the same spirit of composure, and they came from both men and women, from both sides of the hall. Everyone had something to offer that they had learned by questioning the elders in the family. It struck me that the people in the coastal reservations had woken up to a new life after a long period of hibernation. When I was living with the Bella Coola Indians before the war, only the bear hunter Clayton Mack owned a canoe, a red canvas canoe that he had not made himself, but had bought. Now the young men on the reservations were learning from older masters how to carve canoes from cedar logs, decorating them with colourful carvings in the traditional style of their ancestors.

Frank, a young boy who had been kept isolated on a little island for a year because he had stolen and abused drugs, had turned into a wonderful man. It was he who organised the youth of the 'First Nation' along the coast, arranging canoe races and reviving the best of their traditions. Later we also met the Polynesian movie producer, Karen Williams, who came to film the first canoe race. Her father was a Maori, her

mother came from Tonga, and she was so convinced that here
was the homeland of her ancestors that she had stayed behind
to film and record cultural parallels.

Ever since I sat on a quay in the neighbouring valley of
Bella Coola, with my oldest son Thor, who was then two
years old, I had dreamed of finding my way out of the long
and narrow fjord, and out to the open sea, all the way to the
Hakai Straits. That was sixty years ago, but we were now
about to try to land a seaplane there. When the assembly in
the long-house heard where we were going, three of the oldest
members were so eager to join us that we had to leave Don
and Jerome behind on the reservation, while two old men and
an even older woman clambered into the plane and fastened
their seatbelts.

In the overcast weather and wind we bumped our way over
the hillside towards the Bella Coola valley. The pilot took
bearings and we saw the shimmering light of the Hakai Straits
between the larger islands. We descended without changing
course, and with forested wilderness on both sides flew along
the Hakai Straits toward the open ocean. So enclosed by
mountains was the Bella Coola valley, that the only possible
way out was the route we were taking.

And that was precisely the reason for this trip. The Bella
Coola valley, thrusting inland between steep mountains, was
the largest and most fertile valley along the entire coast. Once,
Salish Indians, strangers from the south, had managed to force
their way right into the heart of Kwakiutl territory and conquer the valley, thereby splitting Kwakiutl territory in two.
One of the essential problems in the ethnology of the
Northwest coast was how this could have happened. Most
likely they had avoided detection on the coast by stealing into
the valley from the land side. But what had happened to those
who had fled the valley?

I hoped to find traces of earlier settlements along the uninhabited Hakai Straits. With the three elders well secured, we flew just above the wave tops, with Calvert Island on one side and the two islands Nalau and Hecate on the other.

The pilot landed in a calm cove protected by a small headland where the Hakai Straits opened up to the Pacific Ocean.

It was a peculiar experience. Except for Bella Bella, we had not seen a single house on the whole flight. We flew over an endless expanse of forested islands spread out like pieces of a puzzle on a mirror. But on the spot where I had hoped to find some trace of prehistoric settlement, there was a newly built house. A single man lived here and he was just as surprised as I was by our unexpected meeting. He was from Pitcairn in Polynesia, where all the inhabitants are descendants of the mutineers on the *Bounty*. I had been there with my expedition ship after the Easter Island expedition. At that time I took the entire island's male population on a two-day trip to the uninhabited and forested island of Henderson. The object of the exercise was to find timber for wood-carving, their main source of income. This man was housesitting, temporarily. The house had been built for tourism, but owing to the storms it would remain closed until the summer.

No sooner had I recovered from my disappointment, when I spotted a giant tree that had toppled over close to the house wall. All the roots were showing, and beneath the turf, which was open like a lid on a treasure chest, something white appeared: a huge kitchen refuse heap full of shells. The new house had been built on top of an ancient settlement, which had remained undiscovered by archaeologists. With our three aging guests we climbed through undergrowth, scrambled over rocks, between gigantic trees, and finally through a forest which opened to the sea. Here, we stumbled upon a wide beach, the widest and most beautiful sandy beach I

have ever seen in America. It was the outward face of the
Hakai Straits.

We sat down on some enormous logs of Canadian driftwood. It was a powerful sight and a great moment. Here, the
old people said, in the olden days the 'First Nation' people
from along the coastline had gathered annually for celebrations
and masked dances. One of them had been told by his grand-
mother that there had been so many people, that when they
arrived in their canoes from north and south they could hear
the drums playing from far out at sea. The stories contained
such vivid detail that they must have taken part in some of the
celebrations themselves when they were young. We learned
that beyond the mouth of the Straits the offshore wind and the
south-west current were so strong that even modern fishing
boats were swept off course and had to be picked up by rescue
vessels from Victoria.

We listened and listened, and as proof of the wealth of the
ocean the two old salts beckoned us over to a smooth, polished
wall of rock that looked like a curtain flanking one side of the
beach. Vertical fissures in the cliff were filled with starfish,
colourful sea anemones and other live, glittering creatures that
live in the sea and were suspended decoratively while waiting
for the tide to come in. I felt as if I were in a gigantic theatre.
Stepping out from the forest was like opening a curtain and
suddenly finding oneself on a stage, blinded by the limelight,
hearing the sound of the surf from the rows of benches in the
great blue ocean theatre. And then my eyesight took over and
all the rows of benches were nothing but empty waves. And
we were only a small group of people sitting on driftwood
feeling that this theatre was ours. But we from the outside
world had arrived too late for the great show itself.

As we sat there, I thought I heard a prompter's calm voice.
You feel more at home here, sitting and listening to the stillness,

*or to three aging Kwakiutl Indians, than when you yourself are on
the podium, wearing a black gown and a cap with a tassel . . .*

One learns more from listening than speaking, I thought.
And both the wind and the people who continue to live close
to nature still have much to tell us which we cannot hear inside
university walls.

A scientist has to distinguish between legends and myths,
and make use of both. Before the last generation, the legend
surrounding the bearer of culture, Kane Akwea, had been the
most important one on this coast. When he reappears with the
same name as the ancestor of the royal family in Polynesia, the
legend breathes a spirit into the archaeological skeletons and
the ethnological stone axes. It does not qualify as myth just
because Kane in his own time was considered a deity in human
form. The Pharaohs, the Incas, the Emperor of Japan and the
wandering god Odin of the Vikings were also regarded in the
same way.

That Kane went to heaven and lives on the sun is a myth.
But when the myth is exactly the same for the worshippers of
Kane among the Kwakiutl people and also on the nearest
Hawaiian islands, then it is science to consider the myth a
cultural parallel in the grand puzzle of migration routes in the
Pacific Ocean.

Home again in the old house in Tenerife, the *aku-aku* had
become so familiar that it marched straight into the living
room as soon as I lay down to collect my thoughts after a day's
work. Jacqueline had turned on the television, but instead of
interesting news about the conflict in the Middle East or
nuclear tests in Pakistan, it was screening the World Cup. I
closed my eyes demonstratively, but suddenly Jacqueline
jumped out of the chair and cheered. Norway had beaten
Brazil 2–1.

People were completely crazy at the close of the twentieth century. The whole world talked about football. Tens of thousands sat on rows of benches with painted faces and screamed, while the ball was kicked back and forth by someone running around on the grass.

Football is not for you?

I've never been interested, but now I'm beginning to wonder.

The tiny voice was persistent. I supported the UN and One World and everything that represented peaceful coexistence between nations. Did I not see that here people had finally made something happen that was not controlled by politicians? People from all nations met and played together peacefully, without a thought for politics or weapons. Here, in a healthy sporting conflict, a small nation from Africa could compete with the superpowers without the millions needed for an arms race or a race into space.

I should have kept in touch with what was going on. I began to understand something as I sat in the centre of the arena at the Lillehammer Olympics, welcoming all nations to the opening ceremony. It cannot be denied that ping-pong and football reach more people and can do more for peace than political slogans or a five-year agreement between the United States and Cuba about archaeological co-operation.

But it is the past that interests you most.

No – the future. But it is too soon to study that. We must not mistake that for the present. The present is not real. Grab it and it's gone. It is a short, yet eternal transformation from what has been to what will be. We can't build on it. We are all explorers of the unknown, and by looking back, at our wake or our footprints, we can see the course we are taking.

The most important thing we can learn from the past is that no earlier civilisation has survived. And the larger the pyramids and temples and statues they build in honour of their god or themselves, the harder is the fall. Most civilisations have been so completely erased that archaeologists are required to bring them to light again. Neither the sun god nor the creative power behind the Big Bang smiles upon the huge buildings or powerful armies of mankind. They smile on the civilisations that respect their creation and who show appreciation for it.

Where people have constructed great buildings they have also fought great wars. When the archaeologist digs deep below the ruins of an extinct civilisation, more often than not he will find the remains of an even older one beneath it. And we would be wise to note that the most advanced culture is rarely the one at the top.

While civilisations come and go, primitive people live on undisturbed.

Yes, and shoot at one another with bows and arrows. They have lived on this planet just as long as we have, and deep within ourselves we have changed just as little. We think we have made enormous strides, but, at best, done so periodically between world wars, by changing the environment, not ourselves. Today's civilisation is so advanced that we can see through walls and roofs with the aid of an antenna, we can change everything from the ozone layer and weather and wind to the life that pulsed before us in the oceans and the forests. We attempt to improve our physique with gymnastics and a healthy diet, and at best we manage to maintain the muscles and the health our forefathers had. They lived in what we call a wilderness.

As so often before, when the television was turned off and Jacqueline grabbed a book from the shelf, I remained on the sofa, thinking. During my whole life I have tried to wheedle secrets out of the people who smile the most. The smile is a God-given gift that comes from within. And we have something strange within us that science cannot dissect because it disappears before the autopsy; some sort of receiver and transmitter with different frequencies from the television but also able to pass through walls and roofs, and controlling things such as instinct and intuition and conscience.

We have inherited certain things from the animal kingdom. Every species is instructed in how to use its sensory horns, its wings, legs or genitals. We call it instinct and intuition. But mankind is born with responsibility for his actions; we call this conscience. And since the time of Adam we have had the ability of two-way communication, and those who still master this art ask or pray for advice and help. Civilised people believe they have to build churches and temples in order to get closer or be heard better by the creator of heaven and earth. But when I think of what I have learned from those we call heathens, I often get the feeling that their transmitters and receivers were in good working order long before we taught them to believe that the creator of nature preferred the indoors.

When we left the long-house in Bella Bella, a Kwakiutl Indian pressed a small pamphlet about totem poles into my hand. The Kwakiutl chief Mum-Xiou, whose Christian name was James Sewid, wrote: 'Our ancestors have a deep philosophy of life, and it is with their faith and laws that we have been raised. They saw the beauty in nature that surrounded them, with all its wealth, and tried to capture some of all this beauty in their daily life, in their legends, dances and art. My people believed in an almighty power that created everything, and they were in awe and filled with reverence at the greatness of creation.'

Jacqueline had a private hideaway for her favourite literature and old Indian art that she had collected all her life and that bears witness to the fact that, in most respects, we all like the same things. I asked her to find one of her books that reveals much of our joint view on life: *Touch the Earth: A Self-Portrait of the Indian Existence.*

In it the plains Indian Tatanga Mani from the Stoney tribe in North America wrote: 'Oh yes, I went to a white man's school, I learned to read school books, newspapers and the Bible. But as time went on, I discovered that this wasn't enough. Civilised people become too dependent on their own printed pages. I turn to the Great Spirit's book, which is his whole creation. You can read a lot from that book if you study nature. You know that if you leave all your books out in the sun, to be eroded by rain and snow and insects, there will be nothing left. But the Great Spirit has given you and me the possibility to study in the university of nature, the forests, rivers, mountains and animals, ourselves included.'

Our Lord was there before the Big Bang and before Buddha, Jesus and Mohammed were born, I thought. But civilised people see nothing but roofs and walls and indoor television screens and outdoor traffic jams. How can we believe that anyone has created us when all we see around us are things we have created ourselves?

The Sioux Indian Ohiyesa tried to teach us some of what took place deep within his people: 'In an Indian's life there was only one unavoidable duty – the duty of prayer – the daily recognition of the Invisible and Eternal. His daily time of prayer was more important to him than his daily food. He awakened at dawn, put on his moccasins and went down to the edge of the water. Here he either threw a few handfuls of clean, clear water into his face, or dived in. After the bath he stood facing the dawn, and stared toward the sun as it rose over the horizon while he prayed his prayer without a word. His wife could go and pray by herself, but never with him.

Every soul had to meet the morning sun, the fresh aroma of soil and the Great Silence alone.

'At any time during the course of the day, when the red hunter caught sight of something that was strikingly beautiful or captivating – a black thunder cloud with the rainbow arched in glowing colours over the mountain, a foaming waterfall in a green canyon, an endless prairie blushing in the sunset – he would stop for a moment and stand as if in prayer. He saw no reason to reserve the seventh day as a holy day, because to him all days belonged to God.'

I also think that the sun is a well-chosen symbol for everyone to fix their eyes upon in prayer to an invisible Creator – not least to those who neither know, nor understand why the Christians pray to a cross. The Incas, for example, directed their prayers to the highest, invisible Viracocha, who was represented in the sky by the sun, *inti*, and on earth by the Inca peoples' own priest king. What has made an impression on me is that the Incas only looked upon the sun as the highest forefather of all life here on earth, while they called the ocean Mama-Ocllo, Mother Ocean.

And that is what we have come back to, even in modern research. The sun fertilised the ocean with its rays and created life in the ocean; fertilised particles of salt and minerals that floated about without genes or chromosomes on the undulating surface of the ocean. The first child of the sun in the ocean became the ancestor of all life on earth. St. Francis of Assisi touched upon the same idea in the European Middle Ages, but it was in the wake of Darwin that modern science finally admitted that animals and humans have the same progenitor, and a visible ancestor that still lights up the sky. The halo around the head of a saint is merely visible inheritance.

Does that mean that man's forefathers came down from the trees?

I don't think so. Personally I think they go back to the water's edge. If mankind had first managed to find safety in the trees, they would never have come down to earth again voluntarily. All the wild animals were already in place on the ground. As biologists say, all the niches in the ecosystem were occupied. If we had come to life on a branch in the trees, we would have remained there and groomed our tails and our climbing claws, rather than expose ourselves to everything that ran and jumped on the ground, with horns and talons and sharp teeth. We would have been stampeded to death on the animal trails, and in the bush we would have wanted our fur coats back. I know from my own experience that in the jungle the treetops are where one finds fruit and nuts. Hardly anything grows on the ground because the sun's rays cannot break through.

We were born naked – except for hair – to enable us to wade with our heads above water. We stood upright with totally free arm movements in order to dive and swim away from enemy attacks on land. We left climbing monkeys and gorillas to share the jungle with the wild animals of the forest, and kept to the beaches and rivers where we could jump in, and where there was an endless amount of food reserved for the last of nature's children. The table was set at the water's edge and waited for the fingers of the walking ape; shells and shellfish of all sorts, cleverly hidden behind lids and locked doors and in endless amounts.

Do you believe in creation?

One is bound to. One cannot avoid the conclusion that there must have been something almighty behind the Big Bang that managed to create everything from nothing. There must have been something supernatural that made the universe natural for us, who were placed on a sterile planet by the rays of the sun.

Even in *On the Origin of the Species*, Darwin admitted that believing that something as complex as the eye could have its origins in natural development would have been totally absurd.

Do you believe in God?

I believe in the same god as Abraham, Jesus and Mohammed; the Great Spirit of the Indians. I think it would be a tragedy for the civilised world if churches, synagogues and mosques were to close their doors. Not everyone can manage two-way communication with his inner being in the midst of traffic jams and TV programmes in a modern urban society. We need something to remind us of another dimension in our existence.

Are you Christian?

I am a Christian if Christianity began with the living Jesus of Nazareth, and not others who came after him. I am a Christian if that simply means seeing him as the most important person in history and the greatest thinker. I believe he had more two-way contact with conscience, intelligence and intuition than anyone else, ever since the possibility of such contact was instilled into the human brain.

But do you believe in the Trinity?

I don't think that God can be counted. One cannot count anything other than the tangible – apostles, popes and Bibles. Abraham did not count his God, nor did Mohammed, and certainly not Jesus, who protested when someone reverently addressed him as Father. There is only one Father, he said, and that is our common father in Heaven. We are all brothers.

Do you believe in the Bible?

I have read it as an immensely interesting collection of well-preserved scriptures from ancient times, not all equally valuable today. I have been most attentive to the first chapters of both the New and the Old Testaments. The story of creation begins with light and the ocean and it is chronologically correct as we see it today, from fish and fowl to animals on land and human beings at the end. This could not have been a coincidence, and must be a result of sound ingenuity or keen intuition.

Do you believe in the Holy Spirit?

I think it is the name the church chose for what I call conscience. I conceive of it as a form of two-way contact with one's own inner being. Science does not have a better word for something so strange and important, something we all have that no one can find.

Do you believe in the future?

We create the future ourselves, now, while we still have time. Science has advanced to the point where it can dissect nature and its atoms. It would be smart if we learned to put it all correctly back together again as well, before nature itself takes drastic steps to save itself and us. If there were something I could wish for in the future, it would be that there would be an end to all the conflicts between the different religions, and that everyone who believes in a creative force behind nature would use intelligence, conscience, intuition, the Holy Spirit and everything that is in our collective power to get advice and help to preserve nature before we completely disrupt the great day of rest.

Do you believe in me?

He who does not believe in himself will get nowhere.

Appendix

Leitmotif

What a life! I am completely confused. Do you understand what has driven you on?

Others have also asked me. I can only answer by referring to my expeditions. They have provided a leitmotif throughout my unsettled life.

It started with the **Marquesas Islands** in 1937–8, a journey that had two goals. As an experimental philosopher I wanted to try to return to mankind's original existence to look at civilisation from the perspective of an outsider. As a cautious scientist I wanted to study the beginning of biological life in islands that had once emerged lifeless from the bottom of the ocean. The philosophical answer was that man cannot return to the natural state, but neither can he continue safely without planning the course of civilisation. The scientific answer was that wind and sea currents were the key to the riddle of all life in the Polynesian islands.

I went to **British Columbia** in 1939 to search for traces left by seafarers who had sailed from South-East Asia in the early Stone Age and failed to reach Polynesia before the beginning of our own millennium. I found that the North-West American coastal Indians provided the missing link between Asia and Polynesia.

The *Kon-Tiki* expedition started in 1947 to refute the dogma that South American balsa rafts were unable to transport people and cultivated plants live over the ocean from Peru to Polynesia. I proved that the balsa raft could manage the voyage and was more seaworthy than any pre-European vessel, and that the Polynesians might be right to insist that their ancestors found an earlier population on the islands.

I organised the **Galapagos** expedition in 1952–3 in order to introduce professional archaeologists to a group of islands that no one believed had been visited by any human beings before the arrival of the Europeans. We found pot shards that specialists at the American Museum of Natural History identified as the remains of at least 131 different pre-Incan jars from Ecuador and Peru.

I took a team of archaeologists to **Easter Island** in 1955–6 to search for possible traces of raft voyagers from Peru who could have been there before the Polynesians. We found traces of older civilisations that were previously unknown, suggesting the possibility of a South American point of origin. Excavations and legends on the island also sparked my interest in the importance of the reed ship in the spreading of ancient culture.

I sailed from Morocco with the reed ship *Ra I* in 1969 to

discount the dogma that papyrus reed could only be used on rivers because the reed would sink within two weeks. We found that papyrus ships could float for months provided the reed bundles were properly tied.

I sailed on the **Ra II** in 1970 from Morocco to Barbados to show that a papyrus ship, properly built, could cross the Atlantic Ocean. We proved that the oldest known form of vessel in North Africa and the Mediterranean area could have reached America just as easily as a Viking ship or a caravel.

The *Tigris* expedition in 1977–8 was, like the two *Ra* journeys, an experiment with both crew and vessel. I wanted to show that even in cramped space and under stress, peaceful co-operation was possible between people of different colour, nationality and faith, and that Mesopotamian *berdi* reed was just as good for boat building as papyrus, and that when harvested in the right season *berdi* reed maintained its buoyancy, and would have enabled the Sumerian boat-builders to visit both the Indus valley and the Red Sea on the same voyage.

The expeditions to the **Maldives** in 1983 and 1984 were organised to confirm a suspicion that ancient seafarers had been in contact with remote coral reefs in the middle of the Indian Ocean long before Vasco da Gama and the Arabs. Our excavations showed that before the Arabs discovered the group of islands in 1153, the Buddhists had built *stupas* on the ruins of earlier Hindu temples. From even earlier times we found stone sculptures of unknown seafarers with elegant moustaches and elongated ears, like those on Easter Island.

The expeditions to **Easter Island** in 1986, 1987 and 1988 had two main goals; we wanted to experiment with the theory held by the Czechoslovak engineer Pavel Pavel that the Easter Island statues were moved in an upright position, as the island dwellers claimed when they said that they 'walked'. In addition we wanted to reintroduce the Easter Island *toromiro* tree, a species that would have been extinct on our planet if I had not brought the last seeds from a dying tree on Easter Island in 1956 and planted them in the botanical garden in Gothenburg. With the aid of a rope tied to the top and the bottom of a statue, a handful of Easter Island residents managed to wriggle a statue forward in an upright position. The first *toromiro* trees we planted did not survive, but the species was saved and later reintroduced by other seeds from Gothenburg.

The archaeological project in **Túcume** in Peru in 1988–93, organised in co-operation with the Peruvian authorities and the Kon-Tiki Museum, aimed to search among the pyramids for possible proof that seafaring in Peru did not begin with the Spanish conquest. We found proof that the coastal population in Peru had based their subsistence on ocean fishing and ocean trade from the earliest settlements until the Inca Yupanqi conquered the coast with his mountain Indians, three generations before the arrival of the Spaniards. We also found clear links with Easter Island in the form of reed ships crewed by mythical men with bird heads, and symbolic motifs that have otherwise only been seen in religious art on Easter Island.

I arrived in the Canary Islands in 1990 and decided to stay permanently. I came to explore the step pyramids in **Guimar** on Tenerife, which people thought were piles of stones left by the first Spaniards to have cleared the ground. I found that they were astronomically oriented temple pyramids built of quarried stone from a solidified flow of lava and with steps from the west facing the sunrise, which led up to a pebbled platform. They were in the valley where the last Guancho king surrendered to the Spaniards after Columbus' first voyage to America. He was the last of the white and bearded seafarers to survive in the legends of Mexico and Peru.

Index